THE HARMONY
OF HEAVEN

For Mom and Dad,

   Lent, 2004

with love from Claude + Hilary

GORDON GILES

THE HARMONY
OF HEAVEN

MUSICAL MEDITATIONS FOR LENT AND EASTER

Published by
The Bible Reading Fellowship
First Floor, Elsfield Hall
15–17 Elsfield Way, Oxford OX2 8FG
ISBN 1 84101 334 X

First published 2003
10 9 8 7 6 5 4 3 2 1 0

Acknowledgments
Unless otherwise stated, scripture quotations are taken from The New Revised
Standard Version of the Bible, Anglicized Edition, copyright © 1989, 1995 by the
Division of Christian Education of the National Council of the Churches of Christ in
the USA, and are used by permission. All rights reserved.

English translations of the 'Kyrie', 'Gloria in Excelsis', Nicene Creed, 'Sanctus',
'Benedictus' and 'Agnus Dei' are copyright © English Language Liturgical
Consultation, and are used by permission.

Extracts from The Book of Common Prayer of 1662, the rights of which are vested in
the Crown in perpetuity within the United Kingdom, are reproduced by permission of
Cambridge University Press, Her Majesty's Printers.

A catalogue record for this book is available from the British Library

Printed and bound in Great Britain by
Bookmarque, Croydon

CONTENTS

LENT 4

LENT 5

HOLY WEEK

EASTER WEEK

PRELUDE

It was St Augustine who is supposed to have said that anyone who sings prays twice. He also wrote:

In the Psalms it says 'O sing to the Lord a new song; sing his praise in the assembly of the saints'. We are urged to sing to the Lord a new song. It is a new person who sings a new song. A song is a joyful thing, and if we reflect more deeply, it is also a matter of love. Thus anyone who has learned how to love a new life will also have learned how to sing a new song. For the sake of the new song however, we need to be reminded what the nature of the new life is. Indeed a new person, a new song and the new covenant are all manifestations of the one kingdom: a new person will both sing a new song and belong to the new covenant.

AUGUSTINE OF HIPPO, SERMON 34.1

Lent is a time for prayer, and for music. Some of the greatest sacred music ever written was written for this season: consider Bach's great Passions; Allegri's *Miserere*; Handel's *Messiah*. Other music, even if not written with Lent in mind, lends itself to Lenten consideration, by virtue of its vocal content or theme. Operas, for example, like much great art, often touch upon profound questions of truth, beauty and love, or on right and wrong. These are the things that matter, the questions which help us understand ourselves and the world in which we live.

The much-loved art commentator Sister Wendy Beckett, whose television programmes and books opened up the world of religious art to so many people, suggested that religious art falls into three categories: religious art, spiritual art and sacred art. These types need not be thought of as mutually exclusive, for some great works are certainly all three. Religious art is that which takes as its theme subjects or doctrines of the faith. Thus, a painting of Christ, an icon or statue of a saint is religious art. A spiritual work of art is one which goes beyond religious subject-matter (if it touches on religious subject-matter at all) and, as an act of creation in itself, speaks to us on a deeper level than mere doctrine or exposition of something verbal. Spiritual works of art need not be religious in subject-matter or flavour. Examples of spiritual art might be still-life paintings by Turner or Constable, or they might be religious too. Much spiritual art is also religious, such as the powerful religious paintings of Rubens, Grünewald or Sutherland.

Sacred art goes one step further and, again, need not be 'religious' in appearance. Sacred artworks depict reality as it is 'beneath the surface', and they need not therefore be instantly recognizable, nor 'pretty', but they might be. It is said of some of the works of Fra Angelico, that he wept as he painted, because he truly entered into the spirit of what he was painting, and it affected him. Sister Wendy Beckett says of the painter Mark Rothko (whose large, apparently plain canvases cause as much confusion as admiration) that he was able to express pain that points us towards God.

If we translate these distinctions into the musical realm we may want to say that Bach's *St Matthew Passion* is religious music because it has a religious theme (the last week of Christ's life). It is also spiritual because it speaks of salvation, forgiveness and suffering in a distinctively Christian way. And it is sacred music because it introduces and explores themes that transcend the distinctive message of Christ, pointing us to God, and speaking to us of salvation and eternity in a way that cannot be expressed simply in words. This may well help us understand why people of no confessed faith are moved by Bach's Passions. Some say that they almost believe in God when they hear them. This is important, because it reminds us that faith is not simply a verbal matter, and it also tells us of the power of music to witness to faith. Music that does so is more than religious, more than spiritual even, and should be valued as sacred.

If we have these three kinds of musical types in mind, then there is certainly a wealth of material we might contemplate in Lent (or at any other time, for that matter!). For we need not confine ourselves to Bach's cantatas, Mozart's masses or Britten's anthems in order to reflect and pray musically in Lent. There are great works of music which help us to reflect ethically or spiritually, whether on the situations presented on stage, or on the text, or also in other contexts which the music causes us to think about. Thus, for example, Benjamin Britten's *War Requiem* sets poetry from the First World War allied to the Latin text of the requiem mass, but when we hear it today it can move us to think not only of the First World War tragedy, but also about other wars that have happened or may yet happen. The particular context of the work inspires us to reflect on the more general issue of war, its spiritual and moral implications, and how we should respond to the threat of war or its prevention.

Some works can surprise us when we tune in to them with a theological ear. Works that do not have a religious text (or no text at all), nor a religious theme, can still enlighten us when filtered spiritually. Thus, Mozart's *The Marriage of Figaro* turns out to be quite a treatise on the cost and value of forgiveness, and forgiveness lies at the heart of the Christian gospel. Other works, such as Berg's *Wozzeck*, Britten's *Billy Budd*, Schönberg's *Verklärte Nacht* and Holst's *The Planets* can be examined and appreciated in terms of the opportunities for spiritual reflection they offer. Sometimes, what they do have to offer is not immediately obvious.

Some music is quite unattractive, even unpleasant to some ears. While, as the eighteenth-century philosopher David Hume famously declared: 'Degustibus non disputandem est' ('In matters of taste there is no disputing'), there is music which is less well-liked, and less understood than other more tuneful fare. Sometimes, with a guiding hand, we can learn to appreciate 'hard' music, or we can prefer to ignore its sound, its power and its significance.

This can also be true in the life of faith: we can so easily prefer the bits we like (which is hardly difficult!), and generally ignore issues that confront us in areas of our life we like to keep cocooned in melodious secrecy. So often we want to be heard to be playing a loud, jolly tune to drown the bass line of our lives, in an attempt to convince ourselves, others and even God, that all is well. Lent is a good time to listen to the deep voices of our hearts, to let the lower melodies speak to us, and to learn from them. Lent is a time for self-examination, for learning, for spiritual growth, all achieved through a kind of humility which allows God to do new things in us. But we have to be open to that, just as we have to be open to new music if we hope to broaden our musical knowledge and appreciation.

Readers of this book will no doubt approach it from all kinds of different musical and even spiritual locations. Some people will find here exactly what they might expect from a book that takes pieces of music and reflects on them for Lent. They may well know most of the music, and even have access to a recording of each work discussed. They may also find that there are works which they think I ought to have included, or should not have included. Inevitably, my choice of music is something for which only I can take responsibility. But I hope and believe that there is something for us in each day's choice.

Other readers may be perplexed by some of the music, if they can even lay their hands on it. To them I would want to say that I hope it is possible to join in this musical Lenten journey without actually listening to any of the music. I hope that the textual passages and Bible readings, with the commentaries, will provide an adequate thought for the day, even if they are read unaccompanied, as it were! Nevertheless, this book is intended to be read with some musical accompaniment, and some of the music discussed is widely available and well-known.

I imagine and expect that for most readers the marriage of text and music will combine novelty and familiarity. On our musical journey there will be some old friends to accompany us, but also some new acquaintances. Where the music is familiar, do listen to it if you have access to it. If the music or the work is unfamiliar, then here is an invitation to get to know it a little. For in doing so, we may discover something about ourselves and our relationship with God. Sometimes it can be good to meet in groups, to listen and discuss, and for any considering using the book as a Lent course, there are some suggestions for listening and discussion at the end of the book. Such a Lent course could be conducted either in church or in someone's home. In order to get the music, there is now such a wide range of recordings available that it would be impossible to make recommendations here, but also unnecessary, as a good record shop, or a surf of the Internet should provide the goods! Further to that, of course, one should not forget local libraries. Many of the pieces disussed are often broadcast on the radio. Thus, I hope that most people will be able to become at least a little familiar with most of the music.

Each day, a work is suggested and discussed, and a particular part of it is highlighted for personal or corporate listening. A specially written prayer concludes each chapter, and there is also a recommendation for further biblical reading for those who wish to do so. Sometimes the main text provided comes from the music for the day, rather than from the Bible, but there is always a biblical passage to refer to.

The purpose of this book is similar to that of so many Lent books, even if the method of spiritual journey is a little different. In Lent we are invited by the Church, and therefore, by each other (for we are the body of Christ), to enter into a six-week pilgrimage. We travel little distance, but may explore great depths. Our journey has no practical purpose and takes only a little time each day, but it does have direction and destination. Our direction in Lent is towards the cross, and our destination is Easter. This is a journey which some make every year, while others may never have made it before. Perhaps with music, we may follow a different route, and will therefore see things (and hear things) that are new to us.

Any pilgrimage, whether it involves a physical distance or not, contains within it a microcosm of our lives, as we journey through life towards the end-point that we call death. The end-point is not the end, full stop, though, for in Christ's resurrection we believe that a new dimension of life, and new direction and a new destination become possible for mortal humans. We journey, therefore, not so much towards the end of life, but towards the gate of heaven, through which we seek admission, by virtue of the salvation wrought for us by our Lord Jesus Christ. No one has put this idea of earthly pilgrimage better than St Augustine, who describes it in these terms:

How happy will be our shout of 'Alleluia' as we enter heaven, how carefree, how secure from any assault, where no enemy lurks and no friend dies. There praise is offered to God, and here also, but here it is offered by anxious people and there by those who will live for ever. Here praise is offered in hope, there by those who enjoy the reality; here by pilgrims in transit, there by those who have reached their homeland.

So, my friends, let us sing 'Alleluia', albeit not in the enjoyment of the heavenly rest, but in order to sweeten our toil in this life. Let us sing as travellers sing on a journey; but keep on walking. Lighten your toil by singing, and never be idle. Sing, but keep on walking. And what do I mean by walking? I mean press on from good to better. The apostle says that there are some who go from bad to worse, but if you persevere you will keep on walking. Advance in virtue, in true faith and in right conduct. Sing up—and keep on walking!

AUGUSTINE OF HIPPO, SERMON 256.1

Therefore I invite you to join in this musical pilgrimage through Lent. Let us sing through Lent, towards the cross and beyond into the realm of Easter joy and light, where in the power of the Spirit and in union with Christ we may sing that new song of redemption, of love and of praise.

MUSICAL NOTES

In writing this book, I have tried to assume as little background knowledge as possible, but in case there is any confusion, I hope the following notes will be helpful as a form of brief glossary.

MASS

Many composers have written settings of the main congregational parts of the eucharist. In doing so, they have often made these parts, usually the 'Kyrie', 'Gloria', 'Creed', 'Sanctus' and 'Benedictus' and 'Agnus Dei' non-participatory. Thus the choir sing on behalf of the congregation. Today this is less often the case, and the text is often set in the local language of each country, but while the approach to the eucharist has changed, the appeal of the music of the past is still strong. The texts of the 'movements' of the mass hardly change, and in many works are sung in Latin. In English they may be referred to as:

- Lord have mercy ('Kyrie')
- Glory to God ('Gloria')
- We believe in one God ('Creed')
- Holy, Holy, Holy, Lord ('Sanctus')
- Blessed is he who comes in the name of the Lord ('Benedictus')
- Lamb of God ('Agnus Dei')

Translations can be found alongside discussions of each of the movements, which make up our reflections for the sixth week of Lent. Some of the movements of the mass are also found in requiems (see below). Other parts of the eucharistic celebration in which we often participate today were not generally set by the composers. Often the original plainsong would be used at these points, or they would be said. Thus the Lord's prayer, the acclamations ('Christ has died'), the intercessions, and the peace were not set to music. The collect, gospel, and eucharistic prayer itself were often sung to a simple plainsong chant; this practice has continued to this day, and in some churches can still be heard.

OPERA

The first acknowledged operas date from Italy in the early seventeenth century. Basically speaking, they are musical stage dramas, with some or all of the text set to music. Early opera contained a great deal of recitative—recited vocal music, which is not unlike plainsong, with sparse accompaniment. During recitative, the story would move on, often narrated by one of the characters. Dialogue was often set in this fast-moving form. When the composer wanted to reflect at length on what was going on, or explore the emotions of some of the characters, an aria would appear. An aria ('air' in English) is a song, written with a defined structure, containing few words, giving the composer opportunity to write flowing, expressive melodies. It tends to be the arias that have survived in popular appeal. Broadly speaking, opera owes a lot to the ancient Greek approach to drama, and so it is not surprising that in opera we find not only recitatives and arias, but also choruses. The chorus comments on the action, and sometimes also provides the 'crowd' material in staged settings. Oratorios also adopted these musical forms (see below).

Through time, opera composers became more ambitious, gradually abandoning the recitative, in favour of 'through-composed' music, such that the action, dialogue and any commentary on the action is all joined by a seamless thread. In Mozart and Rossini we find the beginnings of this, Verdi and Puccini carried the approach further, and eventually in Wagner we find lengthy 'music-dramas' that seem a long way from the early days of Monteverdi and Caccini.

ORATORIO

Oratorios evolved from opera during the time of Handel, when it was not permitted to perform opera during penitential seasons. The same structures are to be found, such that oratorios can be considered to be unstaged operas, in which the drama is religious and the central characters are biblical heroes, apostles or even divine beings. *Messiah*, *Elijah*, *The Creation* and *Belshazzar's Feast* are all good examples. A recently composed example is John Taverner's *Fall and Resurrection*, first performed in 2000 for the Millennium.

PASSION

The Passions, notably those by Bach (but also by Schütz, Handel, Penderecki and Arvo Pärt), are basically oratorios drawing exclusively on the accounts of holy week. In Bach's great examples, recitatives take us through the story, narrated by the Evangelist John or Matthew, and some of the dialogue is also in recitative form. Arias convey a personal response to the action described, and the chorus comments on the action with devotional chorales (in which the congregation or audience might join in). The chorus also act as the crowd, berating Pilate and singing the words of the Roman Centurion when Christ dies. In the Passions, Christ, Pilate and Peter are *dramatis personae*.

REQUIEM

The requiem mass (*Missa pro defunctis*) is an augmented eucharist, containing extra movements appropriate for a funeral. Thus, the 'Kyrie', 'Sanctus' and 'Agnus Dei' are still to be found (see above). The 'Gloria' and 'Creed' are omitted. Requiems are still sung or said today in Roman Catholic and some Anglican churches when someone dies, although the splendour and scale of some of the great requiems is rarely possible. Where requiems are sung, the eucharist is an integral part of the liturgy. Traditionally there were special plainsong chants that were used at requiems, especially the 'Dies irae', and this chant was often incorporated by composers of later requiems. It is recognized most often today in Saint-Saëns' *Danse macabre*, where it is the main theme. The 'Dies irae' itself is a distinctive part of the requiem, in which the torments of hell are articulated, and the soul of the departed is prayed for. The usual movements of a requiem are as follows:

- Introit: Rest eternal grant unto them ('Requiem aeternam')
- Lord have mercy ('Kyrie')
- Day of wrath (Dies irae) including the following sections:
  - Day of Wrath ('Dies irae')
  - Hark the trumpet ('Tuba mirum')
  - Now the record ('Liber scriptus')
  - What affliction ('Quid sum miser')
  - King of glory ('Rex tremendae')
  - Remember ('Recordare')
  - Sadly groaning ('Ingemisco')
  - From the accursed ('Confutatis')
  - What weeping ('Lacrimosa')
- Lord Jesus ('Domine Jesu Christe')
- Holy, holy, holy Lord ('Sanctus')
- Lamb of God ('Agnus Dei')
- Light eternal ('Lux aeterna')
- Deliver me ('Libera me')

Not all settings of the requiem employ all these texts; some translate them into other languages, while others almost ignore them, borrowing the title 'requiem' to merely indicate a musical and textual offering for the dead. The reflections for the third and fourth weeks of Lent offer some more detail on this.

'HAVE MERCY ON ME, O GOD'

GREGORIO ALLEGRI—*MISERERE* (PART ONE)

Have mercy on me, O God, according to your steadfast love; according to your abundant mercy blot out my transgressions. Wash me thoroughly from my iniquity, and cleanse me from my sin. For I know my transgressions, and my sin is ever before me. Against you, you alone, have I sinned, and done what is evil in your sight, so that you are justified in your sentence and blameless when you pass judgement. Indeed, I was born guilty, a sinner when my mother conceived me. You desire truth in the inward being; therefore teach me wisdom in my secret heart. Purge me with hyssop, and I shall be clean; wash me, and I shall be whiter than snow. Let me hear joy and gladness; let the bones that you have crushed rejoice. Hide your face from my sins, and blot out all my iniquities.

PSALM 51:1–9

We begin, as we traditionally begin Lent, with Psalm 51, and there can be no more appropriate a piece of music to illustrate the purpose and meaning of Lent than that exquisitely beautiful, famous, and most over-exposed piece of sacred music, the *Miserere* by Gregorio Allegri (1582–1652). This setting of Psalm 51 is known to many merely by the first word of the Latin translation of the psalm—*Miserere*. Even that Latin title has overtones in English: 'Miserere mei, Domine', 'have mercy on me, O Lord'. It hints at misery, a word we hardly associate with mercy these days, and yet the English word is derived from the Latin. In the Litany found in the 1662 Book of Common Prayer, and often said or sung on Good Friday, we find the phrase 'have mercy upon us miserable sinners'. This does not mean that we are unhappy in general, nor even that we are particularly unhappy about our sinfulness. What it means is that we are people in need of mercy, and are therefore to be pitied, most of all by God the Trinity, to whom we make our plea. In the first eight lines of the Litany, the phrase 'us miserable sinners' is repeatedly used to emphasize guilt, and to remind us of our need of mercy.

The words and music of the *Miserere* epitomize Lent, and for many people Ash Wednesday does not feel like Ash Wednesday if this piece is not sung. Psalm 51 has been associated with Ash Wednesday and the Lenten penitential season by virtue of its opening words: 'Have mercy on me O God, according to your steadfast love'. Here is Lent in microcosm; this is what Lent is all about: penitence, seeking mercy, and having the hope of receiving it because of God's already established record of being firm in love. The psalm is all about the seeking of mercy and the hope of obtaining it; pleading gives way to assurance, and in Lent we hold the two together. We know that heartfelt penitence yields forgiveness from God, and so even as we seek forgiveness, we know we are not only to be forgiven, but are already forgiven. God knows the secrets of our hearts, the desires of our hearts, and the sins of our hearts before we articulate them in his presence, yet he also knows that we need to articulate them, and it is important that we do so. Confession of sin is not a mechanistic procedure, leading to forgiveness just as putting water in the freezer leads to the formation of ice. Saying sorry is not a means to an end; it is a value in itself, because it is better, not only to be forgiven, but also to have prepared oneself to accept the gift of forgiveness, and thus to appreciate, feel and value the forgiveness when it is inevitably given.

King David is reckoned to be the author of Psalm 51, and the forgiveness that he seeks follows confession of his most famous sin: the taking of Bathsheba from Uriah the Hittite (2 Samuel 11–12). David sees the beautiful Bathsheba bathing and is smitten. Adultery is committed and she becomes pregnant. The deceitful David tries to get Bathsheba's husband Uriah to spend time with her, so that the child will appear legitimate, but Uriah, whose goodness contrasts with David's wickedness, refuses to visit his wife when his military comrades cannot do the same, and so David's cunning plan comes to nothing. David raises the stakes of sin for, unable to fool Uriah, he decides to have him killed in battle. At David's instruction, as the fighting gets intense, he is deserted by the same comrades with whom he sought solidarity in denying himself his wife's company. This, ironically, leads to his death, as he finds himself fighting alone, outnumbered by the enemy. Uriah's loyalty to his king and country thus brings him a violent, unjust end, and all for the sins of another.

The Christly irony of the death of Uriah is probably a coincidence, but it does lead to repentance in David, just as Christ's innocent death for us should lead to our repentance. Of course, David's involvement in Uriah's death was much more concrete, more deliberate and more conscious than ours in Christ's, but we can readily see something of everyone in David, and it is one of the duties of the Lenten penitent to actively engage in the spiritual experiences of penitence, temptation, passion and crucifixion. And just as we know that with confession there is always forgiveness, so too, as we reach the end of Lent, we are able to be aware that with passion and crucifixion there is always resurrection. We hold these in opposition and together, simultaneously. With any period of the Christian year, we cannot help but know how the story ends up, and yet, at the same time, the story continues beyond us and in us. It changes and yet it is the same. As we return each year to the season of self-examination, we find, not surprisingly, that we have changed, but the promises of forgiveness and healing have not. Each year we return with different wounds, and as different selves, a year wiser perhaps, and also a year more foolish. We are more damaged perhaps, and may find that what we thought was healed isn't healed any more. Scars may have opened up, and painful areas of ourselves we have ceased to examine. Old ghosts return, or new ones arrive, as if from nowhere, creeping in, as if by some inadvertent invitation. Thus we return to Lent each year, differently fragile, newly haunted, strangers to ourselves, but not strangers to God.

And that is why we need Lent, and that is why David needed to repent. On self-examination, he found that he was encountering someone he no longer knew. In the psalm he introduces himself again to himself, and does not like what he meets. Thus, he, and we, must also reintroduce ourselves to God, even though we know very well that God knows us perfectly. Lent is the time to get to know ourselves again, and to get to know God again.

To do so we sometimes have to break through the protective layer with which we surround ourselves. We keep ourselves secret, under wraps, not only from other people, who often never really know us for what we truly are, but also we protect ourselves from ourselves. The psychoanalyst Sigmund Freud spoke of our minds as having a 'West End' and an 'East End', which (with no disrespect to Londoners) meant that there is the glitzy, outward facing, exciting personality, which everyone is supposed to like, but there is also the dark, dingy part of the mind where all the murders take place. This idea may have a spiritual dimension, in that we have a sense of our own mind and spirit, and may present ourselves as holy, kind and loving people, and may even convince ourselves that we are such, but in so doing we may be rejecting some of what we are fighting within. Lent is a time to open up to ourselves, and to God.

PRAYER

As we prepare to enter into your most holy season of Lent, O Lord, have mercy upon us, and grant to us Christ's truth in our inner being, that we may turn away from sin and be faithful to Jesus Christ our Lord. Amen.

For further reading: 2 Samuel 11:2–26
For listening: The first half, or all of Allegri's *Miserere*

'CREATE IN ME A CLEAN HEART, O GOD'

GREGORIO ALLEGRI—*MISERERE* (PART TWO)

Create in me a clean heart, O God, and put a new and right spirit within me. Do not cast me away from your presence, and do not take your holy spirit from me. Restore to me the joy of your salvation, and sustain in me a willing spirit. Then I will teach transgressors your ways, and sinners will return to you. Deliver me from bloodshed, O God, O God of my salvation, and my tongue will sing aloud of your deliverance. O Lord, open my lips, and my mouth will declare your praise. For you have no delight in sacrifice; if I were to give a burnt-offering, you would not be pleased. The sacrifice acceptable to God is a broken spirit; a broken and contrite heart, O God, you will not despise. Do good to Zion in your good pleasure; rebuild the walls of Jerusalem, then you will delight in right sacrifices, in burnt-offerings and whole burnt-offerings; then bulls will be offered on your altar.

PSALM 51:10–19

Lent is the time when we encounter ourselves and our sin. It is a special period in which to get right with God. In medieval times, Psalm 51 was a text by which someone could literally save their neck. If a priest committed a capital offence, he could have his case heard in a special ecclesiastical court, where he might just get a favourable result. In order to gain this apparent privilege, the accused had to prove he was a priest, and one of the ways to do so was to recite scripture. Psalm 51 was one of the texts that could save you if you knew it by heart, and indeed everyone ought to have known it, because it was widely used at the deathbed and execution block. It is perhaps no coincidence then, as we begin Lent, that as well as being reminded of sin, confession and forgiveness, we are also encountering death and judgment on a personal level.

If Allegri's famous *Miserere* is a good piece of music to remind us of this, then the place where it was always sung, is even better. Allegri was a priest, who was born and lived in Rome from 1582 to 1652. The latter part of his life was spent as a musician in the Sistine Chapel in the Vatican. The chapel, originally built between 1475 and 1480 and now restored to its former glory, is a beautiful place, and even though it is hard as a tourist to get any sense of peace and quiet there, the amazing wall paintings by Perugino, Botticelli, Ghirlandaio, Rosselli, and Signorelli create an atmosphere of reverence and awe at the depictions of scenes from the Old Testament and the life of Christ.

On the ceiling are nine scenes painted between 1508 and 1512 by Michelangelo. They depict Old Testament scenes, among them the story of creation (the finger of God famously touches Adam, giving him life), the drunkenness of Noah, and the story of David and Goliath. Twenty-one years later, in 1533, Pope Clement VII asked Michelangelo to return to the Sistine Chapel to paint *The Last Judgement* on the wall behind the altar. Finally revealed to the world in 1541, it is perhaps Michelangelo's greatest work. In its centre is Christ as judge of the world. Angels carry his cross, the symbol of redemption, and Saints Andrew, John the Baptist and Lawrence, and Peter, Paul, Catherine and Sebastian are seen nearby. In the bottom of the picture, angels with trumpets proclaim the day of judgment, and are standing by with the books in which are written the deeds of the good and evil. Meanwhile, demons drag the condemned into hell. As a work of art it is magnificent. It took seven years to paint, and crowns the artistic glory of the pope's private chapel. Against this background of beauty and creation and of judgment and redemption, Allegri's setting of Psalm 51 was sung each year at the beginning of Lent.

Until relatively recently, it was not possible to see these pictures unless one visited the Sistine Chapel in Rome. Even when the chapel was opened to the public, before the days of photography, there was no experience of the work to be had, save for the real one of standing before it. Now, with plenty of books beautifully reproducing details from it—and the Internet—allowing us to view a copy of it from anywhere in the world, we are sometimes forgetful of the privilege of open access that we have. The Church of Michelangelo's day, and of Allegri's day, was much more protective of its art, and indeed of its music.

By the time the 14-year-old Mozart visited Rome, in order to receive a knighthood from the pope, Allegri's piece was known to exist, being sung only in the Sistine Chapel. Excommunication had been threatened to anyone who performed it elsewhere. To steal Allegri's masterpiece was thus a sin from which the church would offer no protection, but rather condemnation. By Mozart's time, this threat was not so real, but the piece had nonetheless never been heard outside the chapel. The story has it that Mozart, on hearing it in the Sistine Chapel, jotted it down when he got home, presumably having heard it only once. The same was claimed for the young Mendelssohn (1809–47), half a century later.

This is not the miracle that it might appear to be. Allegri's *Miserere* is actually very repetitive, and only has two main elements: a plainsong chant, and a choral response. In the course of a performance, Mozart would have heard these alternating sections sung several times, albeit to different words. The wash of sound that is created ebbs and flows between plainsong and harmony, reminding us of the washing away of sin. The music alternates between rich, sonorous beauty and a simpler, austere single line, which barely moves from a single reciting note.

Two choirs are involved, usually placed at a distance from each other, thus creating an ethereal effect as the sound of the distant choir gives the impression of high-singing angels responding to the earthbound penitent. At the same time that this emphasizes the distance between us and God in heaven, it also links the two, showing us in sound that the gulf can be bridged through penitence and forgiveness.

When the piece is sung in St Paul's Cathedral, the second choir is placed either behind the high altar, or sometimes even way up in the Whispering Gallery. This can only be done if there is time to get up there in the lift, as it would be impossible for a young chorister to run up the stairs and then sing the required top Cs! Apparently, one year the *Miserere* was to be sung on Ash Wednesday, and the lift to the

Whispering Gallery was broken, and an adult singer had to carry one of the choristers up the stairs, so that when they got there, he could still sing! It would certainly be an act of penitence to carry a twelve-year-old up all those stairs!

The ebb and flow of the piece reminds us of the two dimensions of Psalm 51, and of the meaning of Lent. The simple, humble plainchant reminds us of the penitential, 'miserable' sinner, kneeling in prayer and supplication. To each plea for mercy comes the full harmony of response, the extravagant, almost luscious sound of the full choir, bestowing forgiveness. Thus there is question and response, held in balance, not only musically but also theologically. Plea and assurance alternate, reminding us of their dependence upon one another, and of human dependence on God. Without a plea, there can be no assurance, and without the hope of assurance, plea for mercy is pointless. Thus, in the midst of beautiful musical, human creation, we may be helped to see and hear God, the divine Creator, whose handiwork is depicted so sublimely round the Sistine Chapel and in the life and art of his creatures.

And we, his creatures, while we may not have the voice of Allegri, or the ear of Mozart, or the brush of Michelangelo, we all have the ability to praise God, and the capability of sin. This Lent, let us relish the beauty of the former, and be properly penitent about the latter.

PRAYER

Most merciful Lord, who desires not the death of a sinner but eternal salvation, not sacrifices but a contrite heart, and despises no one who turns to you, restore in us the image of your glory, that we may sing your praise and return to the fold of your love, for the sake of that great Shepherd of the faithful, Jesus Christ our Saviour. Amen.

For further reading: 2 Samuel 12:1–13
For listening: The second half, or all of Allegri's *Miserere*

'THERE IS JOY IN THE PRESENCE OF THE ANGELS OF GOD OVER ONE SINNER WHO REPENTS'

WOLFGANG AMADEUS MOZART—*THE MARRIAGE OF FIGARO* (PART ONE)

'… what woman having ten silver coins, if she loses one of them, does not light a lamp, sweep the house, and search carefully until she finds it? When she has found it, she calls together her friends and neighbours, saying, "Rejoice with me, for I have found the coin that I had lost." Just so, I tell you, there is joy in the presence of the angels of God over one sinner who repents.'

LUKE 15:8–10

The Marriage of Figaro is probably Mozart's greatest opera. Along with *Cosi fan tutte* and *Don Giovanni* it forms a set of three he wrote with the Italian librettist Lorenzo da Ponte. First performed in Prague in 1786, *Figaro* is an adaptation of a play by Pierre Beaumarchais. The year of the opera's first performance is significant, because at that time the French Revolution was gaining momentum, and many European monarchs were fearing the future. In Austria, the play had been banned by Emperor Joseph II, following the example of his ill-fated colleague in France, Louis XVI, who had pronounced the play 'detestable' in 1778. It was therefore a controversial choice for Mozart and da Ponte.

The play was a very popular sequel to *The Barber of Seville*, written three years earlier. In that play, Count Almaviva is aided and abetted by his servant, the barber Figaro, in securing as his wife the beautiful and charming Rosina. *The Barber of Seville* survives most successfully in the form of an opera written in 1816 by Rossini as a prequel to Mozart's masterpiece. Thus, in *Figaro* we find that the Count is already married to Rosina, now the Countess, but all is not rosy in the Almaviva household.

Figaro has been promoted, and has fallen in love with Susanna, the Countess' maid. The opera begins with their marriage preparations. However, the Count wants to seduce Susanna, and so the play is ostensibly about how they thwart his intentions. The Countess knows about the Count's philanderings, but is powerless to stop him. At the beginning of the second act, we meet her alone for the first time, as she sings an aria 'Porgi Amor', in which she sings: 'Grant, Love, that restoration to my sorrow, to my sighing. Give me back my treasure, or at least let me die.' The music Mozart gives her is tuneful and mournful, sadness tinged with past joy, as she laments her loss. Her music climbs the scale, reaching a top A flat as she sings: 'Give me back my treasure, or let me die.' The music is held, and the world stops, as the Countess is frozen in misery and regret for the love she has lost. It all seems futile, but Mozart is setting up a musical question that will not be answered for some time. We barely notice this woman, whose marriage appears over, but in both operatic and spiritual terms, this story is not so much about the Count's wickedness, but about how it affects his wife, and what she does about it. Early in the opera, Rosina is a weak-willed, downtrodden wife, but that is all going to change. The unresolved chord of 'Porgi Amor' tells us that this will be so.

All around her, Figaro and Susanna are fighting off classical comic opera situations: Figaro owes Marcellina money, and so may have to marry her instead, but it turns out that she is his mother; the boy, Cherubino (who is invariably played by a woman), is disguised as a woman, thus creating the inevitably comic and confusing situation of a woman playing a man playing a woman! The opera is full of complicated false assignations which go wrong, thus confounding the Count, as all his plans to ensnare Susanna are bombarded with ludicrous distractions. The Countess remains mostly sad and aloof, and the servant girl Susanna appears to be in charge. This is superbly demonstrated in the Finale to Act Two, in which the Countess appears to have been caught out by her husband, while she is dressing Cherubino up for a part he is to play in their plot, and so she has to beg for mercy from him on account that there is a semi-naked man in the next room. The Count is most unforgiving, but Susanna has secretly managed to chuck Cherubino out of the window, so that when the Count finally demands that the stranger emerge from the closet, only the composed Susanna emerges. All he can do is beg forgiveness, which the Countess grants him—even though she has been denied forgiveness by him, when she herself was innocent, only appearing guilty, while he is very guilty and attempts to appear innocent.

The Countess is a very damaged person; her faith in her husband and her faith in herself is at a low ebb, and she allows herself to be led by Susanna. Up to this point much is unresolved and inadequate in her life. She finds herself forgiving her husband for accusing her, but has not managed to confront the main issue in their marriage, and any anger she has expressed for his behaviour has been soothed away by Susanna, who herself does not want to contend with a rejected and angry Count.

Thus when we next meet the Countess alone, we expect nothing more than another lament. But her aria 'Dove Sono' is not merely a lament for lost love. She has agreed to exchange clothes with Susanna, so that when the Count makes advances to her, he will be deceived, which means that Susanna will be protected, and the Count will be caught. As the Countess waits to hear whether the plan is likely to work, she reflects on the fact she has a cruel, jealous, unfaithful husband, and that she has to rely on a servant to teach him a lesson.

She sings: 'Where are those sweet moments of peace and pleasure, and what happened to the promises made by those unfaithful lips? But why didn't the memories disappear when my life became so painful and tearful?' Her music then changes character, and she sings: 'Ah, if my constancy still loves through its sorrow, then there is still hope of changing his ungrateful heart.' This becomes her new motto, and the theme of the rest of her life. Suddenly she takes control of her own situation, and we hear this in the music. As the aria draws to a close, we find the Countess soaring up to those A flats, with confidence, and now they resolve: they go somewhere musically, whereas before, in 'Porgi Amor' they were left hanging, unresolved. And all on the word 'change'.

The Countess has resolved what to do. She has identified the problem and seen a solution, which does not depend on Susanna, or Figaro, or anyone else other than herself. And that change comes through forgiveness. She has resolved to forgive the Count, and show him that she still loves him; she believes that her love can change him, just as it is changing her now. The key to her happiness and to her survival lies in being an instrument of forgiveness, and, as we shall see, her difficult decision to forgive brings about true repentance in her husband.

Just as true repentance leads to genuine forgiveness, in which God delights—as the parables of the lost sheep, lost coin and lost son show us (Luke 15)—so true forgiveness can lead to true repentance. The Countess forgives her husband, and consequently he is led towards genuine life-altering repentance. So it is with God and us. Because we have already been shown mercy in Christ, we are able to turn to him in repentance, knowing that if we seek it, it will be granted. This is not necessarily easy, and it may be far less easy to forgive others, especially if they show no sign of remorse, but as Christians we can hardly fail to realize that our calling is to seek forgiveness from God, and offer it to others too.

PRAYER

Heavenly Father, by your Holy Spirit, help those who are resentful or who cannot forgive others, that they may become instruments of your peace. Heal those who have had great wrongs done to them or their loved ones. Have mercy on those who cannot forgive themselves, and lead us all from the darkness of sin to the light of salvation revealed in Jesus Christ our Lord. Amen.

For further reading: Luke 15:11–32
For listening: 'Porgi Amor', from *The Marriage of Figaro*, by Mozart

'I WILL FORGIVE THEIR INIQUITY, AND REMEMBER THEIR SIN NO MORE'

WOLFGANG AMADEUS MOZART—*THE MARRIAGE OF FIGARO* (PART TWO)

The days are surely coming, says the Lord, when I will make a new covenant with the house of Israel and the house of Judah. It will not be like the covenant that I made with their ancestors when I took them by the hand to bring them out of the land of Egypt—a covenant that they broke, though I was their husband, says the Lord. But this is the covenant that I will make with the house of Israel after those days, says the Lord: I will put my law within them, and I will write it on their hearts; and I will be their God, and they shall be my people. No longer shall they teach one another, or say to each other, 'Know the Lord,' for they shall all know me, from the least of them to the greatest, says the Lord; for I will forgive their iniquity, and remember their sin no more.

JEREMIAH 31:31–34

The scene is now set for a final encounter as the Count tries to seduce Susanna, but finds himself propositioning his own wife, while believing himself to have caught his wife with another man. The truth is that the servant Susanna is pretending to be the Countess in order to trick him. Pretending to be the Countess, Susanna asks his forgiveness, which, as before, he refuses. The whole assembly implores him to be merciful, but he refuses, until in a final moment that transcends the comic nature of the opera, the Countess emerges from a different location to seek pardon for herself. She is not at fault though, for all she has done is expose the iniquity of her husband, who is now truly beaten at his own game. Everyone except the Countess is taken aback, and once again the Count has no choice but to get down on his knees and beg forgiveness, again. The Countess is magnanimous, when she feels that the Count's apology is genuine, and so forgives him, bringing the opera to a close.

Figaro, it might be said, is about forgiveness withheld and forgiveness granted. The Countess is a victim of her husband's selfish faithlessness, but she realizes that being a victim is not going to help her, or him. By laying pride aside, she seeks to regain his love by remaining faithful to him, even in the face of his faithlessness.

Here are overtones of God keeping faithful to the Israelites, even when they turned away from him. In the passage from Jeremiah, God speaks of a new covenant and new marriage relationship with his people. Just as the Count has been unfaithful to his wife, Jeremiah portrays the Israelites as having been unfaithful to God. God is not humiliated or beaten though, nor is he forced into forgiving them; he does so because he wants to and because he loves them. God's people continue to sin, of course, being unable to keep the Law, and eventually Christ comes as the new bridegroom, a covenant newer still, in which God gives his own Son for his people. Rather like the Countess, God forgives, and finds that he has to forgive again and again.

The Countess is something of a Christ-figure in that, as a victim, she becomes a saviour to her husband. It is only those whom we have most wronged who can forgive, or, in the human sense, save us from the wrong we have done. Those who are damaged by others sometimes have great power over those who have hurt them, because only they can release the perpetrator of the pain. She continues to forgive, as though following Jesus' injunction to his disciples: '… if there is repentance, you must forgive. And if the same person sins against you seven times a day, and turns back to you seven times and says, "I repent," you must forgive' (Luke 17:3–4).

In Matthew's Gospel, Jesus is recorded as adding: 'Not seven times, but, I tell you, seventy-seven times' (Matthew 18:22). Part of the disciples' call is to be forgiving. The Lord's prayer, in all its forms, speaks of seeking forgiveness as we forgive those who sin against us, and Matthew adds a warning to us all: 'For if you forgive others their trespasses, your heavenly Father will also forgive you; but if you do not forgive others, neither will your Father forgive your trespasses' (Matthew 6:14–15). In Act Two the Countess puts this idea herself: 'perdono non merta chi agli altri non da', which means 'He deserves no forgiveness, he who denies it to others.'

If we think of Mozart's *Figaro* as being a parable about forgiveness, it is not only because the Countess is forgiving, but also because of the change in herself that she undergoes in order to become so. We see her forgive twice, yet the second forgiveness is different to the first. When she is a weak character, a victim, her forgiveness comes from weakness. Sometimes it is easier to forgive a bully because it is less effort, to say: 'Yes, I forgive you', when the forgiving is merely a way of escaping a situation and is barely real. Saying 'sorry' can be superficial, and can be a means to an end, merely to gain an equally superficial pardon. This is what happens midway through the opera, when the Count has to apologize because he is exposed for being wrong, and the Countess has to forgive him, and does so because someone else tells her to. His apology is superficial, and she knows it, and that is why she has to be persuaded by Susanna, for the sake of decency, to publicly forgive him. She does, but it is virtually meaningless, because she knows that he didn't mean it, and nor does she. Their relationship has broken down to that extent.

At the end of the opera, it is as though the Countess has become a different person. By this time, many of the characters, the Countess among them, have disguised themselves, pretending to be someone else. It is ironic that it is only through this disguise that both she and the Count are able to rediscover themselves, and learn the healing power of forgiveness. When the Countess becomes a different person, as it were, her forgiveness costs more and is more genuine. She has consciously decided that loss of pride is the price she must pay, and is willing to pay it to restore her love. It is a brave and noble thing to do. Thus Mozart and Da Ponte ultimately restore to the Countess the dignity of her position. Forgiving people, we see, need not be an act

31

of humiliation, weakness or convenience; forgiveness can make a difference and requires great presence of mind and inner strength.

This is something for which we need not only God's inspiration, but his help. It is perhaps no coincidence that the Countess's first aria 'Porgi Amor' is phrased like a prayer, and some English translations translate the opening phrase as 'God of love, give relief to my sorrow'. The answer to that prayer is found in the Countess' second aria, 'Dove Sono', during which she is given the strength to forgive. Mozart uses the same music for the setting of the 'Agnus Dei' in his Coronation Mass. There again, the music is associated with forgiveness, as during communion we ask the Lamb of God who takes away the sin of the world to have mercy on us. We can see the Countess praying for strength and, later on, gaining it. Just as the prodigal son 'comes to his senses' and returns to his father (Luke 15:17–20), she too has a self-realization that drives her to new, positive and healing action. But as the music shows us, with the unresolved A flat, this process of self-discovery can take time, and it can leave us suspended, like an unresolved melody, until we find the means to resolve the unresolved.

This Lent, may we too 'come to our senses', and gain control of situations that damage us. And may we seek not to destroy or eliminate, or ignore our pain, but with God's help to learn the healing power of human and divine forgiveness given and received.

PRAYER

Merciful God, give us grace to forgive those who have wronged us and to seek the forgiveness of those whom we have hurt. May we bring the damage of our sin and the forgiveness of our hearts before your heavenly throne, so that we may be renewed in virtue and love. Amen.

For further reading: Matthew 18:21–35
For listening: 'Dove Sono', from *The Marriage of Figaro*, by Mozart

'IN THE BEGINNING'

FRANZ JOSEPH HAYDN—*THE CREATION*

In the beginning when God created the heavens and the earth, the earth was a formless void and darkness covered the face of the deep, while a wind from God swept over the face of the waters. Then God said, 'Let there be light'; and there was light. And God saw that the light was good; and God separated the light from the darkness. God called the light Day, and the darkness he called Night. And there was evening and there was morning, the first day.

GENESIS 1:1–5

In 1798 Joseph Haydn (1732–1809) wrote an oratorio all about God's creation, as told in the first chapter of Genesis. The music opens with a 'representation of chaos', in which the composer illustrates the 'formless void', over which God's wind swept, before even the creation of light. It is a daring attempt to depict chaos musically, and to modern ears it sounds rather delightful, with its alternation of drumbeats, scales on wind instruments, and repeated string notes. Musically speaking it is an overture, opening the drama which is to enfold, just as though Haydn were writing one of his 18 operas. Indeed it is an opera—a 'work', the work of God—that the 66-year-old composer was illustrating, and it is the praise of God for his work of creation that Haydn is sharing with us. He wrote, while composing it: 'Never was I as pious as when I was composing this work; I knelt down daily and prayed God to strengthen me for it.'

After the depiction of chaos, the work continues with a gentle bass solo, singing of the spirit of God moving upon the waters, accompanied by some of the quietest choral singing you could ever hear. The angel Raphael, a character borrowed from John Milton's *Paradise Lost*, is narrating the build-up to the creation of light. The hushed choir take over, and the sense of anticipation is almost palpable as they sing: 'And God said, "Let there be light."' And then they sing: 'And there was light', and the word light springs forth from choir and orchestra: a massive C major chord, expected, but blasting in from nowhere. Even when you know it is coming, it is exhilarating, as Haydn tries to show us something of the impact of the first ever light in the world. It is one of the most dramatic moments in all music, even though it is a relatively simple outburst as unison melody becomes a big chord and the *pianissimo* (very quiet) becomes *fortissimo* (very loud) in a fraction of a second. It is the musical equivalent of the 'big bang', even though Haydn could not have imagined it in quite those terms.

Haydn's devotion is clear from his own account, and we also know that he was very moved at the work's first performance, which caused him to fear that he would have a stroke! While the nature of Haydn's devotion was exemplary, the understanding that accompanied it was brand-new in Haydn's time. Although drawing on Milton and the Bible directly for his text, Haydn was also influenced by a theory known as the 'Nebular Hypothesis', which was first put forward by the German philosopher Immanuel Kant in *Universal Natural History and the Theory of the Heavens* (1755).

In that work, which took many years to be distributed properly, Kant proposed that the Solar System originally consisted of a large cloud of gas and dust, which began to rotate. As it did so it flattened, and minuscule versions of the planets combined to form the sun at the centre, and then the planets in orbit around it. In developing these ideas Kant reaches far back into classical Greek thought to claim that the beginning of creation involved a universal diffusion of primitive particles which were then brought together by the forces of gravity. Kant was no atheist, and he believed this to be the way in which the account of creation in Genesis could be explained. Kant's theory combined an understanding of Genesis and Newton's laws of physics. Newton's laws account for how the planets remain in their current state but do not explain how they got there. Kant boldly ventured where Newton had feared to go.

There have been exciting developments in music and science since Haydn wrote *The Creation*, but the basis of our understanding of both can be traced to those enlightenment days of the later eighteenth century. Today, we have electrical instruments of both scientific and musical varieties, pushing forward the boundaries of knowledge and noise alike, and making the music and the theory sound pleasing, even simple. It is so tempting, in our day and age, to look back and see a musical 'progress', as composers do more complex and extravagant things, and to see science as replacing everything in its wake.

Yet through all this survives beauty, enquiry and faith. The early Jewish communities who wrote, taught and believed the accounts of Genesis were able to hold those descriptions of God together with their experience of the world around them, as were Haydn and Kant, both of whom led their fields of music and thought. Still today, we can hold together our experience of the world around us and the scientific knowledge that we glean from writers such as Stephen Hawking. *A Brief History of Time* (1988) and *The Universe in a Nutshell* (2001) are impressive works, drawing on all the latest ideas and descriptions of how the universe came to be and what is likely to happen over the next few billion years. However, even if we really do understand what Hawking is on about, even he has not actually suggested that these ideas are incompatible with Genesis 1. It all depends, of course, on how you read Genesis, and how you read modern astrophysics—and, let's face it, very few people are qualified to do both.

St Anselm famously said that theology was 'faith seeking understanding', and in one sense we are all in that business. But for many today, there is the move from understanding to faith. It can so often seem that the modern world has denied us access to aspects of faith revealed in Old Testament narratives because we have learned how to dismiss them as absurd, mythical stories. We may understand (or think we understand) how the world works, but that understanding need not preclude faith.

There are ways to understanding that do not come through science, nor through the treatment of history as science (a grave mistake). We have the direct revelation of God, and we have art. Haydn, in his art, shows us about creation, illustrating in music everything from light, to a sunrise, to a raging lion and a tiger. Such depictions may well bring a smile, but they also show us that there is another way; we do not live in a two-dimensional world, in which only the oppositions of truth and falsity, or science and religion, have anything to say to us. When we add the third dimension of art, we gain a broader, deeper, picture, giving us new understandings, and ways to see the same truth from different angles.

Thus science and faith can be held together, as they observe the same phenomena from different perspectives. As Haydn's great masterpiece reminds us in its most famous anthem, based on Psalm 19: 'The heavens are telling the glory of God, the wonder of his works displays the firmament... in all the lands resounds the word, never unperceived, ever understood.'

Whether we live in 2000BC, the time of Christ, AD1800 or on this very day, all around us we can see the wonder of God's work. We experience it in sunrise and sunset, animal and plant, and in the joy of human love and friendship. We also encounter it in the beauty of music and the ingenuity and brilliance of scientific discovery.

Part Two of *The Creation* concludes with another choral item, 'Achieved is the glorious work, our song let be the praise of God'. This is Haydn's theory, and it is ours today: that God has done marvellous deeds in creating a beautiful world. For that we offer praise and thanksgiving.

PRAYER

O God our Father, we give you thanks and praise for the beauty of your universe, and for all who help us to understand your creative power. As we encounter the world around us, teach us to find you in all things, and in the light of your supreme gift of life, continually remind us of your love for all creation, for your reign with the Son and the Holy Spirit, ever one God, world without end. Amen.

For further reading: Genesis 1:1—2:3
For listening: The first two movements of Haydn's *The Creation*, also, 'The Heavens are Telling', and 'Achieved is the glorious work'

'LET THE EARTH BRING FORTH LIVING CREATURES OF EVERY KIND'

CAMILLE SAINT-SAËNS—*THE CARNIVAL OF THE ANIMALS*

And God said, 'Let the earth bring forth living creatures of every kind: cattle and creeping things and wild animals of the earth of every kind.' And it was so. God made the wild animals of the earth of every kind, and the cattle of every kind, and everything that creeps upon the ground of every kind. And God saw that it was good. Then God said, 'Let us make humankind in our image, according to our likeness; and let them have dominion over the fish of the sea, and over the birds of the air, and over the cattle, and over all the wild animals of the earth, and over every creeping thing that creeps upon the earth.' So God created humankind in his image, in the image of God he created them; male and female he created them. God blessed them, and God said to them, 'Be fruitful and multiply, and fill the earth and subdue it; and have dominion over the fish of the sea and over the birds of the air and over every living thing that moves upon the earth.'

GENESIS 1:24–28

When we think of creation, we are often drawn to the wide diversity and range of God's creatures, living and extinct. The unique wealth and beauty of the many kinds of creature on this earth delight us, and

37

encourage us in the belief that our rotating planet is in some way special and marked out by God as the object of his creative love. God's creation is not just a range of creatures, though; it is also what those creatures do and how they live.

The skills that we have are all part of God's creative gift, and so it is only right that we should see language, art, friendship and love as part of God's created order. Thus, when we encounter works of art reflecting on the beauties of creation, we are doubly inspired. When human creativity can reflect on creation, and can do so with humour and delight, we are triply blessed, and, as in the case of Camille Saint-Saëns' *Grande Fantasie Zoologique 'Le carnival des Animaux'*, we can rejoice even more at the way in which the composer manages to place humanity and human creativity within the context of divine creation.

Saint-Saëns (1835–1921) was organist at the Madeleine Church in Paris, and is known for his Third 'Organ' Symphony, piano and violin concertos, and for this delightful and immensely popular suite for piano duet and orchestra, written in 1886. He would have been rather embarrassed at the success that his zoological fantasy has had. For while on one level it is a delightful portrayal of God's creation: a happy procession of creatures lovingly illustrated, it is also a satirical work, mercilessly parodying his contemporaries in a more than light-hearted way. The French composers Offenbach (who wrote the famous 'can-can') and Berlioz have their music parodied as the tortoises 'dance' the former (very slowly!), and the elephants stomp all over the latter's 'Sylphs' Dance'! Mendelssohn and Rossini get similar treatment, alongside popular songs of the day. With a certain humility of humour Saint-Saëns also abuses one of his own works, the *Danse Macabre*; this, in its portrayal of rattling bones springing to life (a resonance of Ezekiel's Valley of Dry Bones perhaps!—Ezekiel 37:1–14), is well suited to a xylophonic joke.

The greatest humour, and the greatest significance, is to be found in the portrayal of pianists. Saint-Saëns sees them as a species of animal, up to their tricks, parading their virtuosity and doing their exercises. Many pianists, whether successful or not, will remember the bane of early music lessons—of playing scales and learning fingerings—and may well have felt like some kind of performing monkey in doing so.

Saint-Saëns captures this spirit of piano practice delightfully, and while his tongue is firmly in his cheek, this portrayal of the human animal making music is also indicative of a profound truth.

When we think of pianists as performing animals, we are reminded that all creativity comes from two sources: the divine creator and the human will. Even where there is a creative gift from God, technical brilliance has to be worked at, perfected and kept in trim. The same could be said for a sporting gift. Only practice makes perfect. With life in general, only God makes perfect. For just as in life, even the greatest pianist can trip over notes or scales, we too—no matter how much we try to live the life of faith and love—trip up and make mistakes.

There is a story about the great pianist Artur Rubenstein, who was acting as adjudicator in a piano competition. A young hopeful, performing at a high level, played his recital pieces, and afterwards, with a mixture of pride and apprehension, said to the great man: 'Maestro, how did I do? Did you like my playing?' Rubenstein looked at the nervous pianist, and with a wry smile said: 'There were too many right notes!'

What he meant was that technical brilliance had got in the way of human expression and interpretation of the music. Technique is a means to music, not an end in itself. Saint-Saëns is saying the same kind of thing when he parodies the technical exercises which pupils were expected to learn. Such an approach to music is like the kind of legalistic approach to the law that we find Jesus criticizing in the Pharisees (Luke 11:37–52). Strict adherence to the Law of God but without emotion, without love, is not what the Christian faith is about. Yet we are not called to abandon the Law, any more than a musician is told to stop practising scales and arpeggios. We never 'graduate' from God's Law, even if we find, as time goes by, that it becomes part of the fabric of our music and our life, and we instinctively follow it. But even then, because we are only human, we can slip up, and either play a wrong note here and there, or else play so many right notes that we lose the plot of love.

From Saint-Saëns' delightful 20-minute suite of animal portraits, we can gain amusement; we can admire his satirical touch, and relish how humorous music can be. On another level we can be reminded of our status as divinely created beings, set among and apart from the other animals. We are also reminded that as God's creatures we are uniquely blessed with creative gifts ourselves, but that the full enjoyment and exercise of those gifts also requires human effort. That need for effort on our part reminds us that we are creatures who easily fall short of the mark because we think too readily that we can succeed by following a technical or legalistic approach.

We also fail because there is no perfection on earth that we can attain; even if we are technically brilliant and emotionally mature, we still make those human errors. In life, in love, in music and in faith, we strive for perfection (Matthew 5:48), but must always remember that it is Christ who is made perfect, and that legalistic adherence to God's commandments does not make us so (Hebrews 7:11–19). As we approach God, seeking to be made perfect, through Christ we remember that we are sinners but we are also aware that in Christ all creation shall be redeemed (Romans 8:18–23) in one final, technically brilliant, and creatively beautiful revelation of God's glory.

PRAYER

O God of love, through whom all things living are made, we give you thanks for the beauties of your creation, and especially for the skills and gifts you bestow on musicians and performers. By your Holy Spirit, help us to live your gospel and practise our faith, that we may reflect your perfect love revealed in the death and resurrection of your Son, our Saviour Jesus Christ. Amen.

For further reading: Genesis 6:18–20, Luke 11:37–52
For listening: All or part of Saint-Saëns' *The Carnival of the Animals*

'THE WOLF SHALL LIVE WITH THE LAMB AND A LITTLE CHILD SHALL LEAD THEM'

SERGEI PROKOFIEV—*PETER AND THE WOLF*

The wolf shall live with the lamb, the leopard shall lie down with the kid, the calf and the lion and the fatling together, and a little child shall lead them. The cow and the bear shall graze, their young shall lie down together; and the lion shall eat straw like the ox. The nursing child shall play over the hole of the asp, and the weaned child shall put its hand on the adder's den. They will not hurt or destroy on all my holy mountain; for the earth will be full of the knowledge of the Lord as the waters cover the sea.

ISAIAH 11:6–9

God's world is not only full of delightful cuddly animals. We are justifiably wary of some creatures, especially those with lots of little legs, slimy skins or sharp teeth. Behind Isaiah's vision of the lamb and the wolf lying down together is the recognition that such an occurrence would in some sense be contrary to the natural order of the animal kingdom. The created world, as Charles Darwin put it, is 'red in tooth and claw': there is no shortage of instinctive violence among species. Such violence inevitably contributes to the survival of some and the extinction of others.

As humans, we are little different, even though we have the gift of being able to articulate our human condition. We can reflect on the way we preserve or destroy creation. We can argue about the merits of hunting, whether we are discussing the sport of fox-hunting, or the killing of animals for food. Both practices are long-established and whether we deplore them or not, they remind us that our ancestors were hunters. Nimrod (Genesis 10:8–9) and Esau (Genesis 27) were hunters, founders of a long line of men and women who kill animals for food. Behind that tradition is the assumption, drawn from Genesis 1:28, that all living things are available to humankind, and related to that view is the idea that if one species is hindering human stewardship of flora or fauna, those animals may be disposed of. Thus we have evolved a theology of pest control.

It is the tradition of hunting dangerous, unwanted animals that Sergei Prokofiev draws on in his children's musical story, *Peter and the Wolf*. A narrator guides us through the tale of Peter, a Russian boy, who is warned off straying into the woods by his protective and bossy grandfather, who is represented by a ponderous bassoon tune. Peter is portrayed by airy violins, and a duck and a cat are played by doleful oboe and jaunty clarinet respectively, while the bird is indicated by a fluttery flute. The wolf is played by rich horns, and the hunters who turn up at the end by rumbling timpani. As each character has not only an instrument but a theme tune, the structure of the story determines the musical layout of the piece. Prokofiev blends it all together effortlessly, and it is good to appreciate how cleverly he does so.

In the story, Peter goes out to play in the meadow, where his friends the duck, bird and cat are also to be found. The cat tries to catch the bird, but fails. Grandfather comes out, angry with Peter, and tells him off: 'What if a wolf were to come out of the forest?' Peter ignores him, but is led home, and the gate into the meadow is locked, for Peter's own protection. Immediately, a big, grey wolf does come out of the forest, ominously serenaded by horns. The other animals flee, but the duck panics; she cannot escape the wolf, who catches her and swallows her in one gulp. The bird then annoys the wolf by flying around. Meanwhile, Peter, from across the other side of the gate, manages to catch the wolf by the tail with a rope. Coincidentally, some hunters are on the way, and they are delighted to find the wolf caught. Peter sees them coming, and forbids them from shooting the wolf, insisting that he be taken to the zoo instead. A final procession ends the piece, with the suggestion that the danger has been removed and even the wolf has been saved. The duck, of course, has had a raw deal, but is still alive; in a delightful musical moment, she can be heard plaintively quacking inside the wolf's belly!

There is more to this story than the exploits of a little boy who rashly pursues a wolf which has consumed his feathered friend. In 1936, Europe was on the brink of war and Prokofiev's native Russia was in the grip of Stalin's authoritarian regime. Even musicians found themselves censored by Stalin, and the poet Osip Mandelstam was sent to a labour camp, where he perished because of what he had written. Prokofiev's fellow composer Dmitri Shostakovich was directly criticized by Stalin for his opera *Lady Macbeth of Mtensk District* (now an acknowledged classic), and these attitudes expressed by Stalin were certainly cause for fear at the time. Thus it has been suggested that *Peter and the Wolf* is a parable in which Peter represents Prokofiev himself (the hero); the Grandfather represents the (somewhat overprotective!) Fatherland of Russia, and the duck represents the poor, persecuted Shostakovich, gobbled up by Stalin the wolf. The hunters are the longed-for redeemers of wrongdoing, who arrive to save the day at the end.

Whether this is a parable of 1930s Russian tyranny or not, it is very unlikely that the composer meant the story to contain any Christian symbolism. Yet here we have a situation in which violent animal conflicts are resolved and peace ultimately prevails. The wolf is captured, unharmed, although we have to accept that there probably isn't much hope for the duck in his belly. The wolf carries his past sins with him, as it were, as indeed would the biblical wolf, on the day when he lies down with the lamb in that idyllic scene painted by Isaiah. Animals (and humans) kill each other; this is a sad fact of life and death. Thus, in this children's story, so skilfully and delightfully told in musical form, there are overtones not only of a future vision of peace and reconciliation for creation, but also of the lethally violent current state of nature. This reminds us that in one sense the whole of creation is in a state of sin, and that is why, as St Paul puts it, creation groans, awaiting the redemption revealed and promised in Christ when he comes again.

PRAYER

Creator God, we wait with eager longing for that day when all creation will be redeemed, when the wolf shall lie down with the lamb, and all conflict cease. Until that time comes, give us grace to respect the world around us, and reveal to us your creative purposes. Give us wisdom to understand the world and our place in it, so that all your creatures may dwell together in the glory of your creative love. Amen.

For further reading: Romans 8:18–23
For listening: All or part of Prokofiev's *Peter and the Wolf*

'IN HIM ALL THINGS IN HEAVEN AND ON EARTH WERE CREATED'

GUSTAV HOLST—*THE PLANETS*

May you be made strong with all the strength that comes from his glorious power, and may you be prepared to endure everything with patience, while joyfully giving thanks to the Father, who has enabled you to share in the inheritance of the saints in the light. He has rescued us from the power of darkness and transferred us into the kingdom of his beloved Son, in whom we have redemption, the forgiveness of sins. He is the image of the invisible God, the firstborn of all creation; for in him all things in heaven and on earth were created, things visible and invisible, whether thrones or dominions or rulers or powers—all things have been created through him and for him. He himself is before all things, and in him all things hold together. He is the head of the body, the church; he is the beginning, the firstborn from the dead, so that he might come to have first place in everything. For in him all the fullness of God was pleased to dwell, and through him God was pleased to reconcile to himself all things, whether on earth or in heaven, by making peace through the blood of his cross.

COLOSSIANS 1:11–20

While Haydn's *The Creation* and Saint-Saëns' *Carnival* give us a musical depiction of God's creation, Gustav Holst (1874–1934), writing over a hundred years later, gives us a musical portrait of the solar system. Like Haydn, Holst could only depict what he knew, and so we only find seven movements in his famous suite *The Planets* (he does not include Earth). Uranus had been discovered in Haydn's lifetime, and then in 1845, a Cambridge mathematician, John Couch Adams predicted the existence of Neptune, and French and German astronomers actually identified the 'new' planet the following year. The ninth planet, Pluto, of which Holst was unaware, was spotted for the first time in 1930, by Clyde Tombaugh.

Holst's religious beliefs were not as orthodox as Haydn's had been, and he nourished a particular interest in Hinduism and astrology. *The Planets* is not a 'Christian' depiction of the universe as we know it, but more of an astrological sound portrait. *The Planets* is a musical horoscope, which attributes personality characteristics to each planet, personifying them and giving them significance in the pattern of human life. Many people treat astrology as a joke, or at least as some kind of harmless fun. Astrology, however, used to hold a much greater power over people than now, but this is not to say that millions of people do not read horoscopes weekly or daily, in the English-speaking world alone. Aspects of magic, future prediction and witchcraft con-tinue to hold a fascination for many people.

Holst was mostly interested in the depiction of the planets as having some kind of personality, associated with their supposed astrological significance. A planet, however, of which our own earth is a prime, if special, example, is basically a lump of rock, which orbits around a sun with great regularity. In our solar system, there are nine identified planets, some of which have moons. So far, the only planet known to support any form of life is our own. Thus any qualities or personality traits attributed to a planet amount to a metaphorical description. In our day and age, though, we can see the planets' names as linking them within a range of mythical deities. Thus the names of Holst's planets are also the names of Roman gods, and his portrayal of them blends together the mythological, the astrological, the historical and the scientific.

If we consider 'Mars', the opening movement, subtitled 'The Bringer of War', we are reminded immediately of Mars, the god of war in Roman mythology. Mars was significant in Rome, not only as the war-god, but also as the father of Romulus, after whom the city was named. In many European languages the month of March is named after him.

The movement is march-like, almost belligerent, and marks a striking opening to the suite. Repeated percussion can be menacing (as Shostakovich also demonstrated in his *Seventh Symphony*, where he depicts the siege of Leningrad with a very similar approach), and strident brass and pulsating rhythms all combine to portray the threat of war. (In mythology, trumpets were associated both with war and with Mars.) *The Planets* was written in 1915, when Europe was in the grip of the worst war ever seen, so there is a realism here that should not escape us. In September 1918, Holst was sent by the YMCA to Salonika (Thessalonica) and Constantinople to organize and direct soldiers' music-making, and just before he went, he asked Sir Adrian Boult to conduct *The Planets* at the Queens' Hall in London. The war was soon to end, of course, but Holst departed for the war-ravaged continent with his own depiction of war ringing in his ears.

None of this has anything to do with the 'red planet', nor with any suggestion that if there is life on Mars, it will be violent! Holst had used the idea of a god of war, after whom a planet was named, to portray the menace of war. The idea that there should be a god of war is anachronistic and distasteful, and the idea that the God and Father of our Lord Jesus Christ should be a bringer of war is no less abhorrent. Nevertheless, war and violence always were, and still are part of this planet's daily routine, tragic as that is. Perhaps now we are better able to admit that the causes of war are invariably human error and sin, and that war is not brought upon us by some malevolent deity with a will to destroy part of creation. When we listen to 'Mars, the Bringer of War', we must remember that *we* are the bringer of war, not God. As a society, we must repent of that, and be faithful to Christ's calling us to peace.

Holst is not only interested in Mars and war, of course. The even more famous depiction of 'Jupiter, the Bringer of Jollity', from which was taken the tune to 'I vow to thee, my country' (Thaxted), is boisterous, hopeful and lyrical. Holst can be heard enjoying himself, and so can we. Jupiter, also known as Jove (from which the exclamation 'by Jove' is derived), was revered as the special protector of Rome. But as Christians we may want to claim this movement as a depiction of love, friendship and happiness.

The Planets became one of the most popular and well-known musical works of the twentieth century, and is still popular today, but it has not become so because of its astrological basis or its attempt to describe the solar system. It is successful because it is a striking collection of splendid movements, orchestrated superbly for large forces. Holst's astrological or mythological designs, which were a means to an end, have become sidelined, just as have the mythological beliefs associated with Roman gods.

St Paul spoke to the Athenians about an unknown God (Acts 17:22–32), and told them that the God of Jesus Christ made the whole earth, and would one day be revealed as Creator of all. Thus, St Paul told the Greeks that it was time to move on from multiple, statuesque gods, to the knowledge of the one, true, hitherto unknown God. God, who was in Christ, takes over, in both Greek and Roman cultures, from Jupiter, Mars, Zeus, Poseidon and all the rest, and in him we see and recognize some of the qualities which had been attributed individually to them. In Christ is revealed the God of love, the God of joy, the God of hope, the God of peace, all rolled into one, supreme being. For Christ is the very image of the invisible God, and is the firstborn of all creation, the word made flesh, predating and superseding mythical figures. Since, in him, all things in heaven and on earth were made, we have no need of astrology to determine or predict our behaviour, and we certainly do not need to see the alignment of planets as somehow affecting our mental or spiritual lives. Nor do we need gods of jollity, or of the sea, and we certainly do not need gods of war.

The alignment of planets does of course affect the physical world (the moon affects tides, for example), but we must always maintain a grip on the singular truth that we have free will and are responsible for our own actions. We are free to make war or love, free to sin, and free to repent so that we may be freed *from* sin and the eternal damage that it does. Gustav Holst's alignment of *The Planets* produced a creative outpouring of music for his time, sounding chords that still resonate in a pluralistic, war-torn, pleasure-seeking world that is fascinated by the mysterious and the magical. It is nevertheless a sinful world, which we cannot ignore, and in which we all play a part. For us, let the sin be redeemed, let the magic be that of God's infinite love, and let the mystery be of God's creating power, made manifest in earth and universe.

PRAYER

Creator of the ceaseless round of planets in their course, create in us a singular desire for you. Keep us constantly in the orbit of Christ's love, so that he may be always at the centre of our lives, pulling us ever towards your heavenly glory. For you reign, Father of heaven, Christ incarnate, Spirit ever dwelling, one God, here and everywhere. Amen.

For further reading: Acts 17
For listening: A movement from Holst's *The Planets*, especially 'Mars' or 'Jupiter'

'AGAINST THE COSMIC FORCES OF DARKNESS'

PAUL DUKAS—*THE SORCERER'S APPRENTICE*

Finally, be strong in the Lord and in the strength of his power. Put on the whole armour of God, so that you may be able to stand against the wiles of the devil. For our struggle is not against enemies of blood and flesh, but against the rulers, against the authorities, against the cosmic powers of this present darkness, against the spiritual forces of evil in the heavenly places. Therefore take up the whole armour of God, so that you may be able to withstand on that evil day, and having done everything, to stand firm. Stand therefore, and fasten the belt of truth around your waist, and put on the breastplate of righteousness. As shoes for your feet put on whatever will make you ready to proclaim the gospel of peace. With all of these, take the shield of faith, with which you will be able to quench all the flaming arrows of the evil one. Take the helmet of salvation, and the sword of the Spirit, which is the word of God. Pray in the Spirit at all times in every prayer and supplication. To that end keep alert and always persevere in supplication for all the saints. Pray also for me, so that when I speak, a message may be given to me to make known with boldness the mystery of the gospel.

EPHESIANS 6:10–19

Gustav Holst's interest in astrology is something that many people share today, since horoscopes are still widely consulted. Many would love to believe that they contained some truth, and some do believe that they do. Our society is similarly fascinated by magic and witchcraft. The *Harry Potter* books have not only raised awareness of magic itself, but they have reminded us that we are interested in magic. Many people are interested in magic because the very idea appeals to them or fascinates them, while others are very interested in it because they are concerned about the fact that so many other people are interested in magic for the wrong reasons. This is why Harry Potter and his chums have been both so popular, and so controversial.

Yet, there is nothing new about this. In Shakespeare's time, people were so interested in witches that they even took the trouble to burn them at the stake (although it is doubtful that many of the poor old ladies who suffered in this cruel way were really in league with the devil). *Macbeth* is a prime example of a work of literature involving witchcraft.

Over 100 years later, in 1779, the German writer Goethe wrote the poem called 'The Sorcerer's Apprentice'. In the poem, we hear how a master wizard leaves the apprentice to carry water while he is out, but the boy, who has observed many tricks, thinks he can avoid a bit of hard work by casting a spell on a broom, so that it will do the carrying. All goes well until the requisite amount of water is transferred, but then the apprentice realizes that he cannot stop what he has started. He does not know the spell to stop the broom:

> *Stop, for, lo!*
> *All the measure*
> *Of thy treasure*
> *Now is right!*
> *Ah, I see it! woe, oh woe!*
> *I forget the word of might.*

He successfully chops the broom in half, only to find that he now has a double problem, as both broom-halves start to fetch water! In desperation he cries for his master, who fortuitously returns to end the spell:

> *And they run! and wetter still*
> *Grow the steps and grows the hall.*

Lord and master, hear me call!
Ever seems the flood to fill.
Ah, he's coming! see,
Great is my dismay!
Spirits raised by me
Vainly would I lay!

It is this brief poem of Goethe's which the French composer Paul Dukas represented musically in 1897, and which Walt Disney illustrated in *Fantasia*, casting Mickey Mouse as the hapless student. The music is vivid and lively, and we can hear water rushing in the frenetic string and woodwind writing. There are themes in the work for the conjuring of the spell, and then for the broom rushing about with buckets of water, all brought to comic life by Walt Disney. And yet, this is no comedy; this is a story about a student who bites off more than he can chew. It is a story about a boy who dabbles with magic and nearly drowns in the resulting torrent of chaos, powered by supernatural forces he cannot control.

In the eighteenth, nineteenth and twentieth centuries, Goethe and Dukas and Disney all describe a sorcerer's apprentice who messes up. In the twenty-first century we have witnessed the artistic arrival of Harry Potter, apprentice sorcerer extraordinaire, to whose exploits millions are addicted. He and Mickey Mouse have a lot in common: they experiment, learn, are taught, and get it wrong sometimes. In this much, both, funnily enough, are very human, and endear themselves to us. For many, this makes them harmless, attractive, even exemplary characters.

A cursory surf of the Internet will reveal that many find the exploits of young Master Potter particularly troubling, because he is seen as an advocate of witchcraft. The vehemence with which some critics have attacked him and his creator J.K. Rowling is striking. It is also slightly amusing, for they hurl quotations from the Bible at him as though it were some kind of spell book to be opened and quoted from at will. The problem with opening a book and hurling magic words at people or objects, as the sorcerer's apprentice was to learn, is that there is more to it than that, and if you do not know what you are doing, you can end up in very deep water! We must be very wary of witchcraft, even today, but we must not become obsessed by its presence around us. We must not ignore the devil, nor must we give him too much attention!

The Bible has something to say about witchcraft, and without quoting little chunks of it to support our case, we can be quite clear that a living faith in our Lord Jesus Christ does not encompass sorcery, spiritualism or spell books. There is only one wizard in the New Testament, who was called Simon Magus (Magus means 'magician', see Acts 8:4–24). He wanted to buy the apostles' tricks, as he saw them, and was the first person to commit the sin named after him: that of simony, the selling of the gifts of faith. Peter condemns him harshly for it, and issues what sounds like a curse: 'May your silver perish…'.

Writing in the second century, Justin Martyr says that Simon Magus went to Rome in the time of Emperor Claudius (AD41–54), and Hippolytus, writing in the third century, says that Simon came into conflict with Peter again in Rome, and that he perished dramatically through a failure of one of his magic tricks. According to Clement of Rome, a debate and competition took place between Peter and Simon Magus in the presence of the Emperor Nero, and Simon tried to prove he was God by flying from a tower. He succeeded in doing this until Peter challenged the devil, who was behind it all, and Simon crashed to the ground and was smashed into four pieces.

This part of the story is not in the Bible, but it does go to show how we are continually inspired by our imaginations. Here we see a magician judged and brought to a dramatic end. A battle between good and evil is won by Peter, all to illustrate the victory of light over darkness. In the story, the powers compete for human attention, interest and loyalty, and the light of Christ wins, overcoming the darkness of sin. The story illustrates a desired moral and theological outcome.

Is it so different today? Human beings are just as interested in sorcery, magic and witchcraft as we were in the first century—and indeed in Shakespeare's time, when Macbeth went to the heath to chat up some dodgy hags in thunder, lightning and rain! It is hardly different when the sorcerer's apprentice plays with his master's spell book and is swept away. Harry Potter has the same problem sometimes. This is the same old story, with the cauldron fuelled by renewed imagination, technology, globalization and money. Since time immemorial we have found spiritual evil wherever there has been spiritual goodness, just as there is always darkness wherever there is light in the world. These are recurring themes and ancient realities. And wherever there is a whiff of witchcraft, there will be witch-hunters.

Yet, in Christ, there is no darkness, and if we enter dark places with Christ as our light, we can identify evil, and have no fear of it. That's why we can watch or read *Harry Potter*, or enjoy *The Sorcerer's Apprentice*. But this is also why it is so important that we and our young people are spiritually equipped to walk with Christ and know his ways of goodness and truth. For that we need nothing less than the armour of God, as described in Ephesians 6:10–19.

This Lent, let our hearts not be too troubled by fantastical stories and musical wizardry. But let us ensure that we are not led astray by them, nor that we allow them to become stumbling-blocks to our little ones. And let us all be sharpened in our pursuit of the light of Christ and of all things good and honest and true, so that the real magic of resurrection touches us on Easter day, breaking the spell of death and pointing us all to a better, brighter life with God, Father, Son and Holy Spirit.

PRAYER

O God our master, in whose Book of Life are written all the saints and angels of heaven, protect us in the face of evil, and by your Spirit of wisdom and love, teach us to follow your laws and walk in the footsteps of your Son Jesus, so that we may inherit the eternal kingdom which you have prepared for us by the saving work of the same, Jesus Christ our Lord. Amen.

For further reading: Acts 8:4–24
For listening: Dukas' *The Sorcerer's Apprentice*

'ALL THE PEOPLES, NATIONS, AND LANGUAGES FELL DOWN AND WORSHIPPED'

BENJAMIN BRITTEN—*THE YOUNG PERSON'S GUIDE TO THE ORCHESTRA*

... the herald proclaimed aloud, 'You are commanded, O peoples, nations, and languages, that when you hear the sound of the horn, pipe, lyre, trigon, harp, drum, and entire musical ensemble, you are to fall down and worship the golden statue that King Nebuchadnezzar has set up. Whoever does not fall down and worship shall immediately be thrown into a furnace of blazing fire.' Therefore, as soon as all the peoples heard the sound of the horn, pipe, lyre, trigon, harp, drum, and entire musical ensemble, all the peoples, nations, and languages fell down and worshipped the golden statue that King Nebuchadnezzar had set up.

DANIEL 3:4–7

Benjamin Britten (1913–76) was one of England's greatest composers, and he wrote a great deal of music which draws on biblical and liturgical texts. Today we turn to what is probably his most popular and well-known piece, the theme and variations called *The Young Person's Guide to the Orchestra*.

This piece, which lasts under 20 minutes, was written in 1946 in order to teach the sound and style of the instruments of the orchestra in a demonstrative way. The work can be performed with a narrator explaining what is going on, and is sometimes found coupled with

Saint-Saens' *The Carnival of the Animals* and *Peter and the Wolf*, on recordings or at concerts intended for young people. Educative as it is, *The Young Person's Guide* is not child's play. The instruments of the orchestra are shown off in a dazzling display of virtuosity, with each instrument or group of instruments having a moment of glory as the whole piece builds up to a fantastic finale. This unique composition, like Béla Bartók's *Concerto for Orchestra*, is something of a test piece, providing opportunity to show off brilliance of individual and collective playing, and, by the same token, is full of tricky corners and difficult passages. Pieces like this often sound hard—and they are!

The tune, or theme of the piece, was not composed by Britten, but was lifted from Henry Purcell's incidental music to Aphra Behn's *Abdelazer*, which was performed in Drury Lane and published in 1695. The theme is broad and regal, and lends itself to adaptation and variation. Britten states it at the beginning with full orchestra, then with woodwind, then brass, then strings, and then even percussion alone, all playing the tune in their family groups, giving a hint of what is to come. Next, variations follow for different instruments, first flutes, then oboes, clarinets, bassoons, violins, and so on, as we cruise through the orchestra, with not only varying timbres, but also moving through different moods, different velocities and volumes of sound.

Britten's piece is inevitably, and deliberately, a demonstration of the old adage that the 'sum of the parts is greater than the whole'. The finale is a stunning piece of technical and musical brilliance, with both composer and instrumentalists showing just what can be done with a full orchestra. As the work reaches a climax, we are perhaps not aware that the final section is beginning. Piccolos, playing the highest notes, flutter in the stratosphere, and the other instruments gradually join in. The structure is known as a fugue, a term which derives from the Italian *fuga*, which means 'flight'. And sure enough this is a rollercoaster flight of fancy, as the theme is bounced around the orchestra. Then, the original theme, which has not been heard for about a quarter of an hour, reappears in a blazing fanfare from the brass section of the orchestra, over the top of the other theme, with which the strings are still fiddling. This makes the finale a 'double fugue', with two separate themes competing and collaborating at the same time.

Musically, this is a *tour de force*, a joyous and exhilarating romp through the orchestra. Emotionally it is positive, joyful and expresses *joie de vivre* and delight in creation, musical and divine. On another level, Britten's masterpiece is an allegory of human life, because of the way in which he employs so many different resources to both individual and corporate effect. The individual, unique nature of each instrument is given centre stage, if only briefly, and we can hear what is distinctive about each instrument, as each is demonstrated at the highest level of skill. On the other hand, we hear at the very beginning the full orchestra collaborating in a most harmonious way, and then at the end there is this amazing piece of 'working together'. And yet the finale is not simply about unison—far from it! The fugue involves playing the same music, but in different ways, and while there must be a harmonic and rhythmic togetherness, there is also an individuality which makes the similarity of the music interesting. It takes genius to be able to weave together the parts of a fugue, particularly on such a large scale. Thus, in the orchestra, there really is a sense of the instrumentalists 'playing together', where the emphasis is on 'play'. They are free to dance, as it were, and yet, while it may all sound like some kind of free improvisation, it is tightly and tautly held together by what the composer has written in the score. Britten's *The Young Person's Guide* is a beautiful example of freedom and discipline married musically.

That much we can carry into our lives, as we reflect on the way that God in Christ gives us structures and models for life, but at the same time does not expect us to be rigid, hidebound pilgrims all walking identical roads, and singing in unison. We all sing the same tune perhaps—the song of the Lamb, the song of Jesus, crucified, risen, ascended, but through time and space we sing not in unison but polyphonically—that is, in lots of parts, all blending together, and moving us all forward to the goal that is Christ (Philippians 3:12–16).

We are all on that flight—that roller-coaster of life, with its ups and downs. We are all taking part in that great fugue—not a double fugue, but an infinite fugue, in which God's theme is constantly played and sung by countless followers, all in their own way, but always true to that theme of loving redemption. It is Christ's theme, on which we play out our variations, not so much with skill, but with varying degrees of enthusiasm. There is no such thing as a virtuoso Christian, of course, even though we do have some saints to admire and relish, as we all strive to play our part in the great pilgrimage of the faithful.

Let us therefore relish our diversity, our uniqueness as created, faithful beings, and always strive to sing the song of the Lord in our own distinctive way, but never forgetting the tune that we have been taught in Jesus Christ. Thus, like Daniel, when we hear all the instruments of the orchestra, the 'sound of the horn, pipe, lyre, trigon, harp, drum, and entire musical ensemble', we will fall down on our knees, not to some unknown, humanly imagined God of pleasure and self-justification, but will offer our polyphonic praise to God, Father, Son and Holy Spirit.

PRAYER

God our Father, who has created this world to possess a wealth of diversity, help us to value and witness to our uniqueness, as your creatures and as individuals. Give us grace to turn our differences to joyful and loving ends, so that as we strive towards the perfection only found in your Son Jesus Christ, we may rejoice in our fellowship and inspire others to come and join our song. This we ask for the sake of the same, Jesus Christ our Lord. Amen.

For further reading: Philippians 3:8–17
For listening: All, or the introduction and finale of Britten's *The Young Person's Guide to the Orchestra*

'THERE WAS SILENCE IN HEAVEN
FOR ABOUT HALF AN HOUR'

JOHN CAGE—4'33"

When the Lamb opened the seventh seal, there was silence in heaven for about half an hour. And I saw the seven angels who stand before God, and seven trumpets were given to them. Another angel with a golden censer came and stood at the altar; he was given a great quantity of incense to offer with the prayers of all the saints on the golden altar that is before the throne. And the smoke of the incense, with the prayers of the saints, rose before God from the hand of the angel. Then the angel took the censer and filled it with fire from the altar and threw it on the earth; and there were peals of thunder, rumblings, flashes of lightning, and an earthquake.

REVELATION 8:1–5

No one these days lives amid a great deal of silence. Acoustic ecologists, as they call themselves, tell us that the roar of an airliner can sometimes be heard 32 kilometres away. In 1805 when the American explorers Meriweather Lewis and William Clark first crossed America, they knew they had reached the Pacific Ocean when they heard it raging, even though they were still 29 kilometres away from the seashore.

There is, in fact, no such thing as silence. As well as writing a book on the subject, the American composer John Cage (1912–92) famously composed a work of 'sound organization', as he called it, which involves a performer playing not even a single note. The score of 4'33" is published, and if you have money to spare you can buy a copy which consists of very little except a piece of blank paper with the word 'tacet' written upon it. 'Tacet' means 'keep quiet', and is the kind of instruction that brass or percussion players are used to seeing on their music while the orchestra plays a slow or quiet movement of a symphony. Cage's musical joke instructs all the performers (if there are more than one!) to keep quiet throughout the whole performance, which he has deter-mined should last for precisely four minutes and thirty-three seconds. Some performers open and close a piano lid to mark the beginning and end of the piece, so that the audience knows exactly when to listen.

Cage's piece, whether we want to call it 'music' or not, makes a real point. Cage never claimed that it was a piece of music (he called it 'sound organization'), but insisted on providing the opportunity for listeners to do exactly that—to *listen*, and to listen not to players or singers, but to the sounds that occur involuntarily in any particular place over that period of time. Four minutes and thirty-three seconds is significant, because it adds up to a total of 273 seconds, and minus 273 degrees Celsius is Absolute Zero (zero degrees on the Kelvin scale)—a temperature below which no measurement has been taken. Thus the title of Cage's piece subtly refers to absolute nothingness.

If we do 'listen' for that length of time, under what might be called concert conditions, when we are deliberatively and consciously attentive to the sounds around us, we will hear far from nothing. Not only will we find that four and a half minutes is quite a long time (most hymns take less time than this to sing), but we will find that there are plenty of noises occurring around us, whether in country or city, which are easily heard if we listen to them. Even if we were to retreat to a soundproof room, we would hear the sounds of our own bodies. There is, according to Cage, no such thing as silence where any human being is alive. The only real silence we might encounter is what the psalmist calls the 'silence of the grave': 'The dead do not praise the Lord, nor do any that go down into silence' (Psalm 115:17).

Complete and utter silence is perhaps more of an ideal, only achievable in the context of eternity. We encounter true silence in the book of Revelation when the Lamb opens the seventh seal, and there is silence in heaven, for about half an hour (seven times longer than Cage's piece!). Half an hour is quite a long time, even in eternity, and we would expect heaven to be a very noisy place, with all that praise and singing going on. It certainly becomes so when the angels start blowing their trumpets! But this sole, one-off silence of heaven is an anticipatory silence, stemming the clamour of praise at the momentous opening of the seventh and final seal.

Being silent is not about doing or being nothing. Nor is it about making no noise. The composer Cage knew this, and anyone who prays in silence knows its value and its fullness. Silence is rarely empty spiritually, and spiritual silence for us is rarely characterized by the complete absence of noise. Silence, more today than ever, is a treasured gift. It is a treasure which, if we accept or find it, can give us space for spiritual anticipation. What we consider to be silence can be the space in which we wait for God. We may not be able to achieve complete silence, but we can hope for stillness. We may hear our own heartbeat in the midst of it, but then our heart yearns for God who set it beating in the first place, and who will receive us into perfect silence the moment it stops. We may be reminded of more words from the Psalms: 'For God alone my soul waits in silence; from him comes my salvation' (Psalm 62:1).

Elijah found God in the silence, rather than in the raging of sea, or flames (see 1 Kings 19:11–12). The tradition of silent contemplation continues today, whether in silent monastic orders, silent retreats, or forms of private prayer that are located in deliberate silence. However, a silent environment is almost impossible to find these days, and finding time and space for peace and quiet is not always easy. But if silence is not really about the lack of physical noise, more about a spiritual waiting-place, then there is some hope for us—some hope that in the midst of busy and noisy lives, we may yet find a private corner for holy quiet. And if we succeed, it may yet be a place where four and a half minutes, or even half an hour of silence is not such a long time in the company of God, Father, Son and Holy Spirit.

PRAYER

O God of rushing wind and still silence, by your grace, give us peace and time for prayer, that we may come to know you in the quietness of our own hearts, so that at the last day, when trumpets sound and angels sing, we may rejoice with all the saints and angels, to the honour and glory of your holy name. Amen.

For further reading: 1 Kings 19:9–18
For listening: Perform John Cage's 4'33" either in a group, or yourself in a peaceful and quiet place

'GO FORTH UPON THY JOURNEY, CHRISTIAN SOUL!'

EDWARD ELGAR—*THE DREAM OF GERONTIUS*

Go forth upon thy journey, Christian soul!
Go from this world! Go, in the name of God
The omniscient Father, Who created thee!
Go, in the Name of Jesus Christ our Lord,
Son of the living God, Who bled for thee!
Go, in the name of the Holy Spirit,
Who hath been poured out on thee!
Go in the name
Of Angels and Archangels; in the name
Of Princedoms and of Powers; and in the name
Of Cherubim and Seraphim: go forth!
Go, in the name of Patriarchs and Prophets!
And of Apostles and Evangelists,
Of Martyrs and Confessors, in the name
Of holy Monks and Hermits; in the name
Of holy virgins; and all saints of God,
Both men and women, Go!
Go on thy course;
And may thy dwelling be the Holy Mount
Of Sion; through the Same,
Through Christ our Lord.

FROM *THE DREAM OF GERONTIUS*, 1865, CARDINAL JOHN HENRY NEWMAN (1801–90)

There used to be a tradition at the Royal Albert Hall in London that every Ash Wednesday, Edward Elgar's masterpiece *The Dream of Gerontius* would be performed. It is perhaps surprising that this work found a place at the heart of modern English spirituality, after a very inauspicious opening night at the Birmingham Music Festival on 3 October 1900. In spite of Elgar's conviction, which he inscribed on the original manuscript that 'this is the best of me', the first performance was beset with problems, which meant that *Gerontius* did not get a very fair hearing. The chorus-master died during rehearsals, and the conductor did not know the music well enough. The fact that Elgar left the choice of text undecided until quite late did not help matters.

Popular acclaim soon put *Gerontius* back on the right footing, and it became a staple of the English choral repertoire. It is a very 'English' work, yet it is hardly 'Anglican', as it was written by two Victorian Roman Catholics. It is about an old man dying, and yet it is very popular. Two parts of Newman's text have found their way into the hymn repertoire, as 'Praise to the holiest in the height' and 'Firmly I believe and truly', although in those contexts the words are set to very different music.

Newman's text is not biblical, although it does contain many allusions, particularly to the book of Revelation. Parts of the work are considered by some to be rather mawkish, or over-sentimentalized, and theologically speaking, Newman's commitment to the idea of praying to the Virgin Mary for the souls of the faithful departed raises eyebrows if not hackles in some ecclesiastical circles. The first lines of the oratorio set out this very approach: 'Jesu, Maria—I am near to death, and thou art calling me... (Jesu have mercy, Mary, pray for me)'. Yet there is a very human dimension expressed at the outset that almost transcends theological debate. Whatever we may feel about purgatory, hell and heaven, here is a human being crying out in his 'extremity', and we cannot avoid the knowledge that we too will one day be where he is, even though we do not know how or when death will come to us, nor how we will react, if we will be able to (1 Thessalonians 5:2). Gerontius, whose name means merely 'old man', is Everyman and Everywoman, and that is why we can relate to his predicament immediately.

Gerontius stands apart from numerous requiem masses composed throughout musical history, because here we have the events which precede and follow death creatively presented through the senses of the dying person. There is a small role for the priest, who, in the text printed here, commends Gerontius to God with words which have found their way even into modern funeral services. In *Gerontius* we live and die with the main protagonist, and in doing so we may be helped to realize that in the presence of God, it is not our doctrine of Christ that saves us, but our recognition of his saving power. Our death is not a theological event, but a very human experience. Newman and Elgar help us to understand this, enabling us to travel through the distress, shame, guilt, relief and comfort that the journey of death, judgment and redemption may bring to each and every one of us.

Overall, *Gerontius* is a comforting work. All ends happily, and in showing us the Christian soul's journey to eternal bliss, it encourages us to believe in that journey as being one which we may endure and survive. The idea of death as a journey of endurance is maybe not one we all share, but then, on the other hand, are we really to expect a cosy cuddling-up to God as soon as our time comes? The Christian perspective on the four last things—death, judgment, heaven and hell—needs to accommodate the realities of sin and judgment while at the same time acknowledging a natural fear of them. It is the human lot to fear death and the divine gift to save us from it. It would seem sensible to maintain a balanced perspective that is not overly fearful, nor arrogantly confident. By faith we are assured eternal life, but at the same time we are aware of our own mortality and the inevitability of being called to account. Newman's poem, and consequently Elgar's musical setting of it, locates their particular brand of balancing act in the midst of purgatory, hail Marys and intercession for the dead, but the basic desire to come to terms with death and judgment transcends this distinctively Roman Catholic approach. Ultimately, when we die we meet our Maker, and Elgar's musical dreamwork puts us in touch with the emotional force of that unique event.

There is a sense in which the story of *Gerontius* is mythological. It has little basis in fact, nor even in biblical revelation, for at the end of the work Gerontius is left in purgatory. Such a place has been rejected by Protestant theologians as having no scriptural basis, as well as being a potentially distasteful location in which souls are 'purged' of sins before being made sufficiently clean to enter into the presence of God. Purgatory, as a place, seems to imply that sins are washed away, not so much by love and pure spring waters of heaven, but by fire and torment, all for a later, greater good. The doctrine which points to purgatory was first promulgated by the Roman Catholic Church at the Council of Florence between 1438 and 1445, suggesting a medieval origin. Protestant reformers denounced the idea of purgatory as being not only unnecessary and unhelpful, but barely founded in scripture. It is probably correct to say that purgatory is not fashionable today, but it would be false to say that no one believes in it any more. Whether Elgar and Newman believed in such a spiritual place or not (and they probably did), it certainly held dramatic and musical potential, the fruits of which still move us today.

When we hear that most uplifting rendition of Newman's great hymn 'Praise to the holiest' as set in the oratorio, and when we are stunned by the great percussive crash as Gerontius is 'taken away' towards the end of the work, we can be moved by the realism of the depiction of his experience of death. Interestingly enough, the voice of God is not present in the work; he does not speak, even though faith in him is constantly being expressed. The final encounter with God is left to our own imaginations. Gerontius is prepared by an angel to meet God, Father, Son and Holy Spirit, but this is a private affair which must and does take place beyond the scope of the piece.

Our faith in redemption, our hope in a positive outcome to judgment brought about in Christ, must ultimately consist in a one-to-one relationship between each of us and God. We may be inspired, moved, even helped by the experiences of other, fictional or real, people, but in the end, the only person who stands with us as we stand before Christ, is, paradoxically, Christ. In judgment, Christ stands as judge, but also as Saviour. Only he has authority to judge us, and only he has power to save us. Thus it is he whom we fear and he in whom we put our trust.

PRAYER

O Christ our Friend and Saviour, let not your judgment fall heavy on us and on those whom we love. By the divine love you revealed in your human life, have mercy on us; help us to come to repentance that we may live in the light of your salvation, and reveal yourself to the world as redeemer and rescuer of all who put their trust in you. For you reign with the Father and the Holy Spirit, ever one God, now and in all eternity. Amen.

For further reading: Revelation 20:11—21:8
For listening: The following movements from Elgar's *The Dream of Gerontius*: 'Go forth upon thy journey'; 'Praise to the holiest'; 'Take me away'; 'Softly and gently'

'DO NOT LOOK BACK'

CHRISTOPH WILLIBALD VON GLUCK— *ORPHEUS AND EURYDICE*

When morning dawned, the angels urged Lot, saying, 'Get up, take your wife and your two daughters who are here, or else you will be consumed in the punishment of the city.' But he lingered; so the men seized him and his wife and his two daughters by the hand, the Lord being merciful to him, and they brought him out and left him outside the city. When they had brought them outside, they said, 'Flee for your life; do not look back or stop anywhere in the Plain; flee to the hills, or else you will be consumed.' And Lot said to them, 'Oh, no, my lords; your servant has found favour with you, and you have shown me great kindness in saving my life; but I cannot flee to the hills, for fear the disaster will overtake me and I die. Look, that city is near enough to flee to, and it is a little one. Let me escape there—is it not a little one?—and my life will be saved!' He said to him, 'Very well, I grant you this favour too, and will not overthrow the city of which you have spoken. Hurry, escape there, for I can do nothing until you arrive there.' Therefore the city was called Zoar. The sun had risen on the earth when Lot came to Zoar.

Then the Lord rained on Sodom and Gomorrah sulphur and fire from the Lord out of heaven; and he overthrew those cities, and all the Plain, and all the inhabitants of the cities, and what grew on the ground. But Lot's wife, behind him, looked back, and she became a pillar of salt.
GENESIS 19:15–26

This story from the Old Testament leads up to the destruction of Sodom and Gomorrah, and shares a remarkable feature with the ancient Greek myth of Orpheus. In both stories, the main character is granted a reprieve from grief and despair, but is told not to look back. It is interesting to note that in both Hebrew and Greek cultures, there are stories which deal with obedience and temptation in this way. Both are highly relevant in Lent, when we recall Jesus' temptations, and strive to be more obedient to his will. Particularly at this time of year, we are invited to turn away from sin, and to turn to Christ. When we do so, we should not 'look back', but 'hold fast to what we have attained', and 'press on towards the goal for the prize of the heavenly call of God in Christ' (Philippians 3:14–16).

The story of Orpheus and Eurydice has inspired many generations of musicians and poets because Orpheus was the mythical musician and poet to whose gifts many aspired. Legend held that he was given a lute by the god Apollo, and could charm beasts with it. Orpheus travelled widely, and married the nymph Eurydice. Bitten by a snake, she died, and the action in Gluck's opera begins at her grave.

Orpheus is bereft, and sings a lament as the funeral rite begins. A light, symbolizing their marriage, is deliberately extinguished, to signify that it is over, ended by death. After the funeral, Orpheus is left alone, and his sorrow turns to anger, which he directs at the gods. Amor, the god of love, hears Orpheus; taking pity on him, he allows him to travel to the underworld to fetch Eurydice back. He imposes one condition: that Orpheus must not turn and look at her on their journey away from the place of the dead. Nor is he allowed to show her any affection while in the underworld. Orpheus will have to suppress his natural lover's instincts when he encounters her, until the right time. He accepts the trial, and prepares to enter the world of death.

In the second act, Orpheus journeys to the underworld and meets the furies, who try to scare him away. He plays his lute and they are calmed by his ethereal music; he is allowed to pass through to the Elysian Fields, where blessed souls dance in eternal happiness (accompanied by a delightful flute solo). Elysium represents a pre-Christian vision of heaven, and some of our preconceptions about a special place of enjoyment are undoubtedly rooted in these mythical Greek fields of delight. The *Champs Elysées* in Paris is named after them. Surrounded by the blessed spirits, Eurydice enters, singing about how happy she is there, but Orpheus is able to lead her away by the hand, and according to the bargain, he does not look at her.

Act Three is set in a dark cavern, where we find the two lovers. Orpheus is able to resist looking at her and kissing her, which inevitably means that her joy on seeing him turns to doubt when she encounters his strange and aloof behaviour. He cannot explain, and begs her to trust him. They both become distraught and he succumbs, turning to look at her. As he does so, she dies again. It is a heart-stopping moment, as we realize that he has lost her for the second time. Orpheus sings the lament '*Che faro senza Euridice*' ('What shall I do without Eurydice?'), a beautiful aria which demonstrates that music does not have to be in a minor key to express sadness. It is composed in C major, often considered a 'bright' key, and yet with eloquence and poise, Orpheus' aria displays a mixture of despair and stoicism in the face of loss and defeat. He calls for her, but in vain, and he decides that if she cannot join him in life, he will join her in death. Amor reappears and intervenes, for Orpheus' grief has moved the gods to spare Eurydice again. Thus she springs to life again, this time for good, and with much rejoicing the opera ends.

The story of Orpheus has inspired much art and literature over many centuries, and it is worth noting that this 'happy' ending to the tale is not part of the original myth as handed on by Virgil, Ovid and Seneca, who end their tale with Eurydice returned to Hades and Orpheus finally ripped to pieces by the maenad women, who punish him for his coward-ice. It was Boethius, standing at the intersection of the classical and medieval worlds, who in *The Consolations of Philosophy*, retold the story of Orpheus, giving it a Christian meaning. Boethius was executed on charges of treason around 525 in the Italian city of Pavia, on the orders of the Ostrogoth King Theodoric. Boethius wrote the five books of the *Consolations* while imprisoned awaiting execution. The third book con-cludes with a reflection on Orpheus' story, which contains the passage:

> *Orpheus backwards turned his sight*
> *And, looking, lost and killed her there.*
> *For you I sing this sad affair,*
> *Whoever seek the upward way*
> *To lift your mind into the day;*

For who gives in and turns his eye
Back to darkness from the sky,
Loses while he looks below
All that up with him may go.

Boethius' take on the story is not dissimilar to the way in which a Christian might read the story of Lot's escape from Sodom. Once we have discovered that our salvation is to be found in God, there can be no turning back to former ways, and our way forward can only lie in repentance and forgiveness. Thus the story of Orpheus became Christianized, and because it did so, it was popular in Renaissance and Enlightenment Europe. Monteverdi used the story in his ground-breaking *Orfeo* of 1607, while Christoph Willibald von Gluck (1714–87) broke new ground with his version, first performed in Vienna in 1762. Musically speaking, it was revolutionary, defining new bounds for simplicity of speech-setting and, being less than an hour and a half in duration, it was remarkably short. Ballet and chorus items are part of the action, which all produced an emotional impact hitherto unheard of. Thus, in all respects, Gluck's opera is forward-looking, and embedded in it is the spiritual and moral truth that to look back is death while life is to be found by moving forward with Christ, our spiritual bridegroom, with whom we will be united once the trials of life are over.

PRAYER

O God of all gods, and Lord of all lords, who raised your Son from death to open a new way forward into your eternal presence, without your love we are nothing and without your guidance we are lost. Forgive us when we wander in the wrong direction, and lead us by your Spirit towards our heavenly home, where you reign, Trinity in Unity, now and for ever. Amen.

For further reading: Philippians 3:10–16
For listening: '*Che faro senza Euridice?*' or 'The dance of the Blessed Spirits' from Gluck's *Orpheus and Eurydice*

'ETERNAL REST GRANT UNTO THEM, O LORD'

MAURICE DURUFLÉ—*REQUIEM*

Eternal rest grant unto them, O Lord, and let perpetual light shine upon them. You shall be praised in Sion, O God, and homage shall be paid to you in Jerusalem. Hear my prayer, all flesh shall come before you.

REQUIEM—'REQUIEM AETERNAM'

The French composer Maurice Duruflé (1902–86) is not well-known outside the world of organ music, and where he is known, it is usually because of his *Requiem*, which he completed in 1947. Duruflé, unlike some, was not a composer who could or would write quickly. His widow, and former pupil, Marie-Madeleine Duruflé-Chevalier, once said of him that he would spend a whole morning writing five bars of music (maybe only a few seconds in duration), and would then tear them up in the afternoon. For Duruflé, the creative process was a painstaking, even painful process.

Death, too, is a painful process, and it strains everyone close to it, drawing out a range of emotions and physical effects. Tiredness, lassitude, despair, anger and misery are only a few that we might name when considering the complex nature of grief. Another element of grief is the desire to believe and know that all is well with a loved one who has died. We want to be sure that they have passed to a better place, to be united with our loving God, who, according to John 14:2, has prepared 'many dwelling-places' in 'my Father's house'. It is therefore not surprising that a tradition of praying for those who have died grew up over many centuries, as the bereaved, encouraged by the Church, sought to express hope in eternal life by praying to God for their loved ones who had already died. The reformers of the sixteenth century were uneasy about this approach, particularly where masses for those who were long dead were being said or sung in return for payment, but we must acknowledge the human desires behind such prayers. The desire to pray for deceased loved ones is long-established, is current in both Anglican and Roman Catholic circles, and it is a hard person indeed who condemns such a practice. In the face of grief, it can be unkind to take the view that now a person has died, judgment is up to our Lord, and that there is nothing that anyone can do for the deceased in this respect. On one level, it requires a great deal of certainty to deny the efficacy of prayer for the dead, and on another level we should admit our inadequate understanding of the nature of God, such that if we can pray for someone who is sick, why not for someone who has died? God's time is not our time, we often say.

Various composers who have written musical settings of the requiem text, have brought different understandings and agendas into play, and it is fascinating to consider them. Duruflé approached the traditional text from an early twentieth-century French Roman Catholic position, which honours the tradition of a requiem mass at the time of someone's death, and also acknowledges the fact that a funeral is partly to entrust the beloved to God, but is also a solemn liturgical event that must console the bereaved. A funeral, in this tradition, must also include a eucharist, to remind all present that as the beloved has died, so too did Christ die for him or her, and indeed for all present.

Thus, while Duruflé's *Requiem* is one of the most modern that we might consider, it is also one of the most traditional. The given text is from the Latin Mass of the Dead, which is a eucharist with special texts (propers) added. The title 'Requiem' comes from the opening line of the opening section. 'Requiem' means 'rest', and it sets the tone of any requiem mass. The liturgy begins with a prayer for the dead, by way of stating why the congregation has gathered. The service at which the music is sung is a gathering of those who come to say farewell to the deceased. For Duruflé, writing just after the war, and at a time when the world was in musical as well as physical turmoil, the expression of prayer for the dead comes through the same medium that it had done for hundreds of years. The Gregorian plainsong settings of the requiem mass were well-known and Duruflé employed them in his work extensively (not only in his *Requiem*, but in many organ works that are less well-known). The beginning of the *Requiem* opens with the plainsong chant, and we hear bald statements of plainsong throughout the piece.

Duruflé himself wrote:

My Requiem is entirely based on Gregorian themes from the Mass of the Dead. At times the text is respected in its entirety, the orchestral writing serving merely to support it or comment on it, at other times I simply allowed myself to be inspired by it, or even distanced myself from it completely… I sought above all to immerse myself in the particular style of the Gregorian melodies.

This meant forcing free-flowing melodies into the regimented structures of musical notation, but this he did in a languid and inconspicuous way. In the Introit itself, which opens the work, the plainsong 'Requiem aeterna' is sung in its original form by the men, while the upper voices weave complementary melodies around, creating an ethereal sound world from the very beginning. In one way, Duruflé is drawing on popular perceptions as to what angels might sing like, and what heaven might sound like. For Duruflé, the *Requiem* is an expression of hope in the resurrection, and in it the organ has a special representative role of peace, faith and hope, whereas the orchestra represents the company of humanity remaining on earth.

Duruflé's belief is not in doubt, and this is a work written from a heart deeply embedded in ancient Christian music and faith. Yet it is a relatively modern work, which employs musical techniques and creates sound worlds that are unique to the twentieth century. It is perhaps Duruflé's particular faith and outlook that gives his music a distinctive flavour, which is almost like a halo, bathing listeners in the musical equivalent of light. It is a shame that more of his music is not better known, and a shame that due to his slowness of composition, there is not more with which to become familiar. It is also sad to reflect on what became of this quiet French genius, who was organist at the church of St Etienne-du-Mont in Paris from 1930 until his death. He was also Professor of Harmony at the Paris Musical Conservatory, but his career was curtailed by that most modern of disasters, the car crash. Both he and his wife were injured in an accident in 1975. Maurice was disabled, having borne the brunt of the impact, and he lived another 11 years. His wife, who was known to everyone as 'Madame Duruflé', and whom I had the privilege of meeting when singing in an English Choir at St Etienne-du-Mont, died only a few years ago. Another sadness beset the church community there when the man whom she had appointed to be her successor as organist (she took over from her husband), Hervé Morin, took his own life in 1997. May they all rest in peace.

PRAYER

O God, who holds all creation in life and in death, grant rest to all the faithful departed, and console those of us who remain, with the assurances of your promise of eternal life revealed in and won for us in Jesus Christ our Saviour. Amen.

For further reading: John 14:1–8 and 9–15
For listening: The Introit 'Requiem aeternam' and/or the 'Domine Jesu Christe' from Duruflé's *Requiem*

'TAKE MY ENDING
INTO YOUR CARE'

WOLFGANG AMADEUS MOZART—*REQUIEM*

When the damned are confounded and consigned to keen flames, call me with the blessed. As I kneel in prayer and supplication with a heart as contrite as ashes, take my ending into your care. That day is one of weeping, on which shall rise again from the ashes, the guilty, to be judged. Therefore have pity, O merciful Lord Jesus: give them rest. Amen.

REQUIEM—'CONFUTATIS'

Mozart's famous and beautiful *Requiem* is one of Western culture's greatest unfinished works. In Peter Shaffer's play *Amadeus*, the story is told, with accuracy and embellishment, of how the dying Mozart struggles to complete this final work, which we are led to believe is, to his mind, his own requiem. There is myth mixed in with the truth of Mozart's final months. It was long held that Mozart died poor, supported only by his friends and the members of the Masonic Lodge of which he was a member. It is well-known that he was buried in a pauper's grave in Vienna, such that even today the site of his grave is not exactly known. And yet, the great historian of classical music, H.C. Robbins Landon, wrote a book entitled *1791: Mozart's Final Year* (Schrimer Books, 1988), in which he claims that Mozart was making a fair bit of money as he approached his untimely death. The film of Peter Shaffer's play, also entitled *Amadeus*, brought the events of his life and death into a large public domain, such that it can be hard to distinguish fact from fiction. In that film, we see Mozart being asked to write the *Requiem* by a strange hooded figure, too easily associated with the ghost of his father Leopold, who, with a determination and marketing zeal worthy of today, towed his children Wolfgang and Nannerl around the courts of Europe to gain fame for them and wealth for himself.

If we leave Shaffer's Freudian explorations to one side, we must still notice the dark irony present in the fact that Mozart's last and unfinished work was a requiem. Just as it is hard to distinguish fact from fiction when considering Mozart's final months, it is no less easy to determine which parts of his *Requiem* he composed in full, which parts he sketched, and which parts were written entirely by Franz Xavier Süssmayr (1766–1803), who was Mozart's pupil and frequent companion at the end of his life. Documents of the time suggest that Süssmayr composed the 'Sanctus', 'Benedictus' and 'Agnus Dei', and that Mozart got no further than the 'Hostias' section, only managing the first eight bars of the 'Lacrymosa'. In as much as Mozart's *Requiem* is a game of two halves, it is not easy to distinguish them because, while Mozart's widow Constanze wanted to claim that Mozart had written most of it, and that Süssmayr had merely followed sketches, Süssmayr would have had an advantage in claiming that he had composed more of it, and may not have revealed all of his sketchy sources. The opinion of musicians who know the work of Mozart well is that his hand is evident in the 'Agnus Dei', but not in the 'Benedictus', for example. In one sense it is of little significance, because the work which we have come to know as Mozart's *Requiem* was composed mostly by Mozart and was completed by Süssmayr, and in spite of more historically informed attempts to re-complete the work by Franz Beyer in 1971 and Richard Maunder in 1984, it is the work of Mozart-Süssmayr that we have come to know and love.

From the New Testament we have the idea of John the Baptist as a forerunner of Christ, the one who prepares the way of the Lord, and whose ministry of baptism and preaching of repentance Jesus drives to a conclusion (see Mark 1:2–8). And then, as Jesus' earthly ministry concludes, he leaves unfinished business, which he entrusts to his few fervent disciples, telling them: 'Go therefore and make disciples of all nations... And remember, I am with you always, to the end of the age' (Matthew 28:19–20). The idea of inheriting work from others and handing it on in turn is one which we find in the great traditions of the Church, and through the handing on of truth, wisdom and experience, the Church waxes and wanes, enduring persecution and enjoying popularity, but always moving through time like an eternal melody of truth, albeit harmonized differently in various times and places.

Musical works have a similar journey through history, being popularized and neglected, abandoned and rediscovered. They are performed and adapted in numerous ways. Mozart's *Requiem* is perhaps an extreme case, because it was left unfinished on the composer's deathbed, but that shows how important the 'carrying of the baton' is. Süssmayr picked it up as soon as the dying Mozart dropped it, and the piece has been a popular triumph, in spite of the musically heavy hand that Süssmayr held it with.

There is a tradition, often still honoured at performances today, of marking the death of Mozart in the music. For in spite of recognizing Süssmayer's significant contribution in getting the *Requiem* into performing form, we still want to know which bits are pure Mozart, and at what point he stopped writing. Thus there is a touching, although perhaps mawkish tradition of pausing at some length after the choir have finished singing the languid 'Hostias' section, in order to gently emphasize the fact that Mozart 'died at this point'. If handled well, a brief pause can be moving, as we reflect briefly on the extinguishing of a creative flame, when Mozart was aged only 36. There is a poignancy to the words too, as the text has taken us through the plea for mercy found in the 'Confutatis' (see the start of today's reading), through to the 'Hostias', which contains the prayer: 'We offer to you O Lord, prayers and praises; receive them on behalf of the souls we commemorate today... grant them to pass from death to life'. Thus, where this gesture is made, it turns the performance into a kind of requiem *for* Mozart.

As we have already noted, Protestant churches have long been suspicious of praying for the dead, as are many strands of the Anglican tradition, and it was one of the issues over which the Reformation was wrought. Mozart was a Roman Catholic, who was even employed by the Archbishop of Salzburg at one time, and his *Requiem* was undoubtedly commissioned, like his many masses, for liturgical use. Nowadays the *Requiem* is most often performed in concert. As we see the 'handing on' of the music, and of the faith, constant yet changing in time and place, we may be able to recognize that while the *Requiem* has been moved from church to concert platform, it brings a little liturgy with it. And while the offering of the *Requiem* is not made as a prayer for the repose of Mozart's soul, an act of recognition such as this is an expression of gratitude and respect. That is gratitude for talent and respect for the musical gifts which Mozart displayed and handed on to us. Modern audiences may well not hold the same visions of heaven and hell which the *Requiem* text offers us, nor the awe of God which the music inspires, but the blend of the two still attracts and communicates today. It may well be that through music such as Mozart's *Requiem*, the teachings of the Church are still paraded, if not heard. Yet, something 'goes in', and audiences are believers, if only for the duration of the performance, as they are carried into an Austrian eighteenth-century Roman Catholic world of sin and forgiveness, hell and judgment, peace and eternal joy. There are far less edifying places to be carried to in this day and age, and there is music which has nothing so profound to say to us. Thus, as we observe the death of a musical genius within the notes of Mozart's *Requiem*, we must be grateful to him and to God who blessed him so richly with talent and vision. But we must also be aware of the challenge and opportunity that the continuing performances of works such as these throws up for us, as our music and our faith carry us forward into new encounters with those around us, who may know and love the music but may not feel the same about our Lord Jesus Christ.

PRAYER

As we will leave work unfinished, O Lord, give us grace to sense our own part in the fabric of faith into which our lives are so delicately woven. Help us to reinterpret the past for the future, and to relish the present for the opportunities of adoration, gratitude and enjoyment with which we are so often blessed. For these and all your mercies O Lord, we give you thanks and praise, now and for ever. Amen.

For further reading: Mark 1:2–8.
For listening: 'Confutatis', or 'Hostias', or other movements from Mozart's *Requiem*

'GRANT THEM ETERNAL REST LORD, AND LET PERPETUAL LIGHT SHINE UPON THEM'

GABRIEL FAURÉ—*REQUIEM*

May the angels receive you in Paradise. At your coming may the martyrs receive you, and bring you into the Holy City, Jerusalem. There may the choir of angels receive you, and with Lazarus, once a beggar, may you have eternal rest.

REQUIEM—'IN PARADISUM'

The setting of the *Requiem* by Gabriel Fauré (1845–1924) is one of the most popular and best known. The 'Pie Jesu', sung by a soprano or treble soloist, is a beautiful and simple version of the prayer to 'blessed Jesus', that those who have died might rest in eternal peace. Fauré had no particular reason for writing a requiem when he began it, but when his mother died on the last day of 1887, it took on a very personal dimension.

It was perhaps Fauré's need to assure himself of his mother's safe passage to paradise that prevented him from setting the liturgical texts for the Mass of the Dead in full. Here there is little judgment associated with death, nor is there the clamouring plea for mercy that we find in some of the more dramatic depictions of these ancient rites of burial. The vision of heaven we find in Fauré's work is of a paradise without judgment, where everyone goes, escaping from the rigours of earthly human life. In his own way, Fauré paints a picture of sitting on a cloud in the sky when you die, and this makes for attractive music and attractive theology. This simple and universal hope is appealing, and is largely what we find being expressed at funerals on a daily basis. Fauré was perhaps the first to express musically what many now believe in the face of death: that everything will be all right in the end, and that talk of hell is not only inappropriate, but is unnecessary. For some believe that there is no need to depict the human appeal to be spared the torments of hell, because hell does not exist, and salvation is therefore to be taken for granted. Hell for many is an only slightly biblical construct promulgated by the Roman Catholic Church in the Middle Ages as a means of controlling the living by threatening a terrible afterlife for those who did not conform and behave themselves.

Instead, we have the sweetness of paradise, and a consoling approach to those who are left to mourn. What this gives us, though, is a humanist heaven, populated by everyone who lived a good life, a place more familiar to Aristotle than to Jesus. Many cultures, the ancient Greeks among them, have offered us visions of heaven where tired but noble warriors lay down their arms and sleep, waking only to bodily pleasures translated to a spiritual realm. Salvation, if it may be called that, is through works, not faith, and is earned through living the good life, by being kind, generous and fair, and if religion is involved it matters only that you subscribe to one, and do so with a moderate mixture of commitment and openness (see Romans 3:27–29). In the aftermath of recent terrorist attacks at the beginning of this century and the rise of certain forms of violent fundamentalism, this has become even more significant. What is important now is not what you believe, but what you do not believe—and, whether you believe it or not, it is best not to believe it too much.

It must follow that where societies hold this kind of view, death is a difficulty. Deplorable as it is, a suicide bomber at least thinks he or she knows what he or she is doing, and action in life, in one sense, adds up in death. There is a saying that proposes that we should live each day as though it were our last, but this does not make any sense if we do not have a sense of what our last day might involve. Many Christians actually believe that death is merely the end of life, and that if there really is anything more, it must be something nice. Others more properly see salvation as won, once for all by Christ; therefore, death inspires barely a second thought, as it is all sorted out for us. This is true, but we still have cause to have some fear on the day of judgment, for we are all sinners who have erred and strayed like the proverbial lost sheep. The idea that 'at God's right hand there is pleasure for evermore' is appealing, but it must not beguile us into lack of commitment.

We might want to feel that there was somewhere deeply unpleasant for nasty people to go when they die, even though such a desire is as much vengeful as it is scriptural. The story of the rich man and Lazarus (Luke 16:19–31), which tells of the poor man in heaven being begged by his rich former acquaintance to cool his tongue, and then to warn his family of the impending dangers of hell, helps us to come to terms with deserved suffering, even though we might remember that the rich man's main flaw was that of being rich. The crux of that story comes in the final line: '...neither will they be convinced even if someone rises from the dead' (Luke 16:31). We have all heard the story, but if, having done so, we do not believe it, there is little that can be done.

In Fauré's music, there are always resolutions; the harmony is not controversial, and all is pleasing to the ear. Fauré's is a dream world, where a good life is followed by a good death, and the reverie is barely broken by a passing reference in the 'Libera me' ('set me free') to the 'Dies irae' ('the day of wrath'). Fauré depicts a kind of heaven which we might all fancy going to, and in doing so he wrote some beautiful music, which evokes paradise and soothes the modern soul. Hopefully, eternal life with God will be both pleasant and restful. Eternal life is God's promise to us revealed in and won by Christ, and the decision on who gets saved is not ours but God's. The great twentieth-century theologian Karl Barth admitted this when he acknowledged the power of God to act in ways that might surprise us. God saves whom he wills, and is not bound by any human law. The Christian revelation of life and death is one that speaks of love and salvation, but also of forgiveness and judgment. We may question the ways of God in our hearts, but in this life we will not get answers, other than by looking to Christ. Like Fauré, we can imagine a spiritual realm where there is no judgment, although we must always have that niggling feeling that we are choosing not to see the whole picture.

We cannot say what happens when we die, nor where collectively or individually we 'go' when we do. If we suppose that heaven involves elements of a gentle pleasure-filled paradise, spiritual union with God the Trinity, a refining of our character and a rest—a requiem—from what we understand to be earthly life, then we may not be far from the truth. If we include a notion that the life of faith we have lived in response to Christ's call to walk in his way has bearing on the outcome, then we must be getting nearer to the mark. And then if we remember that it is not so much heaven that we are hoping for but resurrection, then we are truly living, hoping and dying in the realm of Christ.

PRAYER

Our Father in heaven, help us to live our lives on earth in the light of Christ's resurrection and the eternal promises you have made in him. Keep us faithful, and when we do not understand the ways of life and death, show us the way to your kingdom. May we lead good lives, care for those who suffer, and be brought with all your people to our eternal home, where you reign, Trinity in Unity, now and for ever. Amen.

For further reading: Luke 16:19–31
For listening: 'Pie Jesu', or 'In paradisum', or other movements from Fauré's *Requiem*

'GRANT THEM ETERNAL REST LORD, AND LET PERPETUAL LIGHT SHINE UPON THEM'

GIUSEPPE VERDI—*REQUIEM*

And I saw the dead, great and small, standing before the throne, and books were opened. Also another book was opened, the book of life. And the dead were judged according to their works, as recorded in the books. And the sea gave up the dead that were in it, Death and Hades gave up the dead that were in them, and all were judged according to what they had done. Then Death and Hades were thrown into the lake of fire. This is the second death, the lake of fire; and anyone whose name was not found written in the book of life was thrown into the lake of fire.

REVELATION 20:12–15

If Fauré in his *Requiem* played down any mention of hell and judgment, Giuseppe Verdi (1813–1901) took a very different approach. Verdi's *Requiem*, written only a few years before Fauré's, is more than twice the length, and it makes its French counterpart sound like a piece of gentle chamber music. With Verdi's massive work, there is no avoidance of judgment, and the Latin liturgical text is set on a grand scale worthy of any opera house. Verdi is most famous for his many great operas, and his style of composition hardly changed when in 1874 he turned to the requiem text. He did so in response to two occasions which moved him. The first was the death of the composer Rossini and the second was the death of Alessandro Manzoni, the author of Italy's greatest novel, *I promessi sposi* (*The Betrothed*).

Gioacchino Rossini was, in Verdi's lifetime, the greatest Italian composer, and so it was a national blow when he died in 1868. Verdi had an idea at that time that each major Italian composer should compose a movement of a requiem, which could be sung on the anniversary of Rossini's death each year. It was a magnanimous suggestion and reflected the esteem in which Rossini had been held, even though for the last forty years of his life he had written no new operas. Twelve composers, Verdi among them, wrote music, for no fee, and great publicity surrounded the event. Sadly, and with much embarrassment, the planned performance never happened, and the idea was shelved.

On 22 May 1873, the poet and author Manzoni died at the age of 89. Verdi had met him in 1868, when both men were famous, but Verdi maintained a high regard and admiration for this Italian literary hero. Manzoni's death therefore moved Verdi a great deal; he could not bear to attend the funeral in Milan, but visited his grave privately later. Soon afterwards he wrote to his publishers, Riccordi, to say that he wanted to write a requiem in honour of Manzoni, to be performed (as a concert piece, rather than at a service) on the anniversary of his death. This time there was to be no great advance publicity, only assurances that the city of Milan would pay for the performance. Verdi would compose the music for no fee, and likewise conduct the great tribute. Thus on 22 May 1874, Verdi's *Requiem* received its first performance at St Mark's Church, in Milan. It was proclaimed a great success by those present and by those who heard it over the following days at La Scala, Milan's famous opera house. Verdi's own opera *Aida* was being performed at the same time, and some of the same soloists took part.

The *Requiem*'s operatic connections did not go unnoticed, however, and some people today still say that this portrays an operatic death rather than a religious one. The idea that the two should be mutually exclusive is rather strange, as we are accustomed to reading the Bible as a great work of literature as well as God's word of truth. Verdi's musical gestures are certainly large, and his spiritual canvas wide, and even if the *Requiem* is 'Verdi's greatest opera', it is no worse for it. Given the compliments often lavished on Verdi's operas *Aida*, *Otello*,

Falstaff and *La Traviata*, this would be praise indeed. None other than Johannes Brahms said of it that 'this could only be done by a genius'.

Verdi's technique is illustrative, for he seeks to describe the meaning of the text musically. In the second movement, the 'Dies irae', Verdi can be heard at his most dramatic, as he paints for us the day of wrath, the final judgment day referred to in the book of Revelation, at which the Book of Life is opened, and all souls judged. The text for this section is phrased as a statement of what will happen, interspersed with prayers from the deceased, seeking to be spared the lake of fire and the eternal death. It is earth-moving stuff, and Verdi's setting of the phrase 'salva me' ('save me') is almost overbearing in its intensity. Whether Verdi meant it or not, the dramatic impact is one of genuine fear and prayer, even if the whole thing is cloaked in operatic, romantic overstatement. The account of tribulation and judgment in Revelation is also rather melodramatic, and if one is going to set it to music, this kind of approach (also found in Berlioz' *Requiem*) is rather fitting. Thus, it is no surprise, and yet it shakes us out of our seats, when we hear the opening of the 'Dies irae', when the timpani and bass drum crash down to enunciate the day of judgment. As they punctuate the fearful cries of the choir's 'the day of wrath, that day shall dissolve the world in ash', we can literally feel the momentous occasion gathering power, in anticipation of the final trumpet call, which sounds to awake the dead.

When I was at Cambridge University, I played various percussion instruments at lots of concerts, but I shall always remember being telephoned one morning by a friend of mine, who was asking if I could play in a performance of Verdi's *Requiem* that evening. Percussion instruments are expensive to hire, and so it was usual to only get one rehearsal. The prospect of playing the bass drum, pounding out the 'Dies Irae', certainly appealed, but I was a little surprised to find that my friend, who is a better percussionist than I, had reserved that relatively small part for himself, and I had to play the timpani through-out, which was great fun, but much harder work! It is perhaps just a childish fantasy to harbour dreams of bashing a big drum as hard as you can with sticks in both hands, but that is basically what is required by Verdi, for there are no half-measures when it comes to the day of judgment.

The other movements of Verdi's masterpiece are no less engaging, even if they are less terrifying. For Verdi there is death, fear and judgment, but there is also a glorious 'Sanctus', and a beautiful 'Libera me' ('Deliver me'), which may be remembered from the funeral of Diana, Princess of Wales in September 1997. Verdi's *Requiem*, for all its grandeur and operatic dimensions of volume and duration, is in one sense a simple work. It takes the text of the Latin Mass for the Dead, and sets it entire, and does so with a commitment to meaning and power that few have matched. Nineteenth-century Italy, a fledgling nation, knew this text, and it united them to their past, their church and their God. Verdi made sure that his work also linked them to and became part of their national culture, and yet, because it is a requiem, and because it is such good music, Verdi's ever-so-Italian work is a worldwide favourite today. Verdi was also one of the first to take liturgical music such as this and put it firmly on the concert platform. As it continues to remind countless audiences of the saving power of Christ in the face of inevitable divine judgment, Verdi's *Requiem* really is to be applauded.

PRAYER

When you come to judge the world, O Lord, hear the prayers of your sinful servants, and on your healing wings bring to your Church the merciful redemption which you have promised us in Jesus Christ. Strengthen us for service in this life, that at the last we may stand before your throne of judgment with repentance on our lips and the fire of your love in our hearts. Grant this for the sake of the same, Jesus Christ our Saviour! Amen.

For further reading: 2 Peter 3:1–13
For listening: 'Dies irae', or 'Libera me', or other movements from Verdi's *Requiem*

'THE TRUMPET SHALL SEND FORTH
A WONDROUS SOUND'

HECTOR BERLIOZ—*REQUIEM*
(*GRAND MESSE DES MORTS*)

The trumpet shall send forth a wondrous sound, ringing through the tombs of earth, driving all before the throne. Death shall be astounded and creation shall awake to answer to its judge. A book shall be brought forth containing all of that by which the world shall be judged. Therefore when the judge sits, whatever is hidden shall be revealed and nothing shall remain unavenged.

REQUIEM—'TUBA MIRUM'

While Verdi's *Requiem* is a grand, nationalistic piece of liturgical theatre, Berlioz' offering of the same text (the *Grand Messe des Morts*) is grander, bigger and more nationalistic. Like the younger Verdi, Hector Berlioz (1803–69) was also inspired to write a setting of the requiem mass after the death of a significant person, although the circumstances in post-revolutionary Paris were somewhat different.

On the public holiday of 28 July 1835, the entourage of King Louis-Philippe (who later abdicated, in 1848) was attacked in a procession through Paris, and although he survived with only slight wounds, 18 people were killed, including his commander-in-chief, Edouard-Adolphe Mortier. The perpetrator was the Corsican anarchist Fieschi, and he caused a national outrage. The government asked Berlioz to write a requiem for Mortier and the other victims, to be performed at the church of St Louis des Invalides in Paris. Berlioz was honoured and delighted, and set to work immediately, having been given only four months to compose and rehearse the work.

The masterpiece that resulted has a sense of the relish that Berlioz had for this composition. In the 'Tuba mirum' for example, judgment day is announced with trumpets sounding as described in 1 Corinthians 15:52, and Berlioz musters the largest forces and loudest noises imaginable, with multiple brass and timpani. He described this as the moment 'for tears and for gnashing of teeth, where I threw in such a violent stroke of the tam-tam that the church quaked'. But the church had to wait before it could quake according to plan. Only weeks before it was due, the event was cancelled by the government. There was to be a royal wedding, and apparently, Austria and Russia had complained that such an event would glorify revolution, which they particularly feared. It was not until October 1837 that another opportunity arose, this time as a result of the death in action of the governor-general of Algeria, Charles, comte de Damrémont. This time there was money to be found for the funeral of a war hero, and on 5 December 1837 the *Requiem* got its first performance.

That first performance was a great success, in spite of the fact that the conductor took snuff during the crucial 'Tuba mirum'; a member of the choir fainted; the bereaved were moved to tears, as were some of the clergy, while the other priests chanted the liturgy independently throughout the proceedings! As the work is so massive it was not performed very many times in Berlioz' lifetime (he heard it again in 1846, 1850 and 1852), and it is not often heard 'live' today. Hundreds of musicians and singers are required to bring Berlioz' apocalyptic vision to life, but when they do so, the effects are stunning. There are loud climaxes of course, but also moments of quiet beauty, such as the 'Quaerens me' ('seeking me'). The 'Sanctus', perhaps surprisingly, is not a great outburst of angelic praise, but a gentle hymn to God, led by a tenor soloist and conducted as it were in the awesome peace of heaven. Berlioz rearranged the traditional order of the requiem text in order to achieve balance in this respect. His *Requiem* is also a case-study in architectural writing, such that it is carefully planned and orchestrated for a large building with a big acoustic. Thus after the trumpets have announced the day of judgment in the 'Tuba mirum', Berlioz leaves the violins to hold a single note while the building reverberates with the sound, and then, when it has died down, the music continues, having been held in place by a single thread.

This 'architectural' sound that Berlioz was so good at creating brings together the two art forms, and joins the music to the structures of the building. The German philosopher Friedrich von Schelling (1775–1854) wrote in 1809 that 'architecture in general is frozen music', and here we might want to say of Berlioz' music that it is liquid architecture, as it exploits the surfaces from which it bounces sounds which extend across the dynamic range. Thus in the 'Tuba mirum', four distinct groups of brass in different corners of the building consume the total space, forcing an emotional response from the listeners as they are swamped in a terrific, cataclysmic sound.

Evocative and public as Berlioz' music is, it is also very personal, and 'romantic' in the proper sense of the word. For Berlioz, who turned upside down the musical norms of his day, music was about expressing emotions. He had little basic training as a musician, and although he revolutionized the art of orchestration, he was barely competent at an instrument. His father had intended him to be a doctor, but he could not stand the training, and fled the dissection classes, later writing in his autobiography: '… such a feeling of horror possessed me that I leaped out of the window and fled home as though Death and all his hideous crew were at my heels'. Berlioz' love-life was also rather dramatic. He fell in love with the Irish actress Harriet Smithson, and he wrote his *Symphonie Fantastique* in her honour and then pursued her for six years before she acquiesced and entered into what turned out to be a disastrous marriage.

Berlioz' attitudes to society, art, politics and religion were mostly rebellious. He was brought up as a Roman Catholic, but his main religion was his art, which, in true romantic style, could be seen as a doorway into a quasi-heavenly world of beauty, perfection and ecstasy. His mother held a strong Roman Catholic faith, but his father was more liberal-minded, and the young Hector probably took after him, although he did claim that it was at his first communion that he first felt stirred by music. As well as setting liturgical texts, like the *Requiem* and the even more resourceful *Te Deum*, he also wrote an oratorio entitled *The Childhood of Christ*, the 'Shepherds' farewell' from which is still very popular as a Christmas piece. It is unlikely that Berlioz prayed a great deal, for he generally preferred passionate action, and yet it is so ironic that in his music he was able to conjure up musical places where others might pray.

Ultimately we may want to conclude that by substituting faith for art, Berlioz, like many artists after him, succumbed to a form of idolatry. The prophet Isaiah criticizes those who made idols out of lumps of wood: 'They bow down to the work of their hands, to what their own fingers have made' (Isaiah 2:8), and a piece of music can also elicit inappropriate attention. Berlioz' use of scripture and liturgical text can help us to direct our devotions Godward, and can help us to reflect on our own mortality, or to grieve for others in a Christian context. Yet it may be that Berlioz sought mainly to glorify his country, his ideals and himself in music that uses Christian faith as a podium on which to stand and wave about, and church architecture merely as a venue for grand spectacle.

Perhaps this is too harsh a judgment to make of a musical genius, long dead. We should perhaps be more focused on our own faith, rather than question another's. And there can be no mistake that Berlioz' music, in spite of its apparent motivation, can, by its passionate gestures and sounds, inspire us to reflect on the majesty and the power of God's judgment. It can attempt to show us the vastness of creation and the beauty of truth, exposing to us our sinfulness and smallness, even if it may be the case that God speaks to us through it in a way that Berlioz himself might not have wanted to acknowledge. To God be the glory!

PRAYER

Lord Jesus, our Judge and Redeemer, forgive us when we take pride in the work of our own hands, or that of others, and forget to give you the glory. By your gracious Spirit help us each day to see the Father's handiwork in all things of beauty, until that final day when trumpets shall sound and all creation come before your throne of mercy, where you reign with the same Father and Holy Spirit, now and for ever. Amen.

For further reading: Revelation 3:1–6
For listening: 'Tuba mirum', or the 'Sanctus', or other movements from Berlioz' *Requiem*

'LORD MAKE ME TO KNOW MINE END'

JOHANNES BRAHMS—*A GERMAN REQUIEM*

Lord, let me know my end, and what is the measure of my days; let me know how fleeting my life is. You have made my days a few handbreadths, and my lifetime is as nothing in your sight. Surely everyone stands as a mere breath. Surely everyone goes about like a shadow. Surely for nothing they are in turmoil; they heap up, and do not know who will gather. And now, O Lord, what do I wait for? My hope is in you...

'Hear my prayer, O Lord, and give ear to my cry; do not hold your peace at my tears. For I am your passing guest, an alien, like all my forebears. Turn your gaze away from me, that I may smile again, before I depart and am no more.

PSALM 39:4–7, 12–13

The German Requiem (*Ein Deutsches Requiem*) by Johannes Brahms (1833–97) is very different from those which employ the Latin text of the Mass for the Dead. Brahms, who knew the Lutheran Bible inside out, came from the Protestant tradition, and in the work which everyone has come to call his *Requiem*, there is not a single word of Latin. Every word is from the German Bible.

The passages that Brahms used are laid out in seven movements, as follows:

1. Blessed are those who mourn, for they will be comforted (Matthew 5:4)—Those who sow in tears reap with shouts of joy (Psalm 126:5–6)
2. All people are grass, their constancy is like the flower of the field (Isaiah 40:6)—And the ransomed of the Lord shall return (Isaiah 35:10)
3. Lord let me know my end (Psalm 39:4)—The souls of the righteous are in the hand of God (Wisdom 3:1)
4. How lovely is your dwelling-place (Psalm 84:1)
5. So you have pain now, but I will see you again, and your hearts will rejoice (John 16:22)—As a mother comforts her child, so I will comfort you (Isaiah 66:13)
6. For here we have no lasting city (Hebrews 13:14)—I will tell you a mystery (1 Corinthians 15:51)—You are worthy (Revelation 4:11).
7. Blessed are the dead who from now on die in the Lord (Revelation 14:13)

It is clear that this is not a collection of prayers for the faithful departed, but a series of consoling movements, which carry the bereaved through a process of grief. Each movement carries us forward, lifting the musical pitch, pointing us away from the life that is lost, towards the eternal life that is to come. The piece begins and ends with the word 'blessed' (*selig*), initially referring to those who mourn, and finally to those who have died in the faith of Christ. Thus we are moved from grief, through an understanding of human mortality to a contemplation of the heavenly city where God and the righteous dwell together in eternity.

It has been said of Brahms' *Requiem* that it lacks much reference to Christ, quoting him once, and only making a vague reference to the 'last trumpet'. At the first performance, in Bremen Cathedral, on Good Friday 1868, Brahms allowed the aria 'I know that my Redeemer liveth' from Handel's *Messiah* to be inserted into the performance. Two thousand people were present on that occasion, which helped Brahms' reputation immensely. The fifth movement had not been written then, but was added six months later. Written for a soprano soloist, it is the sublime centre of the work.

To a German Lutheran, there is more in this work than we might notice. The musical theme of the second movement is recognizably based upon a Lutheran hymn tune set to the words 'Who all his will to God resigneth'. When familiar tunes are used like this, a juxtaposition of ideas can occur, such that the music conveys two ideas at once, thereby connecting them. A Lutheran listener would be hearing words about the frailty of life, resonating with the idea that salvation in the face of frailty is to be found in submission to God's will.

The third movement sets to music a large chunk of Psalm 39, in which the psalmist seeks to know how long his life will be. This is a question to which we might all want to know the answer, or which we might wish to avoid asking. In our day, doctors and families are often faced with the difficult decision as to what exactly to tell patients who suffer from terminal illness. Should someone who is dying be told? In the Prayer Book Litany, we find the prayer: 'From lightning and tempest; from plague, pestilence and famine; from battle and murder, and from sudden death, Good Lord deliver us', and in the more recent *Common Worship* version, the final phrase is rendered: 'from violence, murder and dying unprepared'. Yet many do not want to know or be told if and when they are dying, nor how long they have to live, and many close to them cannot face telling them. It is a remarkably difficult thing to do.

It may be that we no longer fear death in quite the same way as we used to. Psalm 39 seeks some insight into our life, so that we might prepare for death spiritually, with confession, absolution and a readiness to 'meet our maker'. Yet these days, many fear death because they believe that it amounts to the end of everything for them. This individualistic approach fears death, not judgment, and desires to face neither. A denial of an afterlife makes the fear of death more urgent, and focuses life much more in the present. Any attempt to bring imminent death into the open can therefore prove to be very threatening indeed. When we add suffering into the equation, the fear intensifies. Some people would rather be killed instantly than face a debilitating illness. With that as a driving motive for painless death, the question of euthanasia soon arises, as people seek to avoid pain, even at the loss of some of the number of their days. By referring to our lifespans in terms of a few 'handbreadths' the psalm reminds us that our lives are in the hands of God, and it is the Lord who gives and the Lord who takes away. It is our calling as Christians not so much to influence or alter the span of our lives, but rather to live in such a way that we are ready for death. Suicide is not the only response to pain.

Brahms' *German Requiem* is a comfort-work, a piece of music setting before us the hope and comfort which we find in Jesus Christ our Saviour, who will receive us into everlasting arms at our lives' end, whether that life be short, long, gentle or hard. Sometimes when we look at home or abroad at the conditions of some people's lives, we may feel that life is not fair, either to us or to others. Sometimes we are even tempted to say that someone's life is 'not worth living'. 'Life' of course, has no say in this, and it is invariably human beings who have created some of these conditions. We must acknowledge that nature plays her part too, and many people associate nature with God. But the Creator and creation are independent, for some of the natural phenomena we encounter in the world are the result of the world's freedom with which God has blessed the whole of creation. For example, the same processes of change and mutation in cells which promote human adaptation also lead to malformation of cells, which can turn cancerous.

While the initial movements of Brahms' *Requiem* remind us of our own mortality, the second half of the work directs us heavenward and reminds us that there is more to come, against which a brief or long life can barely be measured. Even though such a hope is often rejected these days, because it cannot be proved or guaranteed in conventional terms, this must be our hope, our only hope, that in Christ God reconciles everyone to himself, so that we might all share in the promise of resurrection life in his heavenly city, where no earthly torment can touch us.

PRAYER

Help us to measure the days of our life in terms of the eternal life you promise us in Jesus Christ. Help us to live each day as though it were our first and our last, that we may love and serve you until we are brought into your heavenly dwelling, where you live and reign, Father, Son and Holy Spirit, now and for ever. Amen.

For further reading: Isaiah 40:1–8
For listening: 'Herr, lehre doch mich' ('Lord, let me know my end') or 'Ihr habt nun Traurigkeit' ('So you have pain now') from Brahms' *German Requiem*, and any other movements.

'I WILL LIFT UP MINE
EYES UNTO THE HILLS'

HERBERT HOWELLS—*REQUIEM*

I will lift up mine eyes unto the hills from whence cometh my help.
My help cometh even from the Lord, who hath made heav'n and
earth. He will not suffer thy foot to be moved; and he that keepeth
thee will not slumber nor sleep. Behold, he that keepeth Israel shall
neither slumber nor sleep. The Lord himself is thy keeper; he is thy
defence upon thy right hand. So that the sun shall not burn thee by
the day, neither the moon by night.

The Lord shall preserve thee from all evil; it is even he that shall
keep thy soul. The Lord shall preserve thy going out and thy coming
in: from this time forth and for evermore. I will lift up mine eyes unto
the hills from whence cometh my help.

PSALM 121 (BOOK OF COMMON PRAYER)

Brahms was not the only composer to construct a requiem out of
vernacular biblical texts. Recently John Rutter has done so, and there
is also the short but exquisite *Requiem* by Herbert Howells
(1892–1983). As much of his output was for choir or organ (or both),
Howells is not as well-known as he deserves to be, but there are many
within the cathedral music world who profess a great fondness for his
music.

Howells is best-known for his hymn tune 'Michael', to which we
sing: 'All my hope on God is founded'. He wrote it for Charterhouse
School in 1930, and named the tune after his son Michael, who died
of meningitis in 1935 when only nine years old. It was thought that

the *Requiem* was a response to Michael's tragic death, but recent research suggests that Howells was drafting the *Requiem* before 1935. Whether Michael's death inspired composition or not, we can hardly separate the music from an appreciation of Michael's life, so tragically cut short. Howells did write the *Hymnus Paradisi*, ('Hymn of Paradise') as a tribute to Michael in 1938, but he was reluctant to have it performed until 1950, when it was instantly recognized as a masterpiece. Howells was similarly reluctant to release the *Requiem*, much of the material for which also appears in the *Hymnus Paradisi*. The *Requiem* was not published until 1980, only a few years before Howells died, but it became part of the church music repertoire immediately.

Howells' *Requiem*, which takes fewer than twenty minutes to perform, is made up of six gentle movements. Each moves us on through loss to consolation, and draws on the Prayer Book Funeral Service of 1927/8 (which was never authorized by Parliament) and the traditional Latin requiem text: '*Requiem aeternam dona eis. Et lux perpetua luceat eis. Requiem aeternam dona eis, Domine*' ('Grant eternal rest to them and let perpetual light shine upon them. Grant eternal rest to them O Lord'). This Latin text is used in both the third and fifth movements, with different music. Interspersed as the fourth movement is a setting of Psalm 121, and we also find Psalm 23 ('The Lord is my Shepherd') as the second movement. The *Requiem* opens with the sentence from the Prayer Book funeral known as *Salvator mundi*: 'Saviour of the world, who by thy cross and precious blood hast redeemed us, save us and help us, we humbly beseech thee, O Lord'. The final movement employs a text from Revelation 14:13—'I heard a voice from heaven saying', which is also found in the Prayer Book service.

The two psalms that Howells uses are now well-established as 'funeral' psalms, but it was not always so. Psalm 23, with its specific reference to the 'valley of death' was formally permitted as an alternative to the already recommended Psalms 39 and 90, in 1928, but Psalm 121, which now seems so appropriate, was not introduced officially until the *Alternative Service Book* of 1980 included it. This means that Howells was pastorally and theologically ahead of his time. The development of the Anglican funeral rite has broadly shifted the emphasis from death and judgment to the plight of the mourners. In the medieval period, the emphasis at funerals was on the fear of judgment. Hell and purgatory were very much in evidence; in order to scare people out of hell the attempt was made to scare the hell out of them! Funerals were a public event at which the Church attempted to discipline the people, and murals and altar paintings also portrayed the torments of the damned and the rewards of the faithful. We find this kind of view in some of the older requiem masses, but not in Howells' brief, intimate work.

Psalm 121, which Howells sets in its entirety, is a psalm of consolation and of hope. The hills to which our eyes are lifted could be threatening or comforting, but it is from them that help comes. Thus, in time of need or danger, we look to the place from which we know help will come, and that place is the place of the Lord, Creator of all, and he will protect his children, for the Lord is our keeper and our strong arm of defence. In our pilgrimage of life, he will walk at our side, protecting us from natural disaster and any kind of evil. The Lord will preserve us whether we come or go—that is, in all circumstances. It is to him that we lift our eyes as we journey onward to our heavenly home.

At times of bereavement, these words are comforting. Not only do they characterize the journey of the deceased, now arrived at those heavenly hills, but they remind us of our own pilgrimage of life and the safe haven for which we hope. Instead of inspiring a quasi-medieval fear of death, now we have a modern comforting. The initial private nature of Howells' *Requiem*, indicated by his reluctance to publish it and the very mood of the music, tells us that it is comfort that he sought. We must hope that he did find some solace in composing this heartfelt music for his poor dead child.

All of the *Requiem* is for unaccompanied choir. The fourth movement opens with a baritone soloist singing the first line, which returns at the end, at a higher pitch, sung by a tenor. Thus during these few minutes, we are musically lifted out of the gloom, up towards those heavenly hills. In both words and music we conclude where we start, but, as T.S. Eliot said in that oft-quoted passage from 'East Coker', which comes from his *Four Quartets*, 'in my beginning is my end' and 'in my end is my beginning' , and '... the end of all of our exploring will be to arrive where we started, and know the place for the first time'. Often we go on circular journeys, but we arrive refreshed, if only to see the same scenery. Thus when loved ones die, we are forced on to a circular journey: our location in grief cannot be altered, for our beloved has died, but we can be helped to experience that spiritual location in different, perhaps hope-filled ways.

In the poem 'Little Gidding', also from the *Four Quartets*, Eliot makes this explicit: 'What we call the beginning is often the end, And to make an end is to make a beginning. The end is where we start from.' 'We are', he says, 'born with the dead'. Psalm 121 can be seen in this way: it helps us to both make and understand the journey of life, giving us a godly framework by which we appreciate our status as God's beloved children, and his status as our Lord and 'keeper'. Howells' soloists state this at beginning and end, and the other singers meditate on the intervening text with rich but quiet harmonies that are so typical of Howells' distinctive style.

Lent is a natural time to reflect on our own mortality, as we approach the passion, death and resurrection of Jesus. Although we can usefully study requiems, we must not become too morbid, or depressed. Death is not pleasant, nor is it in itself comforting. We are not called to suffer death, but rather to pass through it, travelling onward to the resurrection life that follows and which is our eternal hope. We cannot reflect on resurrection without death, and we cannot reflect on death without resurrection. Lent is so often seen as a period when we recall our sins and remind ourselves of our mortality, thereby 'saving up' resurrection for the Easter period. There is a balance to this, which puts holy week and Easter at the heart of our reflections, but we must not ignore our sin during the Easter period, nor forget our inheritance of eternal life during Lent. Whether or not we have a death close at hand to make us reflect, in Lent let us all remember that we are dust, but also rejoice in the redemption from our earthbound nature wrought in and by Jesus Christ.

PRAYER

O Lord on high, from whom comes all our help, preserve and keep us as we journey in this world, and comfort us as we remember those whom we love but see no longer; until that day when we, like them, shall be taken up into your glory, where you reign, Father, Son and Holy Spirit. Amen.

For further reading: 1 Corinthians 15:35–49
For listening: 'I will lift up mine eyes unto the hills' from Herbert Howells' *Requiem*

'HALF THE SEED OF EUROPE,
ONE BY ONE'

BENJAMIN BRITTEN—*WAR REQUIEM*

So Abram rose, and clave the wood, and went,
And took the fire with him, and a knife.
And as they sojourned both of them together,
Isaac the first-born spake and said, 'My Father,
Behold the preparations, fire and iron,
But where is the lamb for this burnt offering?'

Then Abram bound the youth with belts and straps,
And builded parapets and trenches there,
And stretched forth the knife to slay his son.

Whereupon lo, an angel called him out of heav'n,
Saying, 'Lay not thy hand upon the lad,
Neither do anything to him, Behold,
A ram, caught in a thicket by its horns;
Offer the Ram of Pride instead of him.'

But the old man would not so, but slew his son,
And half the seed of Europe, one by one...

'THE PARABLE OF THE OLD MAN AND THE YOUNG'—WILFRED OWEN (1893–1918)

This poem is one of several that Benjamin Britten (1913–76) included in the choral work which he wrote for the consecration of the newly rebuilt Coventry Cathedral in May 1962. The power and greatness of the *War Requiem* were recognized immediately, in virtue of the composer's evident musical skill and creative depth of vision which brings into dialogue the traditional, Latin 'Missa pro defunctis' texts (the Mass for the Dead) and nine poems by Wilfred Owen. Owen was a lieutenant in the Manchester Regiment during the First World War, who was killed at the Sambre Canal on 4 November 1918, only a week before the final armistice on 11 November. His bravery was recognized with the Military Cross.

The ironic timing and futility of Owen's death (he was 25), which wasted yet another human life and lost for ever a poetic mind, was for Benjamin Britten a potent symbol of the arrogance and cruelty of warfare. The *War Requiem* is not a glorification of those who died, nor a celebration of victory, but rather a lament which pleads for good and peace to rise from the ashes of grief and pain. Just as Coventry Cathedral was wrecked by war, and rebuilt as a symbol of remembrance and hope, Britten's musical architecture brings past and present, and lament of war and hope for peace, together. The new Coventry Cathedral was built adjacent to the burned-out shell of the old, so that they might stand together, thereby encouraging us to move on from death to life. For Sir Basil Spence (1907–76), the architect of Coventry Cathedral, and for Britten, the key idea is that reminders are a form of prevention. As living memory fades over time, these architectural and musical edifices stand firm, as if to say: 'Look what we did; let us never let it happen again.' And just as the old cathedral remains are close to the new building, so are the poetic remains of Wilfred Owen immortalized in the *War Requiem*, presented next to the old texts of the Latin Mass for the Dead.

It would have been so easy for Britten to have written a requiem mass just like everyone else's, with Latin texts, mourning the loss of the dead in a traditional way. But he was a master of the setting of English poetry, and so it is that he claps these two strong hands together, creating a musical, pacifist thunderbolt to cut through some of our complacency about war.

Thus, when he sets Owen's poem 'The Parable of the Old Man and the Young', we can see the juxtaposition of poetry and Latin text, combined with devastating effect. Owen's poem is about Abraham and

Isaac, and appears in the work immediately after the choir have sung: '*Quam olim Abrahae promisisti, et semini eius*' ('as was promised to Abraham and his seed'). This is the 'Offertorium' of the eucharist for the dead, the point at which bread and wine are taken, to become for us the body and blood of Christ.

Britten's use of Owen's poem strikes a blow against war itself, as it reminds us that war is a human choice, laden with sin. Owen's poem is a retelling of the story of Abraham and Isaac (Genesis 22:1–13), except that it has that final, chilling twist in the tale. The story from Genesis can be seen to point towards the time when God will not even spare his son in order to forgive the sins of the world, but in Owen's poem the old man ignores the call of the angels, but presses on to commit more cynical, graver sins with the lives of innocent young men in the field of battle. The direct connection with parapets and trenches makes the meaning clear, and reminds us of the extreme, yet carefully planned lengths to which systematic violence can be extended.

The story of Abraham and Isaac is familiar to almost everybody, and it can be interpreted as a myth about acceptance and blind obedience to orders. The Bible story seems to suggest that if God tells you to do something, you should do it. The love of God, as that other pacifist Cecil Spring Rice (1859–1918) put it, is 'the love that asks no questions, the love that stands the test'. It is so easy to interpret the hymn 'I vow to thee my country', and the story of Abraham and Isaac as presenting this unquestioning view of worldly and divine authority. But Owen and Britten return us to more authentic understandings of these concepts.

The story of Abraham and Isaac had an early purpose of revealing to the Hebrew nation that the God of Israel—their God—does not require human sacrifice. Some other religions of the period advocated human sacrifice for divine appeasement, but the Judeo-Christian tradition has not done so. The story of Abraham and Isaac both establishes and accounts for that understanding. As time has passed, Judaism moved away from animal sacrifice as well, such that in that great Lenten Psalm 51, we find the phrase 'the sacrifice acceptable to God is a broken spirit' (Psalm 51:17). Animal sacrifices were known in Jesus' time (Luke 2:22–24), but he never advocated them for his followers, and that is why we now, at best, speak of a 'sacrifice of thanksgiving and praise'. Nowadays we have realized that there is no need to offer the death of God's creatures in return for spiritual life. In Jesus Christ, this has been done once and for all.

The sad beauty and frightening power of Benjamin Britten's *War Requiem* reminds us that it was written recently, and is as relevant and meaningful today as it was in the aftermath of the Second World War. In one sense Christ is still being crucified in many places, no more so than on the battlefield:

For 14 hours yesterday I was at work—teaching Christ to lift his cross by numbers, and how to adjust his crown; and not to imagine he thirst till after the last halt; I attended his Supper to see that there were no complaints; and inspected his feet to see that they should be worthy of the nails. I see to it that he is dumb and stands to attention before his accusers. With a piece of silver I buy him every day, and with maps I make him familiar with the topography of Golgotha.

FROM A LETTER FROM WILFRED OWEN TO OSBERT SITWELL

PRAYER

O God, who sent your Son to suffer for us that we might become dead to sin and alive in Jesus Christ, grant to those who govern the affairs of this world, the wisdom, integrity and compassion to keep always in their sight the vision of unity and love manifested in Jesus Christ, the Prince of peace. Amen.

For further reading: Genesis 22:1–13
For listening: The 'Offertorium' from Britten's *War Requiem*

'EVEN THOUGH I WALK THROUGH THE DARKEST VALLEY, I FEAR NO EVIL'

LEONARD BERNSTEIN—*CHICHESTER PSALMS*

The Lord is my shepherd, I shall not want. He makes me lie down in green pastures; he leads me beside still waters; he restores my soul. He leads me in right paths for his name's sake. Even though I walk through the darkest valley, I fear no evil; for you are with me; your rod and your staff—they comfort me.

Why do the nations conspire, and the peoples plot in vain? The kings of the earth set themselves, and the rulers take counsel together, against the Lord and his anointed, saying, 'Let us burst their bonds asunder, and cast their cords from us.' He who sits in the heavens laughs; the Lord has them in derision.

You prepare a table before me in the presence of my enemies; you anoint my head with oil; my cup overflows. Surely goodness and mercy shall follow me all the days of my life, and I shall dwell in the house of the Lord my whole life long.

PSALM 23:1–4; PSALM 2:1–4; PSALM 23:5–6

This striking juxtaposition of two psalm texts is found in what must surely be one of the most poignantly beautiful works of twentieth-century music. The *Chichester Psalms*, by the American composer Leonard Bernstein (1918–90) was commissioned for the Chichester Festival of 1965 by the then Dean of Chichester Cathedral, Walter Hussey. Previous to that post, Hussey had been Vicar of St Matthew's

Church in Northampton, where he had also commissioned artworks of lasting fame and significance, among them the 'Crucifixion' by the painter Graham Sutherland. Bernstein, who also wrote Broadway musicals such as *On the Town* and *West Side Story*, was a world-class conductor, who led a very busy and full life. But in the mid-1960s he took a break from a rigorous conducting schedule, and in April and May 1965, while contemplating his own place in the fragmented world of twentieth-century music, composed for Chichester three settings of psalms, and in doing so, introduced his own very distinctive style into the choral repertoire.

The 15-minute work has three movements, all of which take their Hebrew texts exclusively from the Psalms. The first movement opens with a brief quotation from Psalm 108:2: 'Awake, O harp and lyre! I will awake the dawn', which seems an appropriate way to start! Psalm 100, also known as the *Jubilate* follows, making up the rest of the declamatory, almost jazzy movement. The time signature is 7/4—it is not often that we hear seven beats in a bar, and this gives a very unusual but not unpleasant flavour to the music. Psalm 100 is an entrance psalm ('Enter his courts with praise'), and it is not surprising that Bernstein should kick off in this way.

The excitement of the first movement gives way to the elegiac and sublime setting of the opening verses of Psalm 23. It is of course one of the most well-known psalms in the Bible, familiar to all and known by heart by many. Thus the fact that Bernstein's text is in Hebrew does not present a great difficulty to hearers, and even creates an ancient and exotic atmosphere as we hear the psalms sung in their original, Old Testament language. Bernstein, whose Jewish parents had moved to America before he was born, uses the language of his faith, but this is by no means a barrier to understanding or inspiration. As singers or hearers, we are reminded of the long and shared traditions of the Jewish and Christian faiths, and Christians should never forget that what we call the Old Testament is first and foremost the Hebrew Bible, the faith-book of the Jews. Thus, the Psalms are a repository of common heritage and truth.

Bernstein's use of Psalm 23 combined with Psalm 2 jolts us out of any mysterious past right up to his day and age. The mid-1960s were plagued by brinkmanship as the Cold War was at its hottest, during the Bay of Pigs fiasco and the Cuban Missile Crisis of 1963. These events made a Third World War seem a very real possibility, and Bernstein's *Chichester Psalms* are a product of that time.

The move from the gentle and reassuring text of Psalm 23 to the frustrated, angry outburst of '*Lamah rag'shu goyim, Ul'umim yeh'gu rik?*' ('Why do the nations rage?'), comes as a surprise, but also reveals a profound truth about the will to destroy which humankind entertains even in the context of sublime beauty. The central section of the second movement involves the basses and baritones singing tongue-twisting words which follow the initial lyrical soprano solo. These opening bars of music, with their ravishing harp accompaniment, are silenced by the clamour of war and the will to destroy. But then, as the lower voices continue their war dance, the soprano (either boy or woman) returns, and eventually the final words of Psalm 23 win the day: 'Surely goodness and mercy shall follow me all the days of my life'. Peace and faith and hope will triumph over war and hate and pain, even if sometimes it feels as if love and joy are trampled upon. The structure of the movement seems to suggest that we move from peace, through war, to peace again, implying that goodness and peace will overcome evil and death, but Bernstein does not kill his war motif completely: it remains present, lurking in the accompaniment, just to remind us that evil may lie just under the surface.

The third movement opens with an extended organ solo, which itself carries us through tempest and calm, before the choir enters with the word *Adonai* ('Lord'), 5/4 time is used, again creating a slightly uneasy feel, but giving Bernstein a freedom to avoid being foursquare and predicable. The text is Psalm 131, and then the movement, and the whole work, draws to a close with Psalm 133:1: 'How very good and pleasant it is when kindred dwell together in unity!' with an added 'Amen'. The final notes of the *Chichester Psalms* are a subdued fanfare, a farewell to arms reminiscent of bugle calls for the fallen of war, and a reminder of the fearful times in which Bernstein lived, and in which we live now.

Bernstein's music rejects warfare, and although he uses a very modern musical idiom, it is nonetheless approachable and distinctive.

He felt strongly that he would not follow the musical paths of Schönberg, through atonalism and minimalism to the weird and wonderful antics of fellow American John Cage, but would rather write in a particular key, composing melodically.

Bernstein was a talented all-rounder, musically speaking, and had an understanding of his own place in the musical world, gained by reflection and deliberation. In his music we hear peace and war almost simultaneously, and are able to focus our desires on the former. But Bernstein's musical 'retreat', in which he took stock of contemporary music in terms of where it had come from, and where it was going, gave him the strength and composure to write music of profound beauty. May we in Lent also take time, perhaps accompanied by beautiful music, to take stock of where we are coming from, and of where we are going, physically and spiritually, so that we too may be honest, and therefore learn to play to our strengths, to stand up for what we believe, and not to be swept along in any tide of convention, ignorance or evil.

PRAYER

O Lord Jesus our Shepherd, whose will is peace and whose gift is love, calm the raging of the nations and break the bonds of sin that bind peoples, races and communities, so that all your children may live in the freedom of your Spirit and the joy of your salvation, for you are the Prince of peace. Amen.

For further reading: Psalm 131
For listening: The Second Movement, or all of Bernstein's *Chichester Psalms*, either in the full orchestral and choral version, or the reduced version for organ, harp and percussion with choir

'BY THE RIVERS OF BABYLON'

GIUSEPPE VERDI—*NABUCCO*

By the rivers of Babylon—there we sat down and there we wept when we remembered Zion. On the willows there we hung up our harps. For there our captors asked us for songs, and our tormentors asked for mirth, saying, 'Sing us one of the songs of Zion!'

How could we sing the Lord's song in a foreign land? If I forget you, O Jerusalem, let my right hand wither! Let my tongue cling to the roof of my mouth, if I do not remember you, if I do not set Jerusalem above my highest joy. Remember, O Lord, against the Edomites the day of Jerusalem's fall, how they said, 'Tear it down! Tear it down! Down to its foundations!' O daughter Babylon, you devastator! Happy shall they be who pay you back what you have done to us! Happy shall they be who take your little ones and dash them against the rock!

PSALM 137

The opera *Nabucco*, by Giuseppe Verdi (1813–1901), is most famous for its nation-inspiring and moving chorus, '*Va pensiero*' ('Fly, thoughts, on wings of gold'), which is to Italians what 'Land of Hope and Glory' or 'Jerusalem' is to the English. While the chorus is well-known, the opera is not as popular as it used to be, and its biblical origins are often overlooked.

Nabucco, or Nabucodonosor in Italian, is Nebuchadnezzar (strictly, Nebuchadrezzar II), King of Babylon 604–562BC. He can be found in 2 Kings 24—25; 2 Chronicles 36; Ezra 1—2 and Daniel 1—4. In 597BC his armies invaded Jerusalem, and installed Zedekiah as king. Within ten years Zedekiah rebelled, provoking a second attack, the destruction of the Temple and the exile of many Jews to Babylonian captivity. It is this story that Verdi and his librettist, Temistocle Solera, portray.

The first of the opera's four acts is set in Jerusalem before the exile, and the rest of the action takes place in Babylon. Each act is headed by a quotation from Jeremiah. The first act, entitled 'Jerusalem', opens inside Solomon's Temple, where prayer for deliverance from the hands of the Babylonians is being offered. Zechariah, the high priest, has taken Fenena, Nabucco's daughter, as a hostage, and he places her in the care of Ishmael, while he leads the defence of the city. Ishmael and Fenena are in love, having met when he was ambassador in Babylon. She had freed him, and now he will free her. They cannot leave, however, because Babylonian solders enter, led by Abigaille, who is believed to be Nabucco's daughter. She also loves Ishmael, so is angry and hurt at finding him with Fenena, but she offers them all freedom in return for Ishmael's love. Ishmael refuses. The fleeing Jews return at this point, pursued by Babylonians, who would enter the Temple, but for the fact that Zechariah threatens to kill Fenena if they do. Nabucco is unimpressed, and as Ishmael saves Fenena's life, Nabucco destroys the Temple. Abigaille curses the Jews and the Jews curse the treacherous Ishmael.

Act Two, 'The unbeliever', is set in the palace in Babylon. Abigaille has found a document revealing that she is not a princess, but a slave. She is furious with Nabucco, because he has appointed Fenena as regent and sent her home. Thus Fenena has not only stolen the man she loves, but blocks her ambition for power. She cheers up, though, when the High Priest of Baal enters and tells her that because Fenena plans to free the Jews, she, Abigaille must assume power on the pretext that Nabucco has been killed. Meanwhile, Zechariah has decided that he must convert Fenena to Judaism. He succeeds, but the Levites don't like it, and soon the false news that Nabucco is dead and the truth that Abigaille has assumed the throne is announced. Abigaille arrives, but so does Nabucco, who reasserts his authority, condemning the god Baal, who led the Babylonians to betray Nabucco. Nabucco proclaims himself as their new god whom all must worship. As he does so, a thunderbolt knocks the crown from his head. Nabucco goes mad, and Abigaille seizes the crown.

In Act Three, entitled 'The prophecy', Abigaille, now in power, receives the homage of her people in the famous Hanging Gardens of Babylon. The High Priest of Baal enters with a death warrant for Fenena and all the Jews, and asks her to approve it. Nabucco, now mentally ill, wanders in, and Abigaille gets him to sign it. Only later does he realize he has signed the warrant for his daughter's execution. It is too late and also too late to reveal Aigaille's slave status, as she holds the relevant document, which she tears up in his face. Nabucco offers her what little power he has left in return for his daughter's life, but Abigaille does not want to know.

The next scene, the second part of Act Three, contains the famous paraphrase of Psalm 137, '*Va pensiero*', as sung by the Jewish slaves whom Abigaille has just sentenced to death. In chains, they sing:

> *Fly, thought on wings of gold;*
> *go settle on the slopes and hills,*
> *where, soft and mild, the sweet airs*
> *of our native land smell sweet!*
> *Salute Jordan's banks*
> *And Sion's fallen towers.*
> *Oh, my country so lovely, yet lost*
> *Oh remembrance so dear yet deathly!*
> *Golden harps of the prophets*
> *Why do you hang on the willow?*
> *Rekindle the memories of our breasts*
> *And of times past!*
> *Mindful of Jerusalem's fate,*
> *give us the music of lamentation*
> *or let the Lord grant us*
> *strength to endure our sufferings.*

The atmosphere of lament is only broken when Zechariah enters, to prophecy the destruction of Babylon.

Act Four, 'The broken idol', returns us to the personal dramas of Nabucco, now a prisoner in his own palace. Looking out of the window he sees Fenena being led in chains to her execution. In desperation, he prays to God and in a spirit of penitence promises to rebuild the Jewish Temple. He becomes calmer, and tries to escape, and some soldiers who are still loyal to him help him, and all run to save Fenena. She is awaiting execution, but with the support of Zechariah, she is composed and brave. Fortunately, Nabucco and his soldiers arrive in time to save them. Nabucco then orders that the image of Baal be destroyed, but it falls and breaks before anyone can touch it. Nabucco releases all the Jewish captives, and worships God alongside them. In the final dramatic moments Abigaille enters, having taken poison; begging forgiveness of Fenena, she entreats Nabucco to protect Ishmael and Fenena. She dies with God's name on her lips.

In this dramatic opera we are invited to associate the Jewish slaves with the Italian nation. The *Risorgimento*, the movement led by Garibaldi, Mazzini and Cavour, secured Italian independence from Austrian and Spanish rule, unifying the nation at the coronation of King Victor Emanuel II in 1861. Verdi chose an Old Testament theme because of its remoteness from real Italian politics, but in doing so he was able to imbue the action with nuances that promoted the unification of Italy. Thus, in the famous 'Va pensiero', one can interpret the parts that are not directly from Psalm 137 as actually referring to the Italian countryside, laden with a vision of freedom for Italians. That vision has been transposed to sixth-century Babylon. Italians, Verdi says, are exiles in their own land, and thus the chorus (which is set mostly in unison), is composed in a learnable, memorable form, facilitating its adoption as a subversive national anthem. The story of Nebuchadnezzar is almost incidental to Verdi's theme, while the plight of the Jews is used as a vehicle for nationalistic sentiment.

This reminds us that the Bible is always relevant, resonating as it does over millennia. Although the Jewish nation was marked out by God as his chosen people, they are also an archetype, with whom we can empathize. Psalm 137, which refers directly to the exile in Babylon, touches us, because we recognize in their situation something which is sadly all too familiar to us today. We need look no further than the Balkans, Africa, Iraq or Palestine today to find its contemporary echoes. Sometimes when the psalm is said or sung liturgically (and certainly in *Nabucco*) the last verses are omitted. It is easy to be queasy about them, with their murderous intent. However, exiled, repressed peoples do really feel like that, and again, we do not need to look far to know that peoples who are dispossessed can think, and even act, murderously against those whom they perceive to be the perpetrators or supporters of their oppression. Such behaviour should be condemned, of course, but in condemning it, those who dispossess others must hear their cries and act to alleviate the problem, in a spirit of peace, reconciliation and international understanding. It is a shame that the spirit of Lent does not always filter through to a national level, at home and abroad. For Lent is not only a personal form of devotion, it is a discipline of penitence, forgiveness and reconciliation that we should seek to extend to the whole world.

PRAYER

Father, hear our prayer for those who are displaced, persecuted or alienated. Grant to all world leaders a spirit of justice and reconciliation that they may pursue what is good and right for the peoples of the world, and give each one of us the perseverance to pray and act for a better world. Amen.

For further reading: Daniel 4:19–37
For listening: '*Va pensiero*' ('The Chorus of the Hebrew Slaves') from *Nabucco* by Verdi

'YOU HAVE BEEN WEIGHED ON THE SCALES AND FOUND WANTING'

WILLIAM WALTON—*BELSHAZZAR'S FEAST*

'And you, Belshazzar his son, have not humbled your heart, even though you knew all this! You have exalted yourself against the Lord of heaven! The vessels of his temple have been brought in before you, and you and your lords, your wives and your concubines have been drinking wine from them. You have praised the gods of silver and gold, of bronze, iron, wood, and stone, which do not see or hear or know; but the God in whose power is your very breath, and to whom belong all your ways, you have not honoured.'

'So from his presence the hand was sent and this writing was inscribed. And this is the writing that was inscribed: MENE, MENE, TEKEL, and PARSIN. This is the interpretation of the matter: MENE, God has numbered the days of your kingdom and brought it to an end; TEKEL, you have been weighed on the scales and found wanting; PERES, your kingdom is divided and given to the Medes and Persians.'

Then Belshazzar gave the command, and Daniel was clothed in purple, a chain of gold was put around his neck, and a proclamation was made concerning him that he should rank third in the kingdom. That very night Belshazzar, the Chaldean king, was killed.

DANIEL 5:22–30

William Walton (1902–83) began his musical career as a chorister at Christ Church, Oxford, the college chapel that is also the cathedral for that very large English diocese. Born in Oldham in Lancashire, the young William went there at the age of ten, having already sung in the parish church choir where his father was choirmaster. By his own admission, Walton enjoyed his time in Oxford and stayed there through his undergraduate years, developing his talents as a composer after his voice broke. The English cathedral music tradition is a very rich vein indeed, and still thrives, providing boys (and more recently in some places, girls) with a tremendous musical, spiritual and intellectual education, often offered free in return for musical services rendered. Thus William Walton could not have had a better grounding in church music than that offered to a cathedral chorister.

It all paid off, for Walton went on to make a name for himself as a composer, not only of choral music, but also film scores, for classics such as *Henry V*. His best-known work is probably the playful suite called *Façade*, which he wrote in 1922 to accompany a set of poems by Edith Sitwell. Each poem is read through a megaphone by a speaker, with the music happening around the words. Walton was then 19 and had met the Sitwell family in Oxford, who nurtured his friendship and his talent. He even lived with them for a while when he failed exams at Oxford (he never graduated, but received an honorary doctorate in music in 1941).

It was Osbert Sitwell, brother of Edith, who compiled the text for Walton's greatest work, *Belshazzar's Feast*. The text is very faithful to the biblical story found in Daniel, which describes the blasphemous party that the drunken king throws for his nobles.

As the piece opens, before the feast is described, Sitwell and Walton offer us a prophecy from Isaiah, which reminds us of how the Israelites got to be in Babylon in the first place: 'Thus spake Isaiah: Thy sons that thou shalt beget, they shall be taken away, and be eunuchs in the palace of the King of Babylon. Howl ye therefore, for the day of the Lord is at hand!' (from Isaiah 39:7). Then we are transported to Babylon, where the captives sing a lyrical but mournful Psalm 137, which includes the oft-omitted verse: 'Happy shall he be that taketh thy children and dasheth them against a stone' (Psalm 137:9).

Having set the scene, we hear of the feast, which is recounted from the perspective of the Jewish slaves: 'Belshazzar, while he tasted the wine, commanded us to bring the gold and silver vessels'. These vessels were stolen from the Jerusalem Temple by Belshazzar's father

Nebuchadnezzar. The horror and outrage of such an insult to the Jews is vividly presented by Walton, the words 'Yea, drank from the silver vessels', are dramatically punctuated, but the Jews can do nothing, for they are conquered captives who must stand by and watch this sacrilege. Then, to add insult to injury, the assembled guests praise their own gods of gold, silver, bronze, iron, wood and stone, which are vividly described in musical terms by brass and percussion instruments.

However, the writing is on the wall: God comes to their rescue. As the wine is drunk, the king is cryptically condemned: 'mene, mene, tekel, and parsin'. Sitwell and Walton ignore the role of Daniel in the story, and move straight from the strange text on the wall to its translation, quoting only: 'Thou art weighed in the balance and found wanting', and then straight to that stark but chilling statement: 'In that night was Belshazzar the King slain'. And in a moment of unique choral drama, the large chorus shouts with one voice: 'Slain!' The message is clear: 'Don't mess with God', and it emerges not only from Walton's deployment of large choral and orchestral forces, but also in his very careful use of silence between and in the midst of the work's movements.

The inevitable response to the death of Belshazzar is one of rejoicing as a second feast swings into action. Psalm 81:1–3 is now the text ('sing aloud to God our strength'), as they give thanks for their deliverance as Babylon, that great city, falls, thus concluding the reign of Belshazzar, and the half-hour oratorio.

Belshazzar's Feast was composed in 1931 for the Leeds Festival, where it was acclaimed and has remained part of the choral repertoire ever since. It is not an easy work to perform, for even if the choir is up to the technical standard, the orchestral parts are fiendishly difficult in places, and it can be quite hard to keep the whole thing together. When a performance is good though, it is often very good, and the vibrancy and virtuosity of Walton's writing shine through. It is about the death of a treacherous king, but also contains exuberant moments of praise out-poured. Like other pieces by Walton, such as the *Te Deum* and *Gloria*, it has a threefold structure, and while we should not assume that Walton intended any Trinitarian meaning, it is interesting to observe this phenomenon. Thus we may feel that this ancient biblical tale of sin, judgment and punishment is overarched by a Trinitarian promise for

God's people. Such a promise is certainly there for us as we listen to this stupendous piece of twentieth-century musical art, for in the story of Belshazzar we are reminded of God's love and care for his people even in the face of ignominious humiliation. For no matter how bad it is, no matter how weak the people of God seem, God is in, above and over all.

This story of a God-insulter reminds us of the powers to which we are allied. The story also reminds us that sin is very real, and can be very hurtful to others as well as to God and to ourselves. The religious intolerance displayed by Belshazzar has a resonance in our world, and teaches us that whether our faith is ascendant or in remnant mode, nothing becomes us so little as to display intolerance to those of a different disposition, culture, race or creed, even if we are convinced about our own worldviews. It is not even that we should love our enemies (Luke 6:27–29), for people of other creeds are not our enemies. All people are created in the image of God, and our calling is to love and care for them, no matter what they believe, or how they behave. Over many centuries the Christian Church has not had a good history of interfaith or ecumenical relations, and in Lent especially we must seek forgiveness from our brothers and sisters and from God.

PRAYER

God our Father, who revealed yourself to Abraham and Moses, to your prophets and finally in Jesus Christ, pour your Spirit upon your Church, that by your mercy shown to us, we may yet be merciful, kind and generous to others, that divisions may be healed and mutual respect abound in our world. This we ask for the sake of the same, Jesus Christ our reconciling Lord. Amen.

For further reading: Daniel 5:1–30 (the whole story!)
For listening: 'Babylon was a great city' or all or other parts of Walton's *Belshazzar's Feast*

'PRAISE THE LORD, O JERUSALEM'

CLAUDIO MONTEVERDI—
VESPRO DELLA BEATA VIRGINE

Praise the Lord, O Jerusalem! Praise your God, O Zion! For he strengthens the bars of your gates; he blesses your children within you. He grants peace within your borders; he fills you with the finest of wheat. He sends out his command to the earth; his word runs swiftly. He gives snow like wool; he scatters frost like ashes. He hurls down hail like crumbs—who can stand before his cold? He sends out his word, and melts them; he makes his wind blow, and the waters flow. He declares his word to Jacob, his statutes and ordinances to Israel. He has not dealt thus with any other nation; they do not know his ordinances.

PSALM 147:12–20

The Basilica of St Mark's in Venice is a remarkably beautiful building, set rather precariously in a remarkably beautiful city. Venice is a city of dialogue, a city that inspires a rapturous, devoted reaction from some, but makes other visitors flee from its smell and dirt, its crowds and its wealth and decadence. St Mark has long been recognized as the patron saint of Venice, and his body was even stolen from Alexandria (where he was martyred) to rest in Venice around the year 828. The symbol of Venice is still the winged lion of St Mark, who, as evangelist, is often represented by that creature. The association between St Mark and Venice predates the theft of his body, for legend has it that when sailing to Rome, St Mark visited Venice, where an angel greeted him with the words: 'Peace be with you, Mark, my evangelist. Here your body will rest' ('*Pax tibi Marce, evangelista meus. Hic requiescet corpus tuum*'). Apocryphal as the story may be, it meant that when his body was brought from Alexandria, it was revered and placed in a special chapel, completed in 832. That chapel was destroyed by fire and a new one was built in 978. However, the current Basilica of St Mark's was built between 1063 and 1073, and is a glorious, opulently decorated church in the Byzantine style. With the completion of this great building, the relationship between the church and state of Venice was thoroughly established, with St Mark as the central figure. Now the cathedral of Venice, St Mark's still houses a shrine of St Mark, even though his body may well have been destroyed by fire in 976.

Up until 1779, the independent state of Venice was a major player on the European stage, after which time it was annexed by the French. Venice was a centre of art, home to Canaletto and Vivaldi, and also to the composer Claudio Monteverdi (1567–1643). Much of that culture served the interests and delights of Venice's rulers: the elected doge, and the council of ten beneath him. St Mark's, which must count as one of the great churches of the world, was effectively the doge's chapel, and as befitted the wealth of the city and its rulers, the church was decorated exquisitely with marble and gold, with paintings adorning the famous altarpiece, the *Pala d'oro*. The treasury of St Mark's still contains valuable and beautiful objects, given by visiting traders, who were required to make a 'gift to St Mark' when passing through Venice. Thus, the church and the city became rich in every way.

Music was very important in 16th- and 17th-century Venice, especially for civic and religious occasions, and particularly for those events which combined both. Thus, a coronation, as took place for Doge Marino Grimani on 27 April 1595, would be sumptuously accompanied with brass music and choral settings. On that occasion the music was mostly composed by Giovanni and Andrea Gabrieli, who had been organists at St Mark's. Giovanni (c1553–1612) was organist in 1595, and his uncle Andrea (1533–85) had been organist before him. Their music was specifically written with St Mark's in mind, and the younger Giovanni placed the musicians in two parts of the church, in order to establish a musical dialogue between them. This approach became distinctive of Venice, and it was into this tradition that Monteverdi stepped.

In the year 1613, St Mark's needed a new *maestro di cappella* (master of the chapel music), and Monteverdi was the main candidate. He did not have time to compose a special piece, but it is very likely that he impressed the powers that were with his recently composed *Vespers for the Blessed Virgin*. He was being examined for the job in August, and on 15 August, the feast day of the Virgin Mary, his *Vespers* (also known as evensong, the seventh service of the day in the Roman Catholic Church), originally written in Mantua in 1610, were performed in St Mark's. Anyone who has been to Venice can imagine the splendour of the event, as the choir was increased from the usual 30 singers to 50, and with instruments too. Recent recreations of the event (notably by Sir John Eliot Gardiner in May 1989, of which a recording exists) give us a good idea of what it might have been like. The doge and his advisers were naturally impressed, and Monteverdi got the job, which he held until his death 30 years later.

These *Vespers* set new bounds for music of its kind. As well as involving the expected dialogue of choirs around the building, there is also a combination of 'standard' vespers texts, such as the Magnificat and Psalms, alongside settings of hymns to the Virgin. Thus there is a dialogue between public, liturgical texts and more private, devotional ones. This was novel, even in Venice. The music is held together by the plainsong tones commonly used for the set psalms; and to perform the whole thing takes about an hour and a half, an unprecedented duration. The use of instruments in worship was not exactly new, but Monteverdi used them to complement and comment upon the text, just as he did in his opera *Orfeo* written in 1607. These innovations endeared Monteverdi to Venice, and the opportunity to try them delighted him greatly.

For example, the movements 'Nigra sum' and 'Pulchra est' both use texts taken from the Song of Songs (1:4–5; 2:10–12 and 6:4–5). Psalm 113 is sung between them, creating a juxtaposition of texts that are about motherhood and sex. It was not long before the Patriarch of Venice was to ban the Song of Songs from liturgical worship! Monteverdi treats the text 'Pulchra est' ('you are beautiful, my love') as a love duet, which is something we might expect to find in one of his operas, such as *The Coronation of Poppea*, which he wrote in 1642.

One of the most stunning movements of the *Vespers* is the 'Lauda Jerusalem'. It opens with a proclamation of the phrase 'Praise the Lord', by the tenors, and then two three-part choirs battle it out to see who can praise God the most! It is not easy to perform, but it is exhilarating for singers and listeners alike. As the piece draws to its closing climax, the top line contains the *cantus firmus* (the plainsong theme that the piece is based upon), while another six parts weave their way towards a great Amen—'let it be so!'

The text comes from Psalm 147, and while we might not expect to consider such a joyful song of praise in Lent, the psalm does remind us of the strength of God, of his protecting power, and of his blessings poured upon us all. For the psalmist, the city is Jerusalem; for Venetians it was their own city, and for us today, we can think of our own places, as we give thanks to God. Lent is about gratitude as well as repentance, because it is the recognition of God's good gifts to us, his love and protection, that drives us to our knees in repentance; we realize that we have not been worthy of such love, revealed in Christ and continued by his spiritual protection ever since. There is also a risk here of assuming that the inhabitants of a particular place have a special place in God's loving care. Old Testament theology is built upon this idea, that the Israelites were the chosen people, as indeed they were. But now, helped perhaps by the Gospel of St Mark, we have witnessed the opening up of God's love and protection for all who believe. Thus, when we think of Jerusalem (or even of Venice), and praise God, we are doing so on behalf of all believers, in every town, city and village, all over the world.

PRAYER

O God and Father of us all, we praise you for your love and protection revealed in Jesus Christ, and continued in your daily presence among us. By your gracious Spirit, continue to pour your blessings upon us, and keep us mindful of our own unworthiness, so that with heart and voice we may be led to repent of our sins and ever sing your praise in every time and place. Amen.

For further reading: Psalms 127 and 128
For listening: 'Lauda Jerusalem', or other movements from Monteverdi's *Vespers*

'I BEAR A CHILD'

ARNOLD SCHÖNBERG—*VERKLÄRTE NACHT*

Two people go through the bare, cold wood;
The moon accompanies them; they gaze at it.
The moon accompanies them above the high oaks.
No cloud obscures the light of heaven,
up to which reach the black treetops.
A woman's voice is heard:

I am carrying a child which is not yours.
In sin I walk beside you.
I have sinned against myself.
I no longer believed in happiness
And yet had a great longing
For life, for the happiness of being a mother,
And duty; therefore I sinned,
And shuddering yielded my body
To the embraces of a stranger,
I even counted myself blessed for doing so
Now life has taken its revenge,
and I have met you, met you.

She walks on awkwardly.
She looks upwards; the moon accompanies them.
Her dark gaze is bathed in light.
A man's voice is heard:

Do not let this child that you have conceived
Be a burden to your soul.
Look how brightly the whole world shines!
There is glory on everything here,
You are floating with me on a cold sea,
But a mutual warmth flickers
from you to me, from me to you.
That will transfigure the strange child;
You will bear it for me, and from me;
You have filled me with splendour;
You have made me a child myself.

He embraces round the waist.
Their breath mingles in the gentle breeze.
Two people walk on through the lofty, bright night.

'VERKLÄRTE NACHT' ('TRANSFIGURED NIGHT'), BY RICHARD DEHMEL, TRANS. GJG

There are striking similarities between this poem, 'Verklärte Nacht' ('Transfigured Night') by Richard Dehmel (1863–1920) and the story of Joseph's reaction to being told that his fiancée Mary is pregnant and that he is not the father (Matthew 1:18–25). There are, of course, crucial differences, but both give us insights into modern human and ancient miraculous child-bearing. Although Arnold Schönberg (1874–1951) did not set Dehmel's words to music, but wrote a piece of 'programme music' based on them, this is an ideal piece to consider on Mothering Sunday.

Mothering Sunday is a day on which Christians sometimes get a bit confused. 'Mothering' raises all kinds of associations, whether we are thinking of the 'mother church' as the physical building of a diocesan cathedral, or of the Christian Church as a whole as 'mother' to our faith. We also remember the Victorian tradition of allowing servants to return to their mothers in mid-Lent in order to present them with simnel cake. More recently, an awareness has crept into 'Mother's Day', as shops call it, that there are many women who find it a difficult day, because they grieve the loss of children, or the inability to conceive. Meanwhile, there are others who have had children against their own intentions or desires, and the day can be hard for them too. Our society sometimes feels bad about those who are excluded when any group of people is celebrated. This is no bad thing, but we should and no doubt will hold on to and celebrate Mothering Sunday, in both churches and gift shops all over the land.

We can combine Arnold Schönberg's remarkable marriage of words and music with our modern understanding of motherhood. *Verklärte Nacht* is a nineteenth-century work, but only just. Schönberg, who was to become a revolutionary figure in the history of Western music, wrote the string sextet in three weeks in 1899, and in many senses it can be seen as the last work of the nineteenth century. The young composer looks over his shoulder at the music of Wagner, Strauss and Brahms, but at the same time hints at what will flow from his pen and those of Webern and Berg who will follow him. This 'crossroads' piece points us in many directions, emotionally, musically, and indeed, spiritually.

Musically speaking, it begins in D minor and ends in D major, carrying us along a very diverse harmonic road, but unlike what was to follow in the twentieth century, this is very much a piece of 'tonal' music, which means that it is always related to a key signature. It is not until halfway through the work though, at the point in the poem when the man speaks to reassure the woman that he will adopt her child as his own, that we hear the first, full-bodied D major chord. Until that point, while the music echoes the poem's uncertain expressions of the woman's lament, the harmony is shifting, rarely resolved. The 25-minute work also contains a chord which the Vienna *Tonkünstlerverein* classified as an 'uncatalogued dissonance': an illegitimate chord, which, they said, did not and therefore should not, exist. The analogy with the soon-to-be single mother's predicament is ironic: in the nineteenth century she would be shamed by the idea that conception did not and therefore should not occur outside wedlock. In first-century Palestine, Joseph had a very similar problem when he discovered that Mary was pregnant, and not by him. It is so easy sometimes to declare that because something should not be so, it is not so. But, as the eighteenth-century philosopher David Hume once said, 'an "ought" does not make an "is"', and how right he was! These are real situations, then and now.

Schönberg illustrates Dehmel's poem in great detail, and it is possible to locate certain parts of the music with lines of the poem. The music has a tight formal plan, which complements the five-part structure of the poem. This structure gives Schönberg freedom within defined boundaries. In a Collect used at Matins in the Book of Common Prayer, there is a reference to Christ, 'whose service is perfect freedom'. In a way, Schönberg's use of strict musical form to convey the emotional and descriptive impact of Dehmel's poem gives him a freedom of expression while serving the musical regulations of his day (which he breaks only once, as we have seen!).

Schönberg and Dehmel raised controversial issues in their work, yet today we do not find Dehmel's subject so risqué, nor Schönberg's illustration of it musically unusual or challenging: how times change! Change, or transfiguration, is what both *Verklärte Nacht* and the story of Mary and Joseph are about. Musically too, we see the beginnings of change, as Schönberg pushes the boundaries of tonal music, such that within a few years, 'atonal' music will have arrived. Atonal music does not depend on a key, as it moves freely amid all the notes of every scale.

The change in and for the woman in the poem is obvious. By her friend's action and word, she is led from pessimism to optimism, and from shame to acceptance. It is not clear whether she has betrayed the relationship, or whether her pregnancy predates this encounter, and that has some bearing on to what extent the man has been wronged. Nevertheless, she feels that her happiness is at stake, because he does not have to accept the consequences of her confession. He does so, and so releases her from sin and shame. The night, and their lives, are transfigured by the combination of confession and absolution found in the poem. The 'bare, cold wood' of the opening, becomes the 'lofty, bright night' of the ending, and Schönberg illustrates this transformation with ethereal writing for the violin.

We must not push the similarities with Matthew 1:18–25 too far: there is no Christ-child in the poem, and Mary did not conceive our Lord 'in sin', as the woman in the poem claims to have done. Mary is 'blessed among women' for the Christ child she bears (Luke 1:42), whereas Dehmel's woman is ashamed. On the other hand, Joseph's reaction to Mary's predicament, and the man's to the woman's are almost identical: the difference is that Joseph's faith in God is not paralleled in Dehmel's poem, even though there is reference to 'heaven' and 'glory'.

The other major difference is that unlike the woman in the poem, who has been unfaithful to herself, and possibly to the man with whom she is walking, Mary was by no means unfaithful, but is rather praised by the angel Gabriel for her faithfulness (Luke 1:28), and she responds with the Magnificat (Luke 1:46–55). Thus, while we may be moved by the encounter between the man and the woman in the woods, and inspired by the change in their relationship, it is Mary whose example of faith, acceptance and self-control inspires us still, as we all aspire to live up to our status as children of God.

PRAYER

O God, whose love finds expression as both father and mother, bless today all who bear the responsibility of motherhood, and all those in their care. Hear our prayer for mothers in difficulty, for those who grieve, and those who cannot be mothers for whatever reason. By the light of your presence, transfigure the lives of us your children, so that we may walk in the confidence and hope of your eternal glory revealed in Jesus Christ, your Son, our Lord. Amen.

For further reading: Matthew 1:18–25
For listening: All, or part of Schönberg's *Verklärte Nacht* (which exists both as an orchestral version of 1917, revised in 1943, and as the original String Sextet of 1899)

'NEITHER DO I CONDEMN YOU'

ALBAN BERG—*WOZZECK*

The scribes and the Pharisees brought a woman who had been caught in adultery; and making her stand before all of them, they said to him, 'Teacher, this woman was caught in the very act of committing adultery. Now in the law Moses commanded us to stone such women. Now what do you say?' They said this to test him, so that they might have some charge to bring against him. Jesus bent down and wrote with his finger on the ground. When they kept on questioning him, he straightened up and said to them, 'Let anyone among you who is without sin be the first to throw a stone at her.' And once again he bent down and wrote on the ground. When they heard it, they went away, one by one, beginning with the elders; and Jesus was left alone with the woman standing before him. Jesus straightened up and said to her, 'Woman, where are they? Has no one condemned you?' She said, 'No one, sir.' And Jesus said, 'Neither do I condemn you. Go your way, and from now on do not sin again.'
JOHN 8:3–11

Between 1915 and 1923 Schönberg wrote no published works, but began to experiment privately with a completely new mode of composition which we have come to call 'serial' or 'twelve-tone' music. Rather than use notes derived from an eight-note octave, with a 'key signature', such as C major, Schönberg developed a system using all the notes, black notes as well as white notes on a typical piano keyboard. This novel and creatively interesting system produced music that many, even today, find very difficult to listen to. Serial music is highly structured and organized, but to an untutored ear it can sound unpleasant. Nevertheless, serial music was a major landmark in Western music, and much twentieth-century music was either inspired by it, or was a reaction to it.

Schönberg had two important pupils, Anton Webern, and Alban Berg (1885–1935), the latter of whom carried serial technique most effectively into the world of opera. *Wozzeck*, first performed in 1925, is the story of a soldier who, experimented upon by a doctor, consequently murders the mother of his child and drowns himself. Its emotional impact is intense, even though it lasts only an hour and 40 minutes, and it is far more draining than three hours of Mozart. The original play, written by Georg Büchner (1813–37), is based on the true story of a demented soldier who, in 1824, was executed for murdering his mistress. Büchner was convinced that the only way to understand humanity was through acceptance of everybody: no matter how depraved, unpleasant or ugly anybody is, they should not be despised.

Büchner's *Wozzeck*, published in 1875, was distilled by Berg from 26 scenes to 15. Wozzeck is a soldier and servant to a captain, and in the opening scene he is criticized by the captain for having an illegitimate child, but Wozzeck says that morality is only for rich people and quotes Jesus: 'Let the little children come to me' (Matthew 19:14). Wozzeck leaves and meets his friend Andres, who, unlike Wozzeck, is cheerful. Wozzeck is disturbed by visions. He then visits Marie, the mother of his child, who has been watching a military march-past and has caught the attention of a drum major. Wozzeck is still gloomy, and leaves Marie worrying about him. He then visits his doctor, who experiments with his diet, allowing him to eat only beans. Wozzeck reveals that he hears voices in his head. The doctor is delighted to hear it, encourages him in his obsession, and pays him. Meanwhile, Marie first resists and then allows herself to be seduced by the drum major she saw earlier.

The second act of the opera is composed as a symphony in five movements. It opens with a touching scene of Marie and her child. Wozzeck enters and gives her money, so when he leaves Marie feels guilty. There follows a sarcastic encounter between the doctor and the captain, but when they find Wozzeck, both taunt him about the drum major and Marie, and as Wozzeck realizes what they are insinuating, the doctor studies his reactions. Wozzeck then goes to see Marie, whom he quizzes about the drum major. She accuses him of being mad, and then, when Wozzeck threatens her, she is defiant, saying that she would rather have a knife in her than a hand on her. Wozzeck is disturbed by these words, and leaves, saying: 'Humanity is an abyss which makes you dizzy if you look into it.' Wozzeck has now reached the edge of this abyss of madness, jealousy and despair. He therefore heads to a tavern, where everybody else is already drunk. Marie is there too, dancing with the drum major. Drinking songs ensue, and Andres wonders if Wozzeck is drunk, but he cannot afford to get drunk. A character called the Idiot approaches Wozzeck, saying he can smell blood, which greatly disturbs Wozzeck, who is now on the verge of breakdown. Back at the barracks, he has nightmares, haunted by visions of a knife. He prays, quoting the Lord's prayer. The drum major wanders in, boasting about Marie, and when Wozzeck objects, the drum major humiliates him and beats him up.

Act Three is made up of six 'inventions', one of which is based on only one note (B). We hear Marie reading the passage about the woman caught in adultery from the Bible (John 8:3–11). The words are not sung conventionally, but are set in a *sprechstimme* style, whereby the music illustrates words spoken in a lilting manner. Marie focuses on the words of Jesus: 'Neither do I condemn you. Go your way, and from now on do not sin again' (John 8:11) and then turns to the story of the woman (whom Marie calls Mary Magdalene) washing Jesus' feet with her hair (Luke 7:36–39). She prays, 'Saviour, you had mercy on her, have mercy on me!' Then follows her final encounter with Wozzeck, who, jealous and demented, stabs her to death by a pool. Berg's use of serial composition techniques here reaches its minimalist climax, as only one note is used to convey the singular horror and tragedy of her death. Wozzeck goes straight to the tavern, where Marie's friend Margret notices blood on his hand, and soon the whole company revile him because he smells of human blood. Wozzeck returns to the pool to search for the knife, for he knows that he is a murderer and will be found out. Finding the knife, he throws it into the water, but scared of the moonlight he wades into the bloodstained pool, and is submerged. Coincidentally, the doctor and captain pass by and hear him groaning as he drowns, but they do nothing, and there is no Good Samaritan to help Wozzeck as the darkness closes over him. The opera ends with children singing and playing, Marie and Wozzeck's child among them. The others tell the boy that his mother is dead, but he does not really understand.

We may well feel that we do not really understand. This is a dark tale, accompanied by profound but challenging music. There is no happy ending, if it could be said that the opera has an ending at all. For some people, life is like that; it is merely something that happens until you die, and then it just stops. Yet the opera is full of religious imagery and direct quotations from the Bible: underneath the torment is a plea for goodness and a recognition of Christ as Saviour. But there is also the dark implication that the real significance and the saving power of Christ through faith, is somehow inaccessible to impoverished people like Wozzeck and Marie. In spite of the fact that Jesus said: 'Blessed are the poor in spirit, for theirs is the kingdom of heaven' (Matthew 5:3), we can only feel at the end that their tragedy has happened beyond Christian reach. In our day, we often hear about people who are driven to kill through madness, and we despair over what can be done to help them and those in danger from them. Such people are incredibly vulnerable, and may be potentially dangerous to themselves and others. As *Wozzeck* shows us, the solution lies neither in religion nor medicine alone. Mental damage needs healing of both kinds.

We may be inclined to ignore mental suffering, but we should not forget the abyss that Wozzeck sees, and towards which any one of us might be led at any time, for any reason. Mental health is as fragile as life itself. As we flinch at the plight of Wozzeck, lamenting the way in which society or authority treats such damaged people, we may well whisper under our breath: 'But for the grace of God, there go I.' In Lent, let us remember those who are so painfully damaged, and pray for spiritual and physical balance to help them in whatever way we can.

PRAYER

Loving God, who rejects no one, and cradles the damaged areas of our souls, grant healing and comfort to all who labour under the strain of mental illness, and give wisdom and understanding to those who minister to them. By the passion of Christ, calm the stresses and strains of our lives, and lead us always from despair to hope. Amen.

For further reading: Mark 1:23–34
For listening: Act Three Scene Two (Variation on One Note) from Berg's *Wozzeck*

'FOR WHAT WILL IT PROFIT THEM TO GAIN THE WHOLE WORLD AND FORFEIT THEIR LIFE?'

CHARLES GOUNOD—*FAUST*

Then he began to teach them that the Son of Man must undergo great suffering, and be rejected by the elders, the chief priests, and the scribes, and be killed, and after three days rise again. He said all this quite openly. And Peter took him aside and began to rebuke him. But turning and looking at his disciples, he rebuked Peter and said, 'Get behind me, Satan! For you are setting your mind not on divine things but on human things.'

He called the crowd with his disciples, and said to them, 'If any want to become my followers, let them deny themselves and take up their cross and follow me. For those who want to save their life will lose it, and those who lose their life for my sake, and for the sake of the gospel, will save it. For what will it profit them to gain the whole world and forfeit their life? Indeed, what can they give in return for their life? Those who are ashamed of me and of my words in this adulterous and sinful generation, of them the Son of Man will also be ashamed when he comes in the glory of his Father with the holy angels.'

MARK 8:31–38

The legend of Faust (or Doctor Faustus) has its origin in the life of Georg Faust, who is thought to have lived in Germany between 1480 and 1538. He was evidently a powerful and boastful man, about whom legends soon circulated after his death. The English dramatist Christopher Marlowe wrote *Dr Faustus* in 1588, but it was Goethe (who also wrote the story of the Sorcerer's Apprentice) who first used the stories about Faust to create the most famous version of the legend. In Part One of that work, published in 1808, Faust, a philosopher seeking not only all knowledge but all experience, finds that he must surrender his soul to Mephistopheles, the agent of Satan. In return, he finds that he can seduce Gretchen, who, when she gives birth to his child, drowns it, thus incurring a death penalty for murder. Faust tries to persuade her to escape with him, but she trusts in God rather than in his devilish temptations, and dies in prison. In this first part of *Faust* we find the main narrative of the story, while in Part Two Goethe presents his views on culture, history and politics. At the end, Faust tries to redeem himself by rescuing land from the sea in order to create an ideal society, but he fails. Finally, in Goethe's play, Faust is saved by angels.

It was only Part One of *Faust* that interested the French composer Charles Gounod (1818–93) for his opera composed in 1859. In German-speaking lands it is often referred to as *Margarethe*, after the name of the heroine in Gounod's version. Gounod and his librettists Michel Carré and Jules Barbier used the love story between Faust and Margarethe (Gretchen) which was almost entirely invented by Goethe.

The opera opens with the disillusioned and aged Faust about to take poison. He is prevented by the sounds of cheerful young people outside, and in frustration invokes Satan to assist him. Mephistopheles appears in a flash of red light and offers him wealth and power. Faust wants more, demanding also the gift of youth. Mephistopheles is happy to grant this, if Faust will sign away his soul, writing in his own blood. This causes Faust to hesitate but he is tempted beyond redemption by a vision of Marguerite (as Gounod calls her) sitting at a spinning-wheel, the very picture of beauty and innocence. Faust drinks from the potion that he is offered and at once he becomes a young man again.

The second of the five acts takes place outside the city walls, where a fair is in full swing. There is much dancing and drinking, and the character of the composer Wagner even appears briefly. He starts to sing a song, but is interrupted by Mephistopheles, who sings in praise of the golden calf (see Exodus 32:1–9). Valentine, Marguerite's brother, is proud of a medallion which she has given him to protect him in battle, but Mephistopheles prophesies that he will die soon and then cuts down a wine barrel and makes the liquid turn to fire. As he does so he drinks to Marguerite; this angers Valentine, who draws his sword. Mephistopheles draws a circle around himself with his own sword and Valentine's sword breaks. Valentine realizes who Mephistopheles is, and he and his companions all extend the hilts of their swords towards him. Confronted by all these 'crosses', Mephistopheles retreats, taking Faust with him. They meet Marguerite, who is carrying a prayer book, and Mephistopheles prevents Valentine's friend Siebel from making advances to her. Instead, Faust is able to meet her.

In order to attract Marguerite, Siebel picks flowers in her garden, but Mephistopheles has cursed them so that they wither. He finds some holy water, which restores them, and he leaves a bouquet outside her door. Faust and Mephistopheles return and Faust extols the humility of Marguerite's lifestyle. Mephistopheles returns with jewels and better flowers, and while they hide she enters and sits down to spin at her wheel. When she discovers the gifts, she is delighted and sings a famous and difficult aria (the 'Jewel Song'). When Martha, her friend, joins her, Faust and Mephistopheles re-appear, and while Mephistopheles flirts with Martha, Faust is able to be alone with Marguerite. Mephistopheles casts a spell and soon she falls into Faust's arms.

In the fourth act, Marguerite is pregnant with Faust's child. He has abandoned her, but in spite of Siebel's love and loyalty to her, she is still hopeful that Faust will return. She goes to church, where Mephistopheles torments her, reminding her of her sin. Demons are heard as the 'Dies irae' ('Day of wrath') is played on the organ. As the singing dies away, Mephistopheles calls out to her, taunting her with the abyss that awaits her. She flees in terror.

The action moves to the street outside her house, where the soldiers Siebel and Valentine return, singing their famous 'Soldiers' Chorus' (which is very well-known). When they have gone into the house, Faust and Mephistopheles arrive; the latter sings a rather insulting serenade to Marguerite. Valentine is outraged and wants to fight. Faust takes up the challenge and kills him, and as he lies dying he curses his sister. (In some productions of the opera, this scene is followed by the scene in church which I have already described, and Act Four opens with the street scene.)

Act Five opens with an extensive ballet section, which is often omitted. Marguerite is in prison, having murdered her baby. Faust breaks into the prison to rescue her, but she is convinced that she is damned and will not leave. Marguerite is already dying, and she begins to pray, but still Faust tries to make her leave with him. As she dies Faust declares that she is damned, but a chorus of angels proclaim that she has been saved. As she is borne away to heaven angels proclaim that 'Christ is risen, Christ is born again!' and Faust himself falls to his knees in prayer. Mephistopheles cannot prevent him because an archangel has struck him with his sword.

This is not a fairy tale in which good triumphs over evil. There are no clear edges, black and white distinctions or simple solutions at the end. With the saving of Marguerite at the end, and the final turning to prayer of Faust it all seems to come right, but there has been much damage, distress and deceit along the way. There is great subtlety here and hard questions posed for any one of us. How much would we sacrifice willingly for eternal youth (or eternal life!)? How often have we actually 'sold out' to Satan, willingly or not? Do we bargain with God, or even with Satan?

If we look more closely at the story we might also ask, 'Is Faust completely evil, or is it more subtle than that?' In Revelation, the number of the beast (the evil number) is 666 (Revelation 13:18). This is so because it falls short of 777, three times. Evil need not be 'completely' evil: it is not always obvious, but disguised, and because it sometimes is as close to goodness as six is to seven, we are so easily deceived into thinking that bad is good, or vice versa.

Gounod turns this kind of story into entertainment, providing rousing choruses, beautiful arias and even a ballet, thereby conforming to contemporaneous Parisian fashion, but in choosing *Faust* he also holds up a mirror to our own lives, reflected in the exaggerated lives of Faust and Marguerite. It is of course unlikely that we should ever find ourselves in a similar position (although there are those who deliberately associate with the devil), yet it is very important that we get the basic message and guard for temptations even in the most subtle of situations. This basic message is found in 1 Peter 5:6–11: we must be vigilant, for the devil prowls like a roaring lion ready to devour us. What seems like an innocuous decision or act can lead us into spiritual danger, or compromise us. The soldier Valentine recognizes Mephistopheles for who he is, and holds his sword up like a crucifix to ward off Satan, but he later pays a high price for it. Even though it appears that goodness has triumphed in Marguerite at the end, which rubs off on Faust, we must notice that Mephistopheles is held at bay only by an archangel. Satan is temporarily defeated, not destroyed.

In the world in which we live, it is very clear that Satan is not destroyed, and sometimes we can see evil gaining an advantage. There are some very nasty people about, and some terrible things going on of which we are barely aware. Where there is such evil we must combat it with prayer and with action, and we cannot expect the decisions we must take, or allow others to take, to be clear cut, black and white moral decisions. For where there is evil, there may be a little goodness to be found, and where there is good, even in the church, Satan may be lurking, and not without effect. This Lent, then, let us be watchful, and prayerful, and active in the pursuit of Christly goodness, in ourselves and in the world.

PRAYER

O God, whom to know and love is salvation, whom to deny is sin, keep us vigilant and level-headed in the pursuit of what is good and righteous and true, and help us to help those who have erred and strayed and whose sin controls their lives. Release them and us from the bonds of evil, and lead all your people by the beacon of your merciful grace revealed in Jesus Christ our Lord. Amen.

For further reading: 1 Peter 5:6–11
For listening: 'The Soldiers' Chorus' from *Faust* by Charles Gounod

'BLESSED ARE YOU WHEN PEOPLE REVILE YOU AND PERSECUTE YOU'

RICHARD STRAUSS—*SALOME*

'Blessed are those who hunger and thirst for righteousness, for they will be filled. Blessed are the merciful, for they will receive mercy. Blessed are the pure in heart, for they will see God. Blessed are the peacemakers, for they will be called children of God. Blessed are those who are persecuted for righteousness' sake, for theirs is the kingdom of heaven. Blessed are you when people revile you and persecute you and utter all kinds of evil against you falsely on my account. Rejoice and be glad, for your reward is great in heaven, for in the same way they persecuted the prophets who were before you.'
MATTHEW 5:6–12

Why did Herod kill John the Baptist? Was it merely because of his promise to his daughter? Perhaps it was as simple as that: Herod's misdirected integrity, his insecure need to adhere to a principle, made him not want to be seen to break his word. Herod was a weak man who would *do* wrong in order not to be *thought* wrong. He was also someone, like many people, who has a deep need to please others, and he wanted to please his step-daughter, whom we have come to call Salome (there is a confusion in the biblical text (Mark 6:17–29), as she is sometimes also called Herodias). He also wanted to impress his guests; and he wanted to please his wife of dubious standing, Herodias. We are told that Herod is frightened of John the Baptist, but surprisingly, it is not his fear of John that leads Herod to kill him, but his fear of his friends, his reputation, and his fear of his wife, who bears grudges easily.

Herod was infatuated with his new wife, and it is through her influence that John the Baptist was imprisoned in the first place, because he spoke out against their adulterous marriage. Herodias fears and dislikes John the Baptist intensely and wants him dead. Herod fears her, not because he dislikes her but because he loves her. People who are obsessed fear the loss of that by which they are obsessed. Thus Herod, it seems, was doubly cursed: first by his obsession for his reputation and the power he held, and second by the obsession he had for his wife.

Herod is forced to act by a pathetic oath. What he believes to be a public statement of power was actually an act of supreme weakness. It revealed that he had very little real power: he was under the thumb of a callous and manipulative wife. He was also vulnerable to the sexual allure of his step-daughter. He was trapped, by his reputation and by his relationships. Both combine in a reaction, at the nucleus of which lies fear and insecurity. In the grip of such fear, Herod acted in what only looks like his own best interest. He protected himself and his own vulnerability, in order to preserve the imagined security he finds in his apparent power, but his obsession with his reputation, his fear of rejection by family and friends, and his false sense of power led to disaster.

This story of power and lust was the inspiration for a French poem of Oscar Wilde's, which, having been turned into a libretto by Anton Lindner, gave the German composer Richard Strauss the material for what some say is his most innovative and influential opera. Richard Strauss (1864–1949) lived through both the first and second world wars in Germany, during which periods he maintained a musical integrity in the inherited tradition of Wagner. His music is often thought to be a little too expressive, too emotional and intense, such that some find him vulgar, yet there is little doubt of his musical genius, or of his ability to explore new realms musically. Oscar Wilde's risqué poem appealed, and became the vehicle for an opera that the Viennese censor said was blasphemous but which was acclaimed with

38 curtain calls on its opening night in Dresden in December 1905. A hint of controversy still surrounds the work a century later, as the character of Salome is required to perform what is effectively a strip-tease, and Wilde portrays Salome as being infatuated with John the Baptist. The Bible passage gives no warrant for this, of course, and here we are in the realm of what might be called 'biblical fantasy'.

Wilde's version of the story, which Strauss' opera follows, begins with John in prison, guarded in solitary confinement. Salome appears and persuades the soldier Narraboth to let her speak to John. John continues to denounce Herod and Herodias for their adultery, and when he realizes who Salome is, he rejects her. She in turn tries to kiss him, and it becomes clear that she is obsessed by him. Narraboth is horrified by all this and kills himself. John tells Salome of Christ, and urges her to turn to Christ and repent.

Then follows a banquet, at which Salome dances for Herod, but only after he has sworn to give her anything as a present. Without direct reference to her mother, she duly asks for John's head, which delights Herodias and appals Herod. He tries to offer even half his kingdom, but she is relentless, and he feels forced to oblige. John is duly executed and his head is brought in on a platter. Salome kisses the lips of the dead John, just as she has tried to do while he was still alive. Herod is so jealous and appalled that he has Salome killed on the spot.

It is not hard to understand why this plot and its musical drama-tization caused controversy. It could be called distasteful, blasphemous, even disgusting. Yet, there is something accurate in the portrayal of the last days and death of a political prisoner such as John the Baptist. He is degraded and humiliated in the opera, and while Wilde's interpretation may not have been accurate, there can be little doubt that John suffered terribly. We might be inclined to think of him as a saintly man, whose memory must be cherished, because of his calling and ministry as forerunner of Christ. Nevertheless he, like Jesus and so many after him, was a victim of brutality and oppression, and Strauss' opera makes this very clear.

We could think of many people like John, who have suffered and died for their faith and for their unpopular opinions. In the century since *Salome* was composed, there have been countless martyrs, only some of whom we know by name. We might think of Dietrich Bonhoeffer, the German theologian who became involved in getting Jews to safety, and in the plot to kill Hitler, for which he was executed (rather like John) only a month before the war ended in 1945. Hitler (rather like Herodias) was not content to let those who spoke out against him merely languish in jail.

Dietrich Bonhoeffer, like John the Baptist, was the victim of a dance of power, prostituted by insecurity and false principles. We do not need to follow the news too closely to be reminded that, like John the Baptist, and Bonhoeffer, we live in a world in which the authoritarian misuse of principle and power is still very real. Political prisoners like John are killed every day for the same reason: no reason. Amnesty International reports that security forces, police or state authorities torture or abuse prisoners in some 117 countries worldwide. We watch for this kind of thing, and pray against it.

This is not only an international issue, for it can infect our own lives too, as it did Herod's. We may not have dinner parties quite as lavish as his, nor may we have such treasures under lock and key. But fear, loss of face, exaggerated loyalty, pride or obsession can equally decapitate what is good in us, and around us, if we are so determined to get what we want, and to prevent others from stopping us.

PRAYER

God of justice and mercy, as we remember the suffering of John the Baptist and of countless others who have laid down their lives in the service of Christ, enable us to cast aside our own selfish desires and speak his name in the cause of truth, righteousness and peace, so that the sacrifice of your servants may not be in vain, but may point to a better world, in which your holy and loving will is honoured in word and deed. Amen.

For further reading: Mark 6:17–29
For listening: 'Salome's Dance', from *Salome* by Richard Strauss

'DO NOT BE OVERCOME WITH EVIL, BUT OVERCOME EVIL WITH GOOD'

CAMILLE SAINT-SAËNS—*SAMSON AND DELILAH*

Bless those who persecute you; bless and do not curse them. Rejoice with those who rejoice, weep with those who weep. Live in harmony with one another; do not be haughty, but associate with the lowly; do not claim to be wiser than you are. Do not repay anyone evil for evil, but take thought for what is noble in the sight of all. If it is possible, so far as it depends on you, live peaceably with all. Beloved, never avenge yourselves, but leave room for the wrath of God; for it is written, 'Vengeance is mine, I will repay, says the Lord.' No, 'if your enemies are hungry, feed them; if they are thirsty, give them something to drink; for by doing this you will heap burning coals on their heads.' Do not be overcome by evil, but overcome evil with good.

ROMANS 12:14–21

The story of Samson and Delilah ranks alongside David and Goliath as one of the most exciting and memorable tales in the Old Testament. It is a truly tragic tale, for it can be read as the story of a hero with a fatal flaw, which leads to his downfall. Samson may not (or should not) be an inspiration to modern humanity, but his story is hardly one we can forget or ignore. It has been set musically as an oratorio by Handel (which we shall consider tomorrow), and also as an opera by the French composer Camille Saint-Saëns (1835–1921).

Saint-Saëns is more well-known for *The Carnival of the Animals*, but he was a talented organist and composer of vocal music. The idea of writing *Samson and Delilah* came to him when he was 32, in 1867, although it took 25 years before it was staged. The French text was created by Ferdinand Lemaire (who was from Martinique), but Saint-Saëns composed erratically and with mixed enthusiasm. Such an enterprise was then controversial, for it was thought sacrilegious to turn a biblical story into a play or opera.

The operatic plot follows the story found in Judges 14—16. At the beginning, the enslaved Israelites are depressed, but Samson encourages them. Abimilech, Philistine satrap of Gaza, arrives and mocks their faith in God. Samson stirs up the crowd, and grabs Abimilech's sword, killing him with it. Delilah, a priestess of the temple of Dagon, enters and Samson is warned about her by an old man, but by the end of Act One she has lured him into the temple of Dagon.

Act Two opens with Delilah apprehensive about her deceitful task, but a priest of Dagon comes to encourage her in her mission, and tells her that Samson does not really love her. Delilah reveals that she has already tried three times to learn his secret, but 'to gratify my hate' she will try again. When the priest of Dagon has gone, Delilah's doubts return. Samson arrives, and he is also doubtful about their relationship, even though he does love her. They sing the duet '*Mon coeur s'ouvre à ta voix*' ('My heart opens to your voice'), but he will not reveal his secret. Delilah unsuccessfully demands his trust, so she leaves him, indicating that the relationship is over. Samson relents and follows her offstage. As Philistine soldiers approach the house, it becomes clear that Delilah has cut his hair.

The final act takes us to the prison of Gaza, where blind Samson laments his fate, chained to a millstone. Other Israelite prisoners berate him for having betrayed them, and Samson apologizes profusely. He is then led away to the temple of Dagon, to be put on show as a trophy of war. A musical interlude, the evocative 'Bacchanale', is heard at this point, and we get a sense of Saint-Saëns' exotic and creative musical imagination. The swirling dance having reached its stunning climax, Samson is led in by a child, emphasizing his new-found weakness.

Delilah and the Philistines mock him, she reminding him of their love, but also of how she is proud of the vengeance she has gained for 'her people, her god and her hatred'. They mock God, and laugh at Samson when he prays for a miracle that he might avenge their insults. Delilah and the priests of Dagon go to the altar to offer a thanksgiving, and Samson is left with the child. Gaining inspiration, he asks the boy to lead him to the central pillars of the temple, and once there he asks God to avenge him for the loss of his sight. His prayer is granted and in a final show of strength, the temple—and the curtain—falls.

The opera manages to hold some of the moral ambiguities of the story, although Saint-Saëns makes more of a character of Delilah, and makes her motives clearer. In the opera, she is out to get Samson, although it is hard to believe that she does not really love him nor ever did. She woos him beautifully, but is also remarkably cruel to him. Samson, in spite of his great strength and reputation as a killer, is her victim. Although he brings the temple down at the end, his victory does appear to be a hollow one, and today we might well be sensitive about Samson, because he could easily be cast as a suicidal terrorist obsessed with ousting an oppressive regime. There are perhaps too many situations like this which make us wonder why we should want to relish this story at all. A man with a record of violence who sacrifices himself while destroying symbols of alien religious power and innocent bystanders is less likely to inspire us after the events of 11 September 2001. How can we praise Samson after the twin towers of New York were brought down by religious fanatics, blind to any perspective but their own?

It took many years for Saint-Saëns' opera to be accepted, liked or understood. Theatres were reluctant to stage it, and many thought the music too progressive Similarly, there are stories in the Bible that we may find difficult: stories that are discordant with our understanding of God. For there is also something distasteful about Samson's story. More about violence than love, more about betrayal than loyalty, no one emerges from it well. If Samson is a hero, it is only because he kills a lot of people, and even if they are worshipping a foreign God, today we would never countenance such behaviour. Sometimes a story like this just seems to be out of tune with the here and now. Violence, vengeance and betrayal are not Christly virtues, and Samson is hardly an exemplary Christ-figure.

This is precisely the point. In Samson we have a hero who is not like Christ. In Christ the old ways are put aside, for Christ and his followers do *not* operate in this way. In Christ there is not revenge, but forgiveness, in return for hate and violence, Christ offers love. Samson and Christ are both betrayed, but they react differently (see Luke 22:47–51, where Jesus tells Peter to put away his sword and heals the damage to the servant's ear). Like Samson, Jesus is taunted and mocked (Mark 14:65, 15:16–20). Jesus does turn the tables over in the Temple (Matthew 21:12–13), but Jesus' anger is symbolic, and there is no harmful violence.

Compelling and disturbing as the story of Samson and Delilah is, whether in text or music, we may find it most helpful when placed in the context of the gospel. It is hard to applaud Samson, or Delilah, but their behaviour helps us see that in Christ there is another, better way. In a violent world these words of John Colet (Dean of St Paul's, 1504–19) still hold true: 'There is nothing that conquers evil but good; and if you aim at returning evil for evil, and endeavour to crush evil by evil, then you yourself descend to evil.'

This Lent, may we strive to return evil with good, and not be led into a downward spiral of getting even for sins committed against us.

PRAYER

O God of goodness and mercy, forgive us our sins, and lead us away from evil to love and peace. Help those who hold great power to wield it not with vengeance, but with hope, integrity and caution, and show to the whole world the pierced and wounded body of your Son, our Lord and Saviour Jesus Christ. Amen.

For further reading: Judges 15:4—16:31
For listening: '*Mon coeur s'ouvre à ta voix*' or the 'Bacchanale' from Saint-Saëns' *Samson and Delilah*

'THOSE HE KILLED AT HIS DEATH WERE MORE THAN THOSE HE HAD KILLED DURING HIS LIFE'

GEORGE FRIDERIC HANDEL—*SAMSON*

Then Samson called to the Lord and said, 'Lord God, remember me and strengthen me only this once, O God, so that with this one act of revenge I may pay back the Philistines for my two eyes.' And Samson grasped the two middle pillars on which the house rested, and he leaned his weight against them, his right hand on the one and his left hand on the other. Then Samson said, 'Let me die with the Philistines.' He strained with all his might; and the house fell on the lords and all the people who were in it. So those he killed at his death were more than those he had killed during his life. Then his brothers and all his family came down and took him and brought him up and buried him between Zorah and Eshtaol in the tomb of his father Manoah. He had judged Israel for twenty years.

JUDGES 16:28–31

Over a hundred years before Camille Saint-Saëns wrote his opera *Samson and Delilah*, George Frideric Handel (1685–1759) composed an oratorio about this rather dubious Old Testament hero. For a text he used the poem *Samson Agonistes* by the great English poet John Milton, and it was Milton who reinterpreted the story of Samson in terms of a classical Greek tragedy. Milton takes the model, epitomized in plays such as *King Oedipus*, *Oedipus at Colonus* and *Antigone*, written by Sophocles, an Athenian who lived four centuries before Christ. In these

146

plays are the forerunners of the tragic heroes who are well-known to us today: Macbeth, Othello and Hamlet (although Shakespeare was influenced as much by the Roman poet Seneca as by the Greeks).

The word 'tragedy' is bandied about these days in various contexts, particularly in news stories, but it has a proper and historical use, which takes us back to ancient Greece. For some obscure reason the word, meaning 'goat's song', denoted a drama with a central character ('hero') who is admirable but who possesses a fatal, 'tragic' flaw, which becomes the means of his or her downfall. As the hero falls, there comes a moment of catharsis, as the full impact of the hero's fall 'purges' the audience. Catharsis is an emotional effect brought on in the observer, and was first identified as an aesthetic phenomenon by Aristotle, in his *Poetics*, where he identifies the tragic moment as the point at which we truly feel pity for the hero. Samson, felt Milton, was like a tragic hero. For it is perhaps as he is betrayed and humiliated, leading to his final act of revenge, that we feel real pity for him, and are moved by his story.

It is all too easy to see Delilah as the bad girl spy who seduces Samson so that she can learn his secret and then humiliate him and his God. Perhaps we should consider what choice she really had, and also remember what Samson did to her people. His wife was taken away from him (see Judges 14–15), and he responded by destroying the Philistines' crops, so they murdered his wife and father-in-law. In turn he killed a thousand men (Judges 15:15). Samson is certainly portrayed as killing people and picking fights, physically or verbally. By the time he meets Delilah (Judges 16:4), he has become public enemy number one, and the Philistines are out to get him. His new girlfriend Delilah hardly stands a chance, for it is imperative that she deliver him to the authorities, who bribe and cajole her. Samson lies to the person he apparently loves. This is morally confusing because we know the outcome, and we can see why he lies: he does not trust her, and we know that he is right not to. Strangely, Delilah's persistence pays off; Samson eventually relents because he is fed up with being pestered about the secret of his strength.

Milton's poem, which Handel's librettist Newburgh Hamilton used, was published in 1671 and was intended to be read rather than performed. Milton had a natural affinity with Samson, for Milton was blind (Samson is blinded by the Philistines: see Judges 16:21). 'Agonistes' indicates that Samson was a strong man or wrestler. The action is set in the period after Samson is captured by the Philistines, and with the presence of a dramatic chorus, Milton draws on the Greek heritage of tragedy, casting Samson as the unfortunate hero. When Handel wrote his oratorio in 1741 (straight after *Messiah*) he did not use the complete text. The action begins with Samson being brought out of prison for show, on a feast day of the god Dagon. He laments his fate, but is soon greeted by his friend Micah, who describes Samson in truly tragic terms:

O mirror of our fickle state!
In birth, in strength, in deeds how great!
From highest glory fall'n so low,
Sunk in the deep abyss of woe!

Samson continues to lament, singing 'Total eclipse!... Sun, moon, and stars are dark to me!', but then his father Manoah appears, intending to ransom Samson. Samson, however, feels that he has deserved his fate. Delilah then comes to see Samson, and she seeks forgiveness from him, but, as she expects, he scorns her, so she redefines her betrayal of him as an act of patriotism. Then a Philistine warrior called Harapha enters and mocks Samson and his God. Micah suggests a trial of strength between them, as champions of their faiths. Samson refuses to humour Harapha, who becomes angry when Samson refers to the 'vain religious rites' of Dagon. Samson then warms to the idea of defeating the Philistines with God's help, and he goes to the feast to show his strength. Offstage we hear the party going on, and then chaos as Samson pulls down the temple upon them all. Micah mourns his friend, whose body is brought in to the accompaniment of a death march. Thus Samson's funeral begins, and as his achievements are praised, the mood changes and his father Manoah sings:

Come, come! No time for lamentation now,
no cause for grief; Samson like Samson fell,

> *both in life and death heroic. To his foes*
> *ruin is left, to him eternal fame.*

This is then followed by the most famous aria from *Samson*:

> *Let the bright Seraphim in burning row*
> *Their loud, uplifted trumpets blow.*
> *Let the Cherubic host, in tuneful choirs,*
> *Touch their immortal harps with golden wires.*

So concludes Milton's (and Handel's) distinctive treatment of Samson's story, which bows to the conventions of Greek tragedy and eighteenth-century oratorio. Dramatically, the plot ends with Samson's tragic death. Musically it must finish in a blaze of glory, and to do this Handel added the ending which we do not find in Milton.

Handel wrote *Samson* as an oratorio because he could not set it as an opera. There was a tradition of singing oratorios in Lent, and in them the drama is located in the music. The chorus propel the action forward by describing events and reflecting upon them, while the characters sing arias and recitatives which convey their feelings, inspiring us to feel for and with them. The oratorio format emerged from the German Passion, of which Bach and Shütz had been major exponents, and Handel, we should remember, was born a German Lutheran, settling in England only in his late twenties.

Handel's depiction of Samson (and of Delilah) is much more sympathetic than Saint-Saëns', and we may feel better about Samson when we experience the oratorio. Samson, we must never forget, was betrayed terribly. He lived in a violent world and he cared passionately about his people. While he himself is known as a 'Judge', today we find ourselves judging him thousands of years later. We must admire his bravery and determination at the end, just as in *Macbeth* where Malcolm says of the Thane of Cawdor:

> *Nothing in his life*
> *Became him like the leaving of it: He died*
> *As one that had been studied in his death*

> *To throw away the dearest thing he ow'd*
> *As t'were a careless trifle.*
>
> MACBETH, ACT ONE, SCENE FOUR

We must leave Samson as an admired and reviled character, a man who crosses boundaries of time and of morality. It was tough living as he did and facing the dilemmas he did. How would you have behaved in his or Delilah's position, and how do you respond today?

PRAYER

O God, whose judgment is forgiving, whose service is freedom and whose power is weakness, help us amid the ambiguities of life to live each day for you such that at our lives' end, we may depart this world as an inspiration to all who follow your Son, our Saviour Jesus Christ. Amen.

For further reading: 1 Thessalonians 5:15–22
For listening: 'The death march' or 'Let the bright Seraphim' from Handel's *Samson*

'MICHAEL AND HIS ANGELS FOUGHT AGAINST THE DRAGON'

OTTORINO RESPIGHI—*CHURCH WINDOWS*

And war broke out in heaven; Michael and his angels fought against the dragon. The dragon and his angels fought back, but they were defeated; and there was no longer any place for them in heaven. The great dragon was thrown down, that ancient serpent, who is called the Devil and Satan, the deceiver of the whole world—he was thrown down to the earth, and his angels were thrown down with him.

REVELATION 12:7 - 9

Many Christians do not really know what to make of angels, and when it comes to the story of the archangel Michael defeating Satan in the great celestial battle, there can be even more reticence to hold a clear view. The *Common Worship* Anglican liturgical provision broadly considers St Michael to be one of the saints, although there is clearly a sense in which he did or does not exist in the same sense that St Peter or St Patrick existed. There are saints whose existence is uncertain, such as St George, but again, they are to be distinguished from St Michael, who is clearly present in the book of Revelation.

Angels are messengers (that is what the word means), and in the Gospels we encounter them visiting Zechariah (Luke 1:11–20) and Mary (Luke 1:26–38), ministering to Jesus after the temptations in the wilderness (Matthew 4:3–11), and finally guarding the empty tomb (Matthew 28:2–7). In the Old Testament we find them meeting Hagar (Genesis 16:7–14), in Sodom (Genesis 19), preventing Abraham from killing Isaac (Genesis 22:11–18) and in Jacob's dream (Genesis 28:12).

Another kind of angel, the guardian angel, has an origin in the apocryphal story of Tobit, in which the angel Raphael takes that role (Tobit 5:4). Let anyone who thinks that a belief in angels is silly read these passages! What is silly, though, is the popular view that angels are like fairies living at the bottom of the garden.

The supernatural status of angels and archangels can be difficult to grasp, or to portray. Paintings often show them as genderless beings, and the archetypal *putto*, or cherub, invariably looks like a rather plump toddler, with or without wings, while other artists prefer to illustrate them as ordinary, human-looking beings. (However, in 1983 a German court decreed that Christmas decorations depicting angels must have wings, in order to be tax-exempt!) Angels are often associated with music, thereby promulgating the ridiculous images of angels sitting on clouds playing harps. The idea that we 'become' angels when we die is unscriptural, as is the idea that in eternal life, we all suddenly become brilliant musicians!

In the light of these traditions of music and art and popular folklore surrounding angels, it is refreshing to encounter the music of Ottorino Respighi (1879–1936). Among his *Four Symphonic Impressions*, *Church Windows* (*Vetrate di Chiese*), published as piano preludes in 1922, is a movement entitled 'St Michael Archangel'. As it happens, these titles were added later (the other movements depict 'The Flight into Egypt', 'The Matins of St Clare' and 'St Gregory the Great') and were what the composer and his wife and friends thought the music evoked. Thus, the second of the four movements was not intended to illustrate St Michael's celestial battle with Satan, but was later felt to do so.

A swirling opening suggests stormy skies, in which war breaks out. It was Respighi's friend Claudio Guastalla, a professor of literature, who thought he could hear in the music a clash of weapons, and then, with the bang of the tam-tam at the end, the announcement of the final victory as Satan is cast down to the earth. The quiet central section of the piece is therefore a little incongruous—why should there be a lull in the battle? Well, in many battles there is a lull, before the final climax of victory, and perhaps we can hear 'into' the work the satanic team fighting back, before their final defeat.

Whether the music illustrates this successfully or not, what we have here is a kind of musical *eisegesis*, rather then *exegesis*. The same phenomenon is found in the way we read scripture; we hope to 'read out' from the biblical text (*exegesis*), to explain it, and not to 'read things into it' (*eisegesis*), endowing it with our own ideas. Respighi and his friends did exactly this with his music (and in the case of 'St Michael Archangel', they did not even get the reference right, attributing the story to St Matthew's Gospel, rather than Revelation!).

The same could be said of angels in general, that it is all too tempting to treat angels as whatever we want them to be, which can make them fantastical or absurd. The book of Revelation lends itself to this kind of interpretation, in which events or stories are 'read into' far too readily. Often people think that the events recounted in Revelation are 'coming true'. Others, like Tim LeHaye and Jerry Jenkins 'use' the story of Revelation for evangelistic purposes: their novels each take as their basis a text from the book of Revelation, reset in the world of today. Lakes and rivers turn to blood, ice caps melt, and the Anti-Christ prepares for the great last battle. Titles in the series include *Tribulation Force*, *Soul Harvest* and *The Mark*, and they have already sold 27 million copies in 30 languages.

The book of Revelation does not contain one single, fantastic story, but rather a collection of visions, and a series of letters. In its later pages it creates for us a world that is strange and fantastical. Some commentators question its place in the Bible, and George Bernard Shaw was even so bold as to describe Revelation as a 'curious record of the visions of a drug addict'! Much fantasy fiction owes a great deal to Revelation, for it is a superb piece of literature containing inspiring passages of description, prophecy and allegory, hinting at deep and significant truths about how things are, how they should be and how they will be.

The problem is, though, that in this day and age it can be so easy to treat it all as either literally true, or as make-believe. Neither approach is satisfactory. It is so easy to treat anything we read or see on television as fictional. We know that, generally speaking, news stories are true, and what we see in films is not, but bombarded with sensory data as we are today, it can be very hard to distinguish between fictional events and news stories. We risk losing the ability to discriminate between what is beautiful and what is terrible, between what is false and what is true. For we all know people who follow a soap opera as though it were the latest news, and the latest news as though it were a soap opera. The 'Big Brother' phenomenon combines these two seamlessly.

We are now used to visiting that strange thought region, where fantasies and realities combine. The tragic death of Diana, Princess of Wales in 1997, and the events of 11 September 2001 took us there, and the media return us there whenever there is a particularly heart-wrenching opportunity. With candles and condolence books, we try to engage with events that seem barely real, reading into them emotions and thoughts that we bring from another, often fictional world.

To some extent this is not new, and some Bible literature specifically does this. For a long time, attempts at self-understanding and moral purpose have been translated into and understood in terms of stories, some of which are fantastic and are found in the Bible. This Lent, let us try to appreciate that stories do not have to be historically true to be truthful; let us try not to fall into the trap of treating fiction as truth, nor of treating truth as fiction, such that we lose sight of the truth contained in fiction. During Lent we seek to know ourselves, but we can only do this if we are in touch with the realities of the world, and of faith. Whether we are reading the newspaper, a fantasy novel, listening to music, or attending to the word of God in scripture and worship, we need God's Holy Spirit to lead us into all truth.

PRAYER

God of truth, send your Holy Spirit into our hearts to inspire and guide us as we negotiate the complex world in which we live. Reveal to us the mysteries of your created order, that we may glimpse holy things and be assured of your care and protection, today and every day. Amen.

For further reading: Daniel 12:1–4
For listening: 'St Michael Archangel', from Respighi's *Church Windows*

'IT IS BETTER TO HAVE ONE MAN DIE FOR THE PEOPLE'

FRANCIS POULENC—*DIALOGUES OF THE CARMELITES*

So the chief priests and the Pharisees called a meeting of the council, and said, 'What are we to do? This man is performing many signs. If we let him go on like this, everyone will believe in him, and the Romans will come and destroy both our holy place and our nation.' But one of them, Caiaphas, who was high priest that year, said to them, 'You know nothing at all! You do not understand that it is better for you to have one man die for the people than to have the whole nation destroyed.' He did not say this on his own, but being high priest that year he prophesied that Jesus was about to die for the nation, and not for the nation only, but to gather into one the dispersed children of God. So from that day on they planned to put him to death.

JOHN 11:47–53

It is always worth remembering that the crucifixion of Christ was, at the time, of little significance. Crucifixion was a common and widely used form of punishment, and Jesus was one of many to die in that painfully prolonged way. Sadly, of course, public execution is still with us in some countries, and countless people, some of whom have committed terrible crimes and some of whom have been entirely innocent, have suffered cruelly and publicly. Many have died for their faith or political opinion, and others for being in the wrong place at the wrong time. Certain periods of history have become notorious for their bloodiness, and we should not assume that the situation has got better as the years have passed. It is sometimes said that there were more Christian martyrs in the twentieth century than in the previous ten centuries added together.

One historical context of particular notoriety is the French revolution. To many, this unfortunate period of European history is synonymous with the guillotine, a device which dispatched its victims with terrifying swiftness, even claiming the life of its inventor. The guillotine was to eighteenth-century France what the cross was to first-century Palestine.

A century and a half later, Francis Poulenc (1899–1963) wrote an opera about a group of Carmelite nuns who were martyred in 1789, at the brutal height of the French revolution. The story can be traced back to the memoirs of Marie de l'Incarnation, who was a Carmelite nun at Compiègne in Paris. These memoirs later formed the basis of a novel by Gertrud von Le Fort entitled *Die letzt am Schafott* ('The Last to the Scaffold'), and that in turn was turned into a film screenplay by Georges Bernanos. This text was also presented as a play, which Poulenc saw twice. He began composing the opera in August 1953, working quickly at first, but he had difficulties over the copyright of the text, and endured a kind of mental breakdown, such that the opera was not complete until 1957.

The plot is quite straightforward: it is April 1789, with a mob roaming Paris, and the Chevalier de la Force is worried about his sister Blanche, who has been out in a carriage. He bursts in on his father, the marquis, expressing his fear, and this upsets his father, who remembers that 20 years earlier a mob knocked the carriage his wife was in, causing her to give premature birth to Blanche and to die thereafter. Blanche enters, unharmed, but shaken, so much so that she is startled by a mere shadow. As a consequence, she resolves to leave the world of which she is so frightened and join a Carmelite convent.

At the convent, the prioress is suspicious of Blanche's desire to flee and challenges her vocation, causing her to cry. Blanche asks to be known as 'Sister Blanche of the Agony of Christ' when she is admitted.

Then we see her working alongside another nun, Constance, who, in spite of the fact that the prioress is now seriously ill, chatters away. Blanche criticizes her, but Constance, rebuked, suggests that they offer their own lives to save the prioress. Blanche rejects the idea, and Constance makes matters worse by describing a dream of hers, in which both she and Blanche die together.

As the prioress is dying, she is being looked after by Mother Marie. In spite of a lifetime of prayer and devotion, she fears death. She asks Marie to look after Blanche, for whom she has a special concern. Blanche comes to see her, and is given wise spiritual advice, but soon the prioress' condition worsens and, delirious, she sees visions of their chapel desecrated. Marie tries to keep everyone else out, but cannot prevent Blanche from witnessing the prioress' fearful and distraught final moments.

In Act Two the dead prioress lies in state in the chapel. Constance and Blanche watch and wait together, but when Constance leaves, Blanche becomes frightened in the presence of the corpse. Mother Marie comforts her. Constance hopes that Marie will become the next prioress, and also believes that the old prioress experienced the wrong kind of death, and that someone else will benefit from a graceful death as a result.

Marie does not become prioress, however (history provides us with the rumour that she was the illegitimate daughter of a king, which would have made her election inappropriate). The nuns are next seen with Madame Lidoine, the new prioress, who reminds them of their calling to pray always, and warns them that there are dark days ahead when even martyrdom may beckon. The nuns then sing a beautiful setting of *Ave Maria* ('Hail Mary').

Next we learn that the Chevalier is fleeing the national crisis, and wants to see his sister first. With Marie also present, he urges Blanche to return home. He accuses her of being frightened of fear, but Blanche insists that she is now dependent on God and intends to stay. He leaves, but the confrontation has drained her.

The priest who serves the convent has been banned from practising his faith and intends to go into hiding. The prioress hints at the possibility of imminent martyrdom, to which Marie declares that it is their duty to be prepared to die so that others may survive. The priest tries to leave but is forced to take shelter as the crowds are battering at the door. Two officials announce that all religious houses must close. Now led by Marie they leave, Blanche clutching a statue of the child Jesus, which she accidentally drops in terror.

At the opening of Act Three, the chapel has been desecrated (as the old prioress foresaw) and in the absence of the new prioress, Marie proposes a vow of martyrdom. All vote, and Blanche is suspected of dissent. To save her embarrassment, Constance claims that hers was the vote against the others; she declares that she has changed her mind, and thus a unanimous decision is reached. As they kneel to take their vow, Blanche escapes.

Outside the house, and now in civilian clothes, the nuns are welcomed as citizens of the new republic by a soldier. They are praised for their public spirit, but ordered not to practise their faith. The prioress warns the priest, who is due to celebrate mass for them the next day, although Marie feels that this contravenes their vow to stand firm in the faith.

Meanwhile Blanche has returned to her father's house, but he has been executed and now there are new occupants, to whom she becomes a servant. Mother Marie comes to take her back to the convent but, ever fearful, Blanche refuses. Soon after Marie leaves, Blanche overhears from the street that all the nuns have been arrested.

In prison, the prioress tries to console the nuns, and takes the vow that they have already taken. They worry about Blanche, but soon the judgment of the revolutionary tribunal is made: they are to be executed. Mother Marie is not in the cell, and only discovers the news when she secretly meets the priest. Distressed, she expresses the desire to die with the others, but he suggests to her that this may not be God's will.

The final scene is terrible and graceful. As the nuns sing *Salve Regina* ('Save us, O Queen'), they are beheaded. At each fall of the blade their choir is diminished, eventually leaving Constance singing alone. She delights in seeing Blanche in the crowd, but as her voice is cut short, Blanche picks up the tune and, finally overcoming her fearfulness, steps up to the scaffold to take her place at the end of the line.

The power of this story is palpable, and it is even more moving for having been based on a true story. As the nuns vow to die for their faith, we cannot help but be reminded of Christ's offering of himself. In the nuns was the same mind as Christ, as they looked not to their own survival but to the glory of God, and they were prepared to pay the ultimate price. In that much they are hardly unique, but along with countless other martyrs, on this Passion Sunday they are to be remembered, respected and revered as ones who took up their cross and walked with Christ even to the point of death.

PRAYER

O Christ, who surrendered your life as a ransom for many, by your holy compassion give comfort and strength to all those who must make the ultimate witness of death, and grant us the grace to live and die for your glory alone. Amen.

For further reading: Philippians 2:1–8
For listening: The final scene (Act Three, Scene Four) from Francis Poulenc's *Dialogues of the Carmelites*

'LORD HAVE MERCY'

LOUIS VIERNE—*MESSE SOLENNELLE*

Kyrie eleison
Christe eleison
Kyrie eleison

Lord have mercy
Christ have mercy
Lord have mercy

THE PROPER OF THE MASS—'KYRIE'

This week I want to spend some time considering some settings of the eucharist that have been composed over the years. The eucharist, or Lord's supper, is the ultimate commemoration of Jesus' suffering and death for our sins, and in Lent we are bound to focus on Jesus' sacrifice of himself. To musicians, the word 'mass' is often used less as a theologically laden term to describe what happens at an altar, but rather as a generic term to describe a related set of compositions by a single composer, which have been composed to accompany and enhance a celebration of the eucharist. Some settings of the mass, such as those by Bach and Beethoven, were not intended to be used in a liturgical setting because they would take too long, and require impossibly expensive or complicated resources which are usually only available to concert halls.

This was not the case with the setting by Louis Vierne (1870–1931), which was written for use in Notre Dame Cathedral, Paris, in 1899–1900. In May 1901, Vierne was appointed organist of Notre Dame, where he played until the day he died, 37 years later (he died while playing the organ). It was first performed in a different church though: Saint-Sulpice in Paris, and Vierne was advised by his teacher Charles-Marie Widor (also a great French organist, and composer of the famous 'toccata' often heard at weddings) that to use an orchestra would be expensive and impractical. Thus, Vierne opted for large choirs, grand organ and chamber organ. The two organs were a long way apart, with Vierne himself playing the smaller organ and Widor playing the great organ. This creation of a dialogue between the grand main organ and the smaller organ in the choir was not a new idea; Berlioz had used the same technique in his *Te Deum*, which placed organ and orchestra at opposite ends of a church ('like pope and emperor in dialogue', as he described it), and the influence of Berlioz is audible in Vierne's work.

The 'solennelle' of the title does not make it solemn in the way in which we often understand the word, but refers to the type of mass or eucharist at which it might be used. Technically speaking, a solemn mass is one at which a deacon and subdeacon are present, and at which the choir sing the 'propers'. The propers are the texts which invariably occur, the 'Kyrie', 'Gloria', 'Sanctus' and 'Benedictus', 'Credo', and 'Agnus Dei'. Communion services in most denominations preserve most of these propers today (although in Advent and Lent it is customary to omit the 'Gloria'). In musical settings, which are often performed apart from any liturgical context, these propers are often treated more as movements in what might be thought of as like a choral symphony.

Vierne's 'Solemn Mass' is no concert piece, however, but was intended for liturgical use, and is still heard in great cathedrals in Europe and America today. It opens with that most Lenten part of the mass, the 'Kyrie eleison'. Loud, rich chords announce the beginning of the piece, which would be heard within minutes of the beginning of a eucharist, and then the smaller organ is heard as the choir begins a *'fugato'* statement of the Latin words. As in a fugue, each part enters one after the other, creating a build-up of sound, and a rising level of intensity, which is punctuated by powerful chords from the grand organ. Thus there is an ebb and flow between gentle imploring and majestic power. The greatness of God's power and mercy are contrasted with the humble plea for mercy with which celebrations of the eucharist rightly begin. This is truly an awesome opening, to which a spacious acoustic contributes a sense of distance. That distance may well be interpreted as representing the gulf between us and God. That distance is created by human sin and is bridged only by Christ. The middle section of the movement is a tender plea to Christ (*Christe eleison*), and then we return to the magnificent petitions with which the movement opened.

The 'Gloria' that follows is a blaze of light and colour and praise. Vierne does not set the 'Credo' (creed), thereby reflecting the French tradition of singing it to a plainsong melody (which takes far less time than a choral setting!). The 'Sanctus' and 'Benedictus' are set separately; in the first, the hymn of praise is bounced around the individual voices before an outburst from the whole choir, portraying the worship of all heaven. The 'Agnus Dei', which is invariably the final movement of choral masses, reminds us of Christ's sacrifice; the music is far from triumphant, but rather serene and gentle. For practical purposes, the 'Agnus Dei' is often sung during the distribution of communion, and the mood of the music reflects this.

The text of the 'Kyrie' is the only part of our communion service which is in Greek. Much of the eucharist was translated into Latin in the early medieval period, but the 'Kyrie' remained untouched. 'Kyrie' means 'Lord' and 'Christe' reminds us that our word 'Christ', which means 'anointed one', is the Greek version of the Hebrew word 'Messiah'. The use of these words can be traced to the fourth century, and has persisted ever since in services of daily prayer, as well as in the eucharist. Often the text is found in English and is so frequent as to be unremarkable. In that, we may have a difficulty: that seeking God's mercy in worship is so common and so instinctive that we barely notice what we are doing. In a similar way, we often sing hymns without thinking about what we are really singing—to ourselves, or to God, or to each other—when we do so.

The 'Kyrie' is for seeking forgiveness, not only for ourselves and for any individual sins we may feel we have knowingly or unknowingly committed, but also for the sins of the world, past and present, which, as we study history or read our newspapers, we very much lament. We make our petition, assured of God's forgiveness already manifested in Christ, but as we prepare to remember his offering of himself which we commemorate in the bread and wine, we need also to remind ourselves of the sins for which he died. This we do in God's presence as we prepare to welcome our Saviour. In this much, there is a bit of Lent in every eucharist, located most obviously in the 'Kyrie'. At the same time, there is also something fundamentally eucharistic about Lent, for Lent is in one sense like a long preparation for communion, that is, a 40-day preparation involving repentance and cleansing, during which time we prepare for that great remembrance of Christ's offering on Maundy Thursday and Good Friday, and that great thanksgiving and celebration of Easter, when the mercy of God is revealed and pronounced most emphatically.

The 'Kyrie' of Vierne's magnificent *Messe Solennelle* reminds us of the magnitude of mercy that we seek and receive, and in this much, it wakes us from any sleepy, unthinking request for mercy that may so easily pass us by at a communion service. The scale of Vierne's writing alerts us to what is going on between us and our merciful, heavenly Father.

Vierne, it should be said, was born almost completely blind. The poignancy of this fact, when allied to the greatness of his musical and technical achievement as organist and composer is humbling. In the face of disability and prejudice, Vierne breaks into our complacent, ungrateful and fortunate lives with a music that makes any plea for mercy very real indeed. May his plea be ours, and that of the whole church, this Lent and always.

PRAYER

Lord have mercy. Christ have mercy. Have mercy on us as we wander through life, often oblivious of our own sins and the afflictions of others. Make us ever thankful of your great mercy and generosity, and by your Holy Spirit, put into our hearts a true recognition of our sinfulness, so that we may be daily renewed by your saving grace. Amen.

For further reading: John 9
For listening: The 'Kyrie' from Vierne's *Messe Solennelle* for choirs and two organs

'WE BELIEVE IN GOD'

LUDWIG VAN BEETHOVEN—*MISSA SOLEMNIS*

We believe in one God,
the Father, the Almighty,
maker of heaven and earth,
of all that is, seen and unseen.

We believe in one Lord, Jesus Christ,
the only Son of God,
eternally begotten of the Father,
God from God, Light from Light,
true God from true God,
begotten, not made,
of one Being with the Father;
through him all things were made.
For us and for our salvation
he came down from heaven,
was incarnate from the Holy Spirit and the Virgin Mary,
and was made man.
For our sake he was crucified under Pontius Pilate;
he suffered death and was buried.
On the third day he rose again
in accordance with the Scriptures;
he ascended into heaven
and is seated at the right hand of the Father.
He will come again in glory
to judge the living and the dead,
and his kingdom will have no end.

We believe in the Holy Spirit,
the Lord, the giver of life,
who proceeds from the Father and the Son,
who with the Father and the Son is worshipped and glo
who has spoken through the prophets.
We believe in one holy catholic and apostolic Church.
We acknowledge one baptism for the forgiveness of sins.
We look for the resurrection of the dead,
and the life of the world to come. Amen.

THE NICENE CREED (*COMMON WORSHIP*)

It is customary in Lent to omit the 'Gloria' in a eucharistic celebration, so we shall save ourselves any discussion of that until Easter, when it takes on an extra special significance for having been unused for more than six weeks. Hence, we now turn to the 'Credo': the Nicene creed, which is said or sung at the eucharist on all Sundays and other holy days. Some churches do not follow this tradition, but it seems right and proper to state the faith together when gathering to worship God, for not only is the creed a sign of orthodoxy and unity in belief, it is also an expression of faith and commitment to our God revealed in Father, Son and Holy Spirit. It has been said or sung at eucharists consistently since the fifth century.

The creed has a varied and interesting history, which takes us back to Jerusalem, on occasions when new Christians were baptized. The sacrament of baptism is still administered directly after a communal or individal statement of the faith. New believers (catechumens) learned the teachings of the Church (catechism) as a preparation and would be exorcised, and immediately before baptism, which would take place outside the main part of the church, would recite a credal statement. Baptism generally occurred at Easter, with the preparation during Lent, and it is from this early practice that we have evolved the idea that Lent is a time for spiritual discipline, self-examination and penitence. Every year, if we keep Lent, we are following in the footsteps of those who were baptized at Easter. The idea that Lent should last 40 days (46 if we include the Sundays!) was first recorded at the Council of Nicea in 325, and from then Lent has become a regular feature of the Church year.

This <u>Council of Nicea</u> was convened by the Emperor Constantine in order to <u>combat various heresies</u> that were causing confusion and discord. Most notably, the followers of Arius were claiming that Jesus, although created by God, was <u>not God</u>, thereby denying that God and Christ are one and the same. Under the guidance of Athanasius, the *Athanasian Creed* Council of Nicea rallied around a credal statement that employed the Greek term *homousios*, which characterizes the inseparability of the Father and the Son. In our modern creed, it is embedded in the phrase 'of one being'. A version of Athanasius' creed can be found in the 1662 Book of Common Prayer, and reading it carries us back to these fourth-century controversies.

The creed which we recite or sing today, and which Beethoven and other composers set to music, is not quite the same as this creed from Nicea. <u>What we call the Nicene creed is in fact an extended version</u>, <u>and should properly be referred to as the Niceno-Constantinopolitan</u> creed. It seems to have been <u>slightly altered</u> at the <u>Council of Constantinople in 381</u> and the revisions only came to light at the Council of Chalcedon in 451. Later, at a <u>Council in Toledo in 589</u>, another part, known as the '*filioque*' <u>clause was added</u>, and there is still controversy about it. The <u>issue is whether it is right to declare that the Holy Spirit proceeds from the Father and the Son</u>. The controversy is not whether or not the phrase is true, but whether such a late insertion can properly be considered as part of the creed. The existence of this extra clause caused divisions, particularly between Orthodox and Roman Catholic churches, but a certain frustration must be acknowledged in the fact that no one actually disputes that the Holy Spirit proceeds from the Father and the Son, togther with whom he is worshipped and glorified!

Ludwig van Beethoven (1770–1827) sets the Latin Nicene creed, with the '*filioque*' clause. He began the *Missa Solemnis* in 1819, intending it for the Austrian Archduke Rudolph's installation as Cardinal Archbishop in Cologne, but it took him four years to write it, by which time, in 1823, he had missed the deadline! It lasts over an hour, and the 'Credo' alone lasts 17 minutes, while the 'Gloria' is almost as long. It is clear, in listening to the *Missa Solemnis*, that Beethoven's music is imbued with a sense of God's glory, contrasted with human insignificance. The key moments of power in the work are those points at which the Godhead is approached and praised.

The 'Credo' movement contains a mixture of brevity and expansiveness. Where he sets the passage of the creed that refers to the belief in the Holy Spirit, we find that the text flies by very quickly, as the singers rattle off the doctrine of the church (including the *'filioque'* clause!), and yet, at the same time, we hear the word 'credo' ('I believe') repeated, emphasizing that we are expressing belief and faith, not just singing words and music. It also reminds us of the helpful (but not defining) fact that the expression of faith is just as important as the content of it. As the choir exclaims 'I believe, I believe', we are reminded of the distraught father who says to Jesus, 'I believe, help my unbelief' (Mark 9:24). Here, Beethoven is expressing a will to believe that is greater than any individual article of faith that is professed. Of course, we cannot simply 'believe' without adhering to particular precepts of faith, but in the *Missa Solemnis*, we are swept away on a tide of fervour which is almost self-dependent.

At the end of the 'Credo', the words 'and the life of the world to come. Amen' take up five minutes of music. Set as a fugue, a structure reserved for technically demanding and climactic music, the format seems appropriate, for musically it points us to the end of the movement, and spiritually to the expectation of life everlasting. Here, the encounter between God's glory and our own eternal life is made palpable in music.

It is well-known that Beethoven suffered with increasing deafness for the latter half of his life. He never married, and must have endured a lonely existence. Visitors would have to write in a conversation book in order to communicate with him, and his piano, around which his life revolved, was wrecked by his attempts to hear his own playing. He lived in relative squalor, but composed until his death, in spite of his ill health. To many, he is one of the greatest composers the world has known. In him was manifested an artistic greatness rarely seen or heard, and yet the bearer of such gifts was undoubtedly a damaged person. Nevertheless, he was able to transcend his various and difficult predicaments to create art which speaks to the depths of our being from the heights of heaven. We can never know the extent or nature of another person's faith or commitment, and should be cautious of judging, but we can say that in the music of Beethoven's great *Missa Solemnis* we have a work which vividly portrays God's greatness and our own smallness. And it does us no harm to remember that, in Lent or at any time.

PRAYER

Help our unbelief, O Lord, and lead us into all truth, that we may be at one in faith and love with your people across time and space. Where there is disunity, bring the singular melody of your mercy; where there is discord, bring harmony and where there is doubt, bring faith, and hope and joy. Amen.

For further reading: Mark 9:14–29
For listening: The 'Credo' from Beethoven's *Missa Solemnis*

'HOLY, HOLY, HOLY'

ANTON BRUCKNER— *MASS IN E MINOR*

Sanctus, sanctus, sanctus
Dominus Deus Sabaoth.
Pleni sunt caeli et terra gloria tua.
Hosanna in excelsis.

Holy, holy, holy Lord
God of power and might.
Heaven and earth are full of your glory.
Hosanna in the highest.

THE PROPER OF THE MASS—'SANCTUS'

The Austrian composer Anton Bruckner (1824–96) began his career as a church organist, and maintained a devout Roman Catholic faith throughout his life. His music is steeped in that faith, which is perhaps why, for some, he has remained on the fringes of nineteenth-century music, recognized only by a few. In recent years though, his symphonies have gained respect and popularity, in spite of their length, but possibly in virtue of their apparent similarity to the works of Mahler. Although contempories working to a certain extent with the same post-Wagnerian musical language, Bruckner and Mahler are not to be confused, not least because of the stance of faith they adopted. Both wrote eight symphonies and an incomplete ninth, but by the end of his life, Mahler had more or less rejected his Jewish roots, whereas Bruckner dedicated his final symphony to God, whom as a composer he served all his life.

Emerging from a rural Austrian church music tradition, Bruckner became organist at Linz cathedral in 1855, a post which he held for 13 years. While in that job he studied composition and encountered the music of Wagner, which was to be so influential, not only on him, but on so many of his contemporaries. In 1864 he wrote his first mass setting, which brought his name to public attention. Around the same time he wrote a symphony, to which he was later to give the numeral zero (Bruckner is therefore the only composer with a 'Symphony Number Nought' to his name!).

Two years later, Bruckner wrote a second mass, for the consecration of a chapel in what was then the new Linz cathedral. The building was begun in 1862, but took many years to complete, and by the time Bruckner had written the mass and the service of consecration took place, the roof was still not complete and so it became effectively an open-air service! For that reason, the instrumental parts are confined to woodwind; Bruckner did not wish to risk strings in the Austrian autumn air, for they would so easily go out of tune. Tuning and pitch are a problem in the vocal parts too, for there are extended passages of unaccompanied (*a capella*) singing, not leastly at the very beginning of the first 'Kyrie' movement. When the woodwind eventually enter, it is always to be hoped that the choir have not wandered off-key. Both the 'Kyrie' and the 'Sanctus' are very slow, and this does not help with the intonation, as when singers begin to run out of breath, the pitch can slip. For this reason, Bruckner's masses are not performed very frequently. Assuming the choir can stay in tune, what we hear is a delightful and unusual combination of brass and wind instruments giving colour to the rich and varied harmony that Bruckner employs. The Russian composer Stravinsky also used only wind instruments with choir in his mass setting.

When we reach the 'Sanctus' movement, we can hear the influence of the great Italian composer Palestrina, whose masses set a standard in the sixteenth century, and which are still heard today. The 'Sanctus' emulates the style of Palestrina, thereby paying homage to him. Ralph Vaughan Williams was to do a similar thing with his *Mass in G Minor*, written nearly 100 years after Bruckner's. A gentle, unaccompanied opening to Bruckner's 'Sanctus' builds up to a central climax on the words 'Pleni sunt caeli' ('Heaven and earth are full of your glory'), and then with brass resplendent, echoing the trumpets of heaven, it concludes with the 'Hosanna'. This Hebrew word means 'please save us' and is most associated with Jesus' triumphal entry into Jerusalem on Palm Sunday. It occurs also in the 'Benedictus', which often follows the 'Sanctus' in liturgical use (more on this tomorrow!). Bruckner, like so many composers, uses the 'Sanctus' to express great joy and praise, and then allows the music to subside for a gentle 'Blessed is he who comes in the name of the Lord', before reiterating the joyful exclamation of 'Hosanna'. The structure of the words when the two texts are juxtaposed lends itself to dramatic musical contrast and recapitulation.

The text of the 'Sanctus' is a very ancient hymn of adoration, which derives from Isaiah 6:3, where the prophet has a vision of angels praising God in heaven: 'And one called to another and said: "Holy, holy, holy is the Lord of hosts; the whole earth is full of his glory"' (Isaiah 6:3). The hymn is generally interspersed between the saying or singing of the eucharistic preface, and the narrative of the institution of holy communion (the story of how Jesus took bread and broke it and shared wine, saying, 'this is my body, this is my blood'). Eastern liturgies of the eucharist included the 'Sanctus' by the fifth century and the Roman West soon followed. It is these Roman, Western rites which the sixteenth-century reformers altered and upon which our English language services are based. While there have been historical changes to the positioning, and even the inclusion of the 'Benedictus', which often follows the 'Sanctus' immediately, the 'Sanctus' itself has largely remained intact and in this position throughout history.

Bruckner did not have the misfortune, like Vierne or Beethoven, to be blind or deaf, but he was blighted by self-doubt and he spent much of his life altering and revising his compositions. When it came to his symphonies he was forced to allow others to edit and shorten them, in order to get them played. The *Mass in E minor* was only performed twice in his lifetime, and there were critics who were far from complimentary of his work. History has vindicated Bruckner, but tracking down his original or preferred version of a work can be a complex business. His masses are very much in the tradition of Haydn and Mozart, and also of Palestrina. Yet, at the same time, they are full of the influence of Wagner, which nowadays makes them both appealing and difficult. It is sometimes said that it is far more rewarding to sing Bruckner's music than to listen to it, and this is a kind of backhanded compliment to the largely self-taught composer who wrote so tellingly for choirs.

One of the most appealing things about Bruckner is the simple, sincere devotion that characterizes the man and the music. In his music he brings the spirit of ages past into a new focus, making it his own and carrying forward the tradition handed on to him. This is partly what the Church does still. We are inheritors of truth, with which we engage throughout life, and at different times, the message of the gospel challenges and encourages us in different ways. Bruckner has sometimes been accused of possessing a childish piety, as though to do so is some kind of disadvantage, but as in other aspects of life, there is sometimes a great deal of pressure to be sophisticated and up to date, when, by doing so, we may lose touch with the realities of what is important in life and faith. We should remember that Jesus was no critic of simple devotion (see Matthew 19:14).

For us, looking back at the life and music of this devout composer, we may find that in him we see how a simple adherence to truth and beauty, allied to the traditions of faith handed on to us by our significant predecessors, can continue to show for us a way to truth and beauty which sustains us throughout our lives, and into the life beyond, where with saints and angels we too shall sing, 'Holy, holy, holy'.

PRAYER

Holy and immortal God, give us a pure heart and a simple faith to praise your name and sing your glory. Touch our lips with the fire of your Spirit that we may enter your presence with confidence and hope, assured always of your mercy and care. Amen.

For further reading: Matthew 19:13–15
For listening: The 'Sanctus' from Bruckner's *Mass No. 2 in E Minor* for choir and wind instruments

'BLESSED IS HE WHO COMES IN THE NAME OF THE LORD'

GIOVANNI DA PALESTRINA—*MISSA PAPAE MARCELLI*

Benedictus qui venit in nomine Domini.
Hosanna in excelsis.

Blessed is he who comes in the name of the Lord.
Hosanna in the highest.

THE PROPER OF THE MASS—'BENEDICTUS'

The 'Benedictus' usually follows the 'Sanctus' directly and immediately precedes the part of the eucharistic prayer in which the celebrant recalls the last supper, at which Jesus first associated the offering of himself with bread and wine. It is important not to confuse it with the Benedictus from Luke 1:68–79, which is the song of thanksgiving uttered by Zechariah on the birth of his son, John the Baptist. While the 'Sanctus' has an unbroken history of inclusion as part of the mass, Thomas Cranmer, in his Prayer Book of 1552, omitted the 'Benedictus', substituting 'Glory be to thee, O Lord most high'. The Prayer Book of 1662, which is still in use today, kept this change. There are some who still prefer not to use any 'Benedictus' at all in a eucharistic celebration.

In Latin settings of the mass it is invariably found, and often in English settings too. The text is a direct quotation from Matthew 21:9 from the account of Jesus' triumphal entry into Jerusalem. These are the words called out by the palm-waving crowd as Jesus enters on a donkey, a humble king, who will soon disappoint them. Within days they will abandon him to his fate at the hands of the chief priests and Roman authorities.

This reminder of Palm Sunday is appropriate for a eucharist. The 'Benedictus' is followed by the account of the last supper, so in one sense holy week is acted out in microcosm at every eucharist. We recall God's creative and saving acts, often referred to in the preface; then we join with angels and archangels in singing: 'Holy, Holy, Holy' and then we move to this acclamation of Christ, which in itself carries us forward to the central sacrifice of Jesus, offered once and for all on the cross.

In practice, it is often advisable to move the singing of the 'Benedictus' to the point when bread and wine are being distributed, as a musical accompaniment to receiving communion. When the setting of the mass is lengthy, this can make a lot of sense, but it tempts us to the view that what we have here is merely nice music, the words of which are not very important. If that nice music were sung in its proper place, then, as in the case of the *Missa Papae Marcelli* by Palestrina, there must be what feels like an eight-minute interruption in the eucharistic prayer.

In the time of Giovanni Pierluigi da Palestrina (1525–94), demand for exquisite, extended settings of the propers of the mass was high, and Palestrina (whose name is taken from the lovely hill town on the slopes outside Rome where he lived) was the finest exponent of this approach to text-setting. His style, perfected in 104 known masses, is contrapuntal, which means that his music is composed of layers of sound, with each melody weaving its way independently of the others. The melodies that are heard in counterpoint are not distinctively different from each other; indeed, the texture of sound is built up by using the same melody in successive voices, turned upside down (inverted) or even sometimes reversed (retrograde). In four- or six- or eight-part choral writing, written for a choir of men and boys, the closeness of harmony and pitch created a mellifluous and rich sound effect. Due to the 'rules' of counterpoint, which forbade consecutive progressions a fifth or a fourth apart (for example), and specified that a melodic line should be played through more or less unaltered (except when avoiding the breaking of the 'consecutive' rules!), there were often some interesting and 'scrunchy' suspended notes, false resolutions of chords and even occasional dissonances. It is these which add a distinctive flavour to the otherwise languid nature of polyphony.

Polyphony simply means 'many sounds together', and it emerged as an elaboration of plainsong (monody). Originally the polyphony would be created by weaving together strands of a familiar plainsong melody, hence a simple tune could become the basis of a major piece of soundscaping. By Palestrina's time composers were turning away from plainsong melodies, and popular songs became a source of inspiration for polyphonic music.

Several composers from the fifteenth to the late seventeenth centuries used the popular French song '*L'homme armé*' ('The armed man') as the basis of a mass. By the mid-sixteenth century, the song was less well-known, and in some settings it became almost unrecognizable. Some people claim that Palestrina's *Missa Papae Marcelli* is based on this very tune, as some resemblance is identifiable in the music.

The pope referred to in the title of the mass is Marcellus II, who held the post for only three weeks in 1555. His fame consists almost entirely in having been the dedicatee of one of Palestrina's best-known masses. At the time, the Roman Catholic Council of Trent were debating the use of music in worship, while in Northern Europe, reformation was rife. While Luther was writing hymns, Rome was discussing the use of polyphony, with many advocating its abolition, for they felt that it was obscuring the words, which, already in Latin, were being rendered incomprehensible. Meanwhile, the reformers were translating the mass into the vernacular. During the English Counter-reformation, between 1553 and 1558, when Queen Mary reigned, she sought a return to the Latin mass, which meant that composers like Thomas Tallis had to turn their coats very quickly, in order to keep their jobs and their heads. This is why there is much good music in both Latin and English by Tallis: he did what he was told!

Back in Rome, where Palestrina was in charge of music in various papal chapels, the debate about polyphony was still raging, and this mass, written for the unfortunate pope, was flaunting some of the council's decrees by its perhaps too subtle references to the French popular song '*L'homme armé*'. It is not hard to imagine that if having more than one melodic line was a problem, then using a bawdy popular song as a basis for the music was beyond the pale. It is possible that Palestrina had a little joke at the expense of the Catholic reformers who, as far as musical development and beauty were concerned, were set to hamper his creativity. If it was his little joke, it was so subtle that they probably did not notice!

It is both easy and difficult for us to appreciate the significance of the debate over polyphony. It is hard because when we enter the beautiful sound world of Palestrina, we can be transported to another plane, on which our encounter with God may be facilitated and nourished. For many, the music of heaven (they hope!) sounds something like Palestrina (others argue for Bach or Mozart!). Thus, the thought that some people tried to ban this beauty is hard to credit. On the other hand, there are still those today who get involved in debates as to what makes appropriate music for worship, and they will sometimes get very wound up about it indeed. We have all heard tales of church organists 'banning' particular kinds of music, and many people will have their opinions. It is only a small step between having an opinion and trying to enforce it in church. When we remember this, we easily recognize that church music, then as now, had the capacity to provoke strong feeling and controversy.

Polyphony, as so gracefully demonstrated by Palestrina, can teach us one important thing: as the strands of music weave together creating a greater whole, each part independent, but each following the rules to create a tight bond of sound, in order to exhibit and express the mercy and love of God, we can identify something of the pilgrim's condition. Each melodic line, woven in fellowship with the others, makes its own journey, finally arriving at a great and unified Amen, towards which it has striven throughout. While each has its part to play in the whole, each is different, making up a greater body. There is much wavering, some discord even, but all is held together by a common purpose, and when the piece comes to its inevitable conclusion, all is resolved in rest and peace.

PRAYER

God of sound and space, who creates and holds us together with bonds of love, guide and guard us as we weave our way on life's pilgrimage, so that whether we resonate with those around us, or even clash with them, we may always be governed by your commandments and live only to reflect your glory and bless your holy name. Amen.

For further reading: 1 Corinthians 12:4–13 (15–26)
For listening: The 'Benedictus' or 'Sanctus' and 'Benedictus' from Palestrina's *Missa Papae Marcelli*

'LAMB OF GOD, HAVE MERCY UPON US'

J.S. BACH—*MASS IN B MINOR*

Agnus Dei qui tollis peccata mundi: miserere nobis.
Agnus Dei, qui tollis peccata mundi: miserere nobis.
Agnus Dei qui tollis peccata mundi: dona nobis pacem.

Lamb of God, who takes away the sins of the world: have mercy on us.
Lamb of God, who takes away the sins of the world: have mercy on us.
Lamb of God, who takes away the sins of the world: grant us peace.

THE PROPER OF THE MASS—'AGNUS DEI'

The final instalment of the great musical drama that makes up any musical setting of the propers of the mass is the 'Agnus Dei'. The text is based on two sayings of John the Baptist found in St John's Gospel, where John exclaims 'here is the Lamb of God who takes away the sin of the world' (John 1:29, 36), which has been used as an acclamation prior to receiving communion ever since the seventh century, when the Syrian Pope Sergius introduced it. Rather like the 'Benedictus', Archbishop Cranmer, in translating and reforming the liturgy for the newly created Church of England at first included this communion anthem in 1549, but omitted it in the much more protestant Prayer Book of 1552. It was not officially 'restored' to Anglican worship until the 1960s!

Nevertheless, it remained popular and prevalent in settings of the mass written for Roman Catholic use. Yet while the Lutheran Church did not include any of the eucharistic texts other than the 'Sanctus',

Johann Sebastian Bach (1685–1750), who was a devout Lutheran, did include them in his great *Mass in B Minor*, which for many is the absolute benchmark piece not only of mass settings but of all choral music, religious or otherwise. For some people, Bach's *B Minor Mass* (as it is so commonly known) is the greatest piece of music ever written.

It was not written for liturgical performance, and indeed would not have been permitted as such in any Lutheran church. Nor, on the other hand, could it have been used in a Roman Catholic setting, because Bach did not set the texts as properly used in that arena. In the 1740s Bach took from a much earlier mass of 1733 the 'Kyrie' and 'Gloria' adding the other historically conventional movements, but splitting the final 'Agnus Dei' into two parts: 'Agnus Dei' and 'Dona nobis pacem' ('grant us peace'). Not only was the *B Minor Mass* unconventionally laid out for practical use, it was also conceived on an unprecedented scale, lasting an hour and a half. It is not entirely clear, therefore, why Bach actually wrote the *B Minor Mass*. It may be that Bach deliberately wrote it as a kind of spiritual, musical and cultural exercise in boundary-pushing. In other senses, the *B Minor Mass* presents us with some of Bach's best choral hits, some drawn from previous works, others written specially. The *B Minor Mass* can be considered to be the culmination of his life's work, and perhaps for that reason some want to consider it to be the greatest work by the greatest composer. The possibilities for performing such a work in Bach's day were minimal, and the work fell into oblivion for many years. But it may have been a deliberate legacy from a composer who knew his own place in the tradition of music, having taken an interest in his own genealogy, which extended backwards through five generations of musicians and composers. His children (notably Johann Christian and Carl Philipp Emanuel Bach) were also musical, and through them the great musical line of Bach survived for another fifty years after his own death.

More significant was Bach's desire to honour God, his Creator and Redeemer, whose Spirit had sustained and blessed his composition throughout his musical life. Even for the protestant Bach, the text of the mass had a deep significance as the archetypal Christian text, and he was no stranger to Gregorian chant and the settings of Palestrina.

The best way to honour God, Bach felt, was to write a mass, and to write a mass like no one had ever written before. Western culture has largely acknowledged that he was successful, as he strove to unite his Christian faith with the challenge of his art. As no one had commissioned this work, and there was therefore no deadline, it took Bach over 15 years to compose; he probably completed it in 1648, just two years before his death. Thus, Bach bequeathed to posterity his greatest act of worship, and although for him it took place through the medium of music, only written on paper, rather than performed, it is our privilege today that we can hear, live or recorded, Bach's ultimate gift to Creator and creation. In this privilege there is also an irony: for we can now play as background music a work of such power, devotion and magnitude that Bach himself could only hear in his head. (This is not to say that no one heard any of it: parts were heard at various times and places, but as far as we know no complete rendition ever took place in Bach's lifetime.)

It is impossible to do justice to the musical content of such a work in these pages, but we may consider the closing minutes, the 'Agnus Dei'. One of the most striking aspects of this setting is the way at the end in which Bach draws on the music used for the opening 'Kyrie', reminding us that it is the Lamb of God who takes away our sins, to whom we first prayed 'Lord have mercy' . This rounding-off of the work reminds us of the continuing journey of mercy of which our earthly pilgrimages are made. As we try to walk in the light and love of Christ, assured of his merciful redemption, we also focus much of our devotion on our inevitable need for mercy day by day. The eucharist also locates us in this pattern of prayer, for in its close association with our daily bread, the bread and wine of Christ act as spiritual sustenance, which we need just as much as food and drink. These days many do not attend a eucharist daily, nor is it necessary to do so, but there is a lot to be said for a regular and worshipful encounter with Christ in bread and wine, as a source of remembrance of his saving grace, as a source of spiritual sustenance, and as a source of fellowship with all those others in different times and places who share, have shared and will share communion with us. Bach's offering of his *B Minor Mass* to generations who might perform it more readily than his own reminds us that when we share holy communion, we are not just sharing with those gathered around the particular table at which we receive bread and wine; we are in communion with Bach himself, and with countless other saints and angels when we join together to remember what our Lord has done for us, and to celebrate his passion, death and resurrection. The fellowship of communion extends beyond our own place and time, and the music, as well as the text, reminds us of this as we hear and sing what our ancestors sang. They lived in a different world, yet worshipped in the same liturgical context. In that much we are united to them in Christ.

The words of the 'Agnus Dei', set by Bach in what can be described as majestic humility, remind us that this is a corporate prayer. In the celebration of the eucharist, so much is done from the standpoint of 'we'. 'We praise you' in the 'Gloria'; 'We believe' in the creed; 'have mercy upon us' in 'Kyrie', creed and 'Agnus Dei'; and finally, the closing words of the 'Agnus Dei' are 'grant us peace'. Thus we are joined together with all who have loved and served our Lord Jesus Christ in this and every age as we gather around his table, and as we depart we pray for peace, not only for Christians, but for all the world. The final section of the *B Minor Mass* sets these profound and necessary words, and there seems no more beautiful, nor more genuine way to express them than from the musical pen of one of history's greatest musical geniuses: J.S. Bach.

PRAYER

God our Father, who allows us to share in your joy of creation, we give thanks for those whom you have blessed with musical gifts and especially those who compose. May the sound of their art always reflect your glory, sustaining and uniting us in praise and worship as we offer ourselves in the service of your gospel revealed in Jesus Christ our Lord. Amen.

For further reading: John 1:29–40
For listening: The 'Agnus Dei' from the *Mass in B Minor* by J.S. Bach

'I AM THE BREAD OF LIFE'

CÉSAR FRANCK—*PANIS ANGELICUS*

'Our ancestors ate the manna in the wilderness; as it is written, "He gave them bread from heaven to eat."' Then Jesus said to them, 'Very truly, I tell you, it was not Moses who gave you the bread from heaven, but it is my Father who gives you the true bread from heaven. For the bread of God is that which comes down from heaven and gives life to the world.' They said to him, 'Sir, give us this bread always.' Jesus said to them, 'I am the bread of life. Whoever comes to me will never be hungry, and whoever believes in me will never be thirsty.'

JOHN 6:31–35

Some people will be familiar with the quiz question that asks us to name six famous Belgians. Unfortunately, not many people get as far as six, and even if they do, they often include Agatha Christie's Hercule Poirot, who never existed. But if we exercise our little grey cells, we may well come up with Marie Curie, who was so important in the twentieth-century battle against cancer, and we might also remember that the composer César Franck (1822–90) was also a famous Belgian, even though he spent much of his life in Paris.

Franck was a devout Roman Catholic, and gave 40 years' service to the Church of St Clotilde, as organist. His performance skills earned him a professorship at the Paris Conservatory when he was 50, but his career as a composer never really took off. It was not until he was 68 that his string quartet got some notice, but he very soon died, after being knocked down by a horse-drawn bus. As well as being a brilliant organist and a composer, Franck was a man of prayer, who spent an hour each day quietly meditating on his faith. This humble, devout man left only a few famous compositions behind, but he is much revered by organists for his organ works, and his *Symphony in D Minor* is quite well-known, as is his virtuosic violin sonata. *Panis Angelicus* is probably his most famous work, even though it lasts barely four minutes.

Whether sung as a solo or as a choral piece, it has a simple beauty that conveys the composer's faithful response to the ancient text of Thomas Aquinas' hymn. St Thomas (1225–74) was one of the most influential theologians of his or any age, and the Roman Catholic Church still reveres him greatly. His unfinished treatise, the *Summa Theologica*, in which he expounds a Christian doctrine inspired by and dependent upon the thought of Aristotle, is still much read and taught. Thomas was a Dominican Friar, living in Paris six centuries before Franck, where he also held an academic post. From Aristotle Thomas learned the importance of reason, but at the same time he never neglected the power of faith to comprehend the Trinity, incarnation and creation. Yet while we need faith to handle these doctrines, they are not alien to reason; indeed, the faculty of reason can help us understand or defend them. In this, Thomas was inventing a scientific approach to philosophy and theology which treats them as comprehensible through study and intellectual endeavour. Thus, what is revealed to us, through scripture and tradition, demands from us an intellectual and moral response, for we are created as rational beings.

Thomas' theology was often focused on the sacraments and particularly on the eucharist. He is often associated with the doctrine of transubstantiation, although he did not invent it (it was first promulgated at the Fourth Lateran Council in 1215). Questions as to what exactly happens to bread and wine at the eucharist have exercised the minds of theologians ever since, and the answers to these questions were pivotal at the time of the various European reformations in the sixteenth century. For Thomas and those who follow him (Thomists), the bread and wine, when consecrated by a priest at the eucharist, retain the appearance of bread and wine, but have truly changed in substance to become the body and blood of Jesus. Obviously they still taste and feel like bread and wine but, according to this view, they have changed in a more fundamental sense. Some people later disputed this unprovable claim, while others have seen little point in making it. For many, the 'real presence' of Christ in the eucharist neither needs nor merits this kind of account, and some prefer the idea that Christ is present spiritually, such that the bread and wine remain as nothing more or less than bread and wine, Christ being present in the gathered community, rather than in the bread and wine themselves.

During Thomas' lifetime the Roman Catholic Church invented the feast of Corpus Christi, which commemorates the institution by Jesus of the holy communion. Inspired by the visions of a nun called Juliana from the Belgian city of Liège, Pope Urban IV declared in 1264 that the feast day should be celebrated, and it soon found a location on the first Thursday after Trinity Sunday, a date on which it is still observed in many churches. There is cause for ambivalence: we might wonder why it is necessary to have a special eucharist to commemorate the eucharist, since every eucharist is a thanksgiving for what Christ has given us. On the other hand, the eucharist is the staple diet of the Church, given and commanded by Christ ('do this in remembrance of me'), and to designate a special date on which to be grateful is equally as valuable as designating a special date on which to celebrate the incarnation (Christmas) or the resurrection (Easter). We should really be celebrating incarnation and resurrection every day!

Thomas was no doubt delighted to be asked by the pope to create the liturgy for the feast of Corpus Christi, although recent scholarship has given us cause to wonder whether he really did compose all of it. However, the poem 'Sacris Solemnis', which formed part of the office of Mattins for Corpus Christi, is generally accepted as being by Thomas. *Panis Angelicus* is only one verse of that hymn, which follows verses invoking praise and reminding us of how Jesus gave his own body to his disciples to sustain them. Then Thomas reflects thus on the bread:

The bread of angels becomes the bread of humanity;
The bread from heaven puts an end to symbols:
O wondrous thing, the poor, the humble, and the lowly
eat their Lord.

Helped by Franck's ethereal music, we can reflect on these words today, which, even removed from their context, remind us of the sacrifice of Christ, made once for all upon the cross, through which he gave up his life to save us from the slavery of sin, that we might be freed to resurrection and eternal life. In the eucharist we are reminded of this each and every time, as the narrative tells the story of the last supper, at which Jesus said to his disciples, while giving them bread and wine: 'This is my body, this is my blood, eat and drink in remembrance of me'. Thomas' text denies a merely symbolic connection between Jesus and the bread and wine, and indeed, even if we did say that the eucharist is a symbolic act, many of us would want to say that it is a very special kind of symbolic act, which, as a sacrament, involves us in a mystery that turns our questions into gratitude, praise and awe. For, as Thomas says in his poem, the eucharist enables all of us who are unworthy so much as to eat the crumbs from under our Lord's table to partake, and be healed.

In Lent, we do well to remind ourselves that the eucharist, while it has inspired much debate, discussion and even dispute, is fundamentally Jesus' gift to us; in it, we recall his saving work, and remember that his work of salvation which encompassed suffering, death and resurrection—is only necessary because of our sinful nature. Thus, all eucharists have a penitential flavour, even though they also 'celebrate' what God has done in Christ. In Lent we may emphasize the penitential aspects of thanksgiving, as we also prepare to welcome the risen Christ at that great eucharistic feast of Easter day.

PRAYER

O God, who gave manna in the wilderness, and gives the bread of Christ's body to your people today, we give you thanks and praise for Christ's sacrifice made for each and every one of us. As we remember him, and join with him in every time and season, help us to live the life of the redeemed, while still repenting, growing, and loving, all for his dear sake. Amen.

For further reading: Luke 22:14–20
For listening: Franck's *Panis Angelicus*

'GOD SAVE THE KING!'

GEORGE FRIDERIC HANDEL—*ZADOK THE PRIEST*

King David said, 'Summon to me the priest Zadok, the prophet Nathan, and Benaiah son of Jehoiada.' When they came before the king, the king said to them, 'Take with you the servants of your lord, and have my son Solomon ride on my own mule, and bring him down to Gihon. There let the priest Zadok and the prophet Nathan anoint him king over Israel; then blow the trumpet, and say, "Long live King Solomon!" You shall go up following him. Let him enter and sit on my throne; he shall be king in my place; for I have appointed him to be ruler over Israel and over Judah.' Benaiah son of Jehoiada answered the king, 'Amen! May the Lord, the God of my lord the king, so ordain. As the Lord has been with my lord the king, so may he be with Solomon, and make his throne greater than the throne of my lord King David.' So the priest Zadok, the prophet Nathan, and Benaiah son of Jehoiada, and the Cherethites and the Pelethites, went down and had Solomon ride on King David's mule, and led him to Gihon. There the priest Zadok took the horn of oil from the tent and anointed Solomon. Then they blew the trumpet, and all the people said, 'Long live King Solomon!' And all the people went up following him, playing on pipes and rejoicing with great joy, so that the earth quaked at their noise.

1 KINGS 1:32 –40

Zadok the Priest by George Frideric Handel (1685–1759) is one of the most famous and popular short works in the choral repertoire. From its opening arpeggios which build to the tumultuous exclamation of the words of the title, it is instantly recognizable, and the sense of anticipation is palpable as singers and audience alike prepare for the choral outburst for which the piece is so famous. Then the mood changes slightly as we move to the jerky dotted rhythms of 'And all the people rejoiced'. A hiatus is reached, at the words 'and said', before the launch into those archetypal coronation words: 'God save the King', and 'may the King live for ever', sentiments emphasized by florid (and difficult) repetitions of 'Alleluia. Amen'. The exuberance, jollity and regal flavour of the setting of these words has made *Zadok* a popular fixture, not only at coronations, but also at countless concerts and in services ever since Handel first wrote it for the Coronation of George II in October 1727.

At that time, Handel, who, like the new king, was also German, wrote four coronation anthems, of which *Zadok* is the best-known (the others are *My heart is inditing*, *The King shall rejoice* and *Let thy hand be strengthened*). Contemporary records tell us that 50 singers and 160 instrumentalists took part, but William Wake, then Archbishop of Canterbury, complained that the music was irregular and confused. *Zadok* survived this early criticism, though, to become immensely successful.

The text is derived from 1 Kings 1:38–40, which describes the coronation of Solomon, the wise biblical king who succeeded David. The words of Handel's anthem are slightly different, but describe the event succinctly:

Zadok the priest and Nathan the prophet anointed Solomon king. And all the people rejoiced and said: 'God save the King, long live the King, God save the King! May the King live for ever. Amen. Alleluia.'

At a coronation, the monarch is not only confirmed as temporal ruler but, in the biblical tradition of David and Solomon, also welcomed, prayed for, anointed and acclaimed as an agent of God. Monarchs in this tradition have a religious as well as human power invested in them.

On Palm Sunday this amalgamation of divine and worldly kingship is poignant. In most churches today, the account of Jesus' triumphal entry into Jerusalem is read (Matthew 21:1–11; Mark 11:1–10; Luke 19:29–40; John 12:12–15). In Mark's Gospel the connection with King

David is explicit, and it is clear that those who waved palm branches rejoiced to hail Jesus not only as divine King, but also as a worldly, powerful leader, to liberate them and restore the throne and realm of their heroes David and Solomon (see Psalm 45).

They were mistaken, and their failure to understand soon led to disappointment, disillusionment, rejection and condemnation of the man who would not be a conventional king. As we follow the story of Christ in the Gospels, we realize that it is not a catalogue of his exercising worldly, judgmental power. Rather it describes how he shows his power, but through his ministry, how he gently, bravely and willingly lays it down. We see, when he is tempted in the wilderness, that Jesus has power to be a very different kind of king: unlike a tyrant who exercises absolute authority, governing through fear and the suppression of any alternative. But no—it is fundamental to Christianity that Christ our King forces no allegiance from us, but rather solicits our freely given love, just as his love is freely given to us.

Jesus also demonstrates his power to heal and deliver, which, to his contemporaries and to us, reveals that his kingship is not earthly but divine. We also see Jesus' intellectual power as he tells parables and confounds the religious leaders of his time, both by asking awkward questions and by evading theirs. Whether it is tax to Caesar, or the fate of a sinner, Jesus conquers their cunning and prejudice. This gives him moral power, as does the idea that he is sinless, both in character and action. However, as we approach the end of Jesus' ministry, we realize, as his disciples did, that 'this is the Christ', 'in whom all things were made, whose name is above every name… in this age… also in the age to come' (Ephesians 1:21). As soon as we realize this, we see it all slip away. Betrayal, arrest, trials, torture, execution, all follow in swift succession. Where then, is this King? Where has his power gone?

He has laid it down, surrendered his loving, divine power to human hatred. Christ our Judge, who is characterized as the Son of Man, judging humans like sheep and goats (Matthew 25:31–46), allows himself to be humanly judged, falsely convicted and killed.

Jesus translates his divine power into what psychologists have called 'nutrient power'. This is a form of power deployed on behalf of another's greater good. It is the power of putting someone else first, of putting one's own abilities, expertise and desires at the service of others. This is the power of giving of self and resources. It is the power demonstrated by Christ as he dies for our sins and opens the gate to eternal life for us.

Christ's kingship offers us a unique model of power, which is in some sense paradoxical because it consists largely in the fact that he laid it down. There is an apparent weakness in this, but it actually points to a far greater strength, that of God's love: love revealed, love laid down, love spent. This kind of kingship and this kind of love is unique in history. It has been beautifully described by the theologian William Vanstone, who in 1977 wrote a book called *Love's Endeavour, Love's Expense*. It concludes with a poem which is often sung as a hymn, in which Vanstone says of Christ that he is 'bound in setting others free... poor in making many rich, weak in giving power to be'.

Christ's love inverts itself for the benefit of others, truly nourishing others. Christ is not a monarch enthroned in luxury: the cost of his kingship not only saves the world but sustains it. It is not easy, nor does it conform to worldly, glorified, wealthy monarchy. Divine kingship and divine love are both about self-giving, and the laying down of power. That is why, if we want to think of Christ as a King, we must think of him as the King of love. And any of us, whether we are kings or not, if we wish to 'live for ever' and be 'saved by God', as Handel's anthem puts it, we must turn to Christ our King of Love, and walk in the ways of his universal, all-embracing kingship.

PRAYER

O Christ our King, as we enter into the mysteries of holy week, rule our hearts with your saving love, and sustain us with your divine power, that we may not be broken by evil nor subdued by suffering, but be borne once more along that road which you trod, which leads through passion and death to the everlasting life which you have prepared for us in your heavenly kingdom. Amen.

For further reading: Mark 11:1–10
For listening: Handel's *Zadok the Priest*

'I DON'T KNOW HOW TO LOVE HIM'

ANDREW LLOYD WEBBER AND TIM RICE—
JESUS CHRIST SUPERSTAR

Now while Jesus was at Bethany in the house of Simon the leper, a woman came to him with an alabaster jar of very costly ointment, and she poured it on his head as he sat at the table. But when the disciples saw it, they were angry and said, 'Why this waste? For this ointment could have been sold for a large sum, and the money given to the poor.' But Jesus, aware of this, said to them, 'Why do you trouble the woman? She has performed a good service for me. For you always have the poor with you, but you will not always have me. By pouring this ointment on my body she has prepared me for burial. Truly I tell you, wherever this good news is proclaimed in the whole world, what she has done will be told in remembrance of her.'

Then one of the twelve, who was called Judas Iscariot, went to the chief priests and said, 'What will you give me if I betray him to you?' They paid him thirty pieces of silver. And from that moment he began to look for an opportunity to betray him.

When it was evening, he took his place with the twelve; and while they were eating, he said, 'Truly I tell you, one of you will betray me.' And they became greatly distressed and began to say to him one after another, 'Surely not I, Lord?' He answered, 'The one who has dipped his hand into the bowl with me will betray me. The Son of Man goes as it is written of him, but woe to that one by whom the Son of Man is betrayed! It would have been better for that one not to have been

born.' Judas, who betrayed him, said, 'Surely not I, Rabbi?' He replied,
'You have said so.'

MATTHEW 26:6–16; 20–25

The story of holy week, the last week of Jesus' life, is well-known, being
described in all four Gospels. In the rock opera *Jesus Christ Superstar*
there are differences, which reward some attention. First, we should
realize that the central character in *Jesus Christ Superstar* is not Jesus but
Judas, and the interest in some of the disciples, particularly in Peter and
Mary Magdalene is greater and more telling than it is in Jesus. The
events of Jesus' passion are the central events around which their
dramas revolve.

The story opens with Judas complaining that Jesus and his disciples
have 'too much heaven on their minds'. Judas is introduced as the critic,
the outsider, who does not believe that 'this talk of God is true'. Then
follows the scene of the woman, who for convenience is Mary Magdalene, wiping Jesus' hair (in Matthew 26:6–16 she is not named). Judas,
who looks after the communal charity box and claims to be Jesus' 'right-
hand man' complains, making Jesus angry, thus introducing the possibility that he cares for Mary. Her response is to give Jesus a massage and
calm him down!

The chief priests want Jesus dead, for the sake of their own safety, for
they have learned to live with Roman occupation. As far as they are
concerned, Jesus is all set to overturn the balance of their security.
In contrast, we encounter the Palm Sunday procession, which is portrayed quite accurately. The crowd love Jesus: 'Hosanna, Heysanna,
sanna sanna ho' they sing. The lyricist Tim Rice inserts quotations from
Matthew 5:1–10: they are all blessed, Jesus sings. Here is Jesus Christ,
the Superstar, turning heads and inspiring a form of idolatry worthy of
any popstar or footballer today.

Soon we meet Simon Zealotes, who wants Jesus to sort out the
Romans, riding on the tide of popular adoration. Jesus does not respond,
but laments over Jerusalem, as in the Gospel narrative (Matthew 24),
predicting its destruction. Then, we meet Pilate, reminiscing about his
wife's dream, singing, incidentally, in the most unusual key of B flat
minor.

Then we move to the Temple, where, at least in the original film version, people are selling postcards, food, drink, and all kinds of souvenirs like those that can be bought at most religious sites today. The irony is strong as Jesus casts out the capitalists and commercial salesmen, all flogging their wares to gullible and bored tourists. After the cleansing of the Temple comes a scene in which Jesus is swamped by people seeking healing, to whom he desperately shouts: 'Heal yourselves!' Mary calms Jesus down again, and when he's fallen asleep, sings that she doesn't know how to love him. This is a love song in the traditional sense; she wonders how to tell him she loves him, and talks of being changed. In one sense this can be seen as an inspirational song, helping us to consider that he can change us too, but the song contains phrases about not being a 'lover's fool', which are hardly biblical! She also sings: 'He's just a man, nothing more'. This is, after all, what Judas sang at the very beginning, but it is not what the Gospels teach us about Christ.

In the second half, we are at the last supper, where the disciples are having a good time discussing what they will do in the future as ex-disciples: 'Always hoped that I'd be an apostle, knew that I would make it if I tried, then when we retire we can write the gospels, so they'll all talk about us when we die.' The cynicism here is poignant. The atmosphere is broken when Jesus and Judas argue, and Judas leaves to betray him. Jesus goes to Gethsemane, where he sings one of the most powerful songs in the work, wrestling with his desires and the will of God. Powerful alternation of moods give us a real insight into what Gethsemane might have been like for a tormented and frightened man, the state of whose mind may be reflected in the use of the unbalanced 5/8 time signature.

Then Judas returns with the guards. James and John are asleep. Judas kisses Jesus, who is seized and led away. On the way, journalists interview Jesus, the disgraced superstar, inviting him to comment. Peter goes into a courtyard, where three women ask him if he knows Jesus. Peter denies Christ three times, and Mary reminds him that Jesus had predicted he would. Suddenly they are frightened and realize that Peter has 'cut him dead' by denying him, and they are aware that it could all go terribly wrong.

Jesus is taken to see Pilate, who is rude and does not care, and on finding him to be a Galilean, packs him off to see King Herod, the Jewish puppet king. 'You're Herod's race—you're Herod's case!' Pilate screams.

Herod is portrayed in a parodied jazz song as a pathetic, unprincipled tyrant. He tries to play games with Jesus: 'Prove to me that you're divine—change my water into wine.' But Jesus says nothing. Herod gets more drunk and angry and sends Jesus back to Pilate, who is not pleased to see him.

Then follow two interludes, dispersing the intensity of emotion that would otherwise build up. Mary and Peter take centre stage in a song added for the film, in which they own up to not having understood, express their fear of having got it all wrong, and ask if they can all start again, please. Then we see Judas, tormented (pursued by Israeli tanks in the film), running to hang himself. Background choirs sing: 'Poor old Judas' until he commits suicide, when they sing: 'Well done, Judas!' This is certainly a disturbing interpretation of the Gospel narratives.

Pilate then offers Jesus for release by the people, but they want him crucified. Jesus is flogged, and then Pilate tries to help, claiming the power to let him live or die. Jesus says Pilate has no power at all, and the crowd remind him what Caesar might say if there was an insurrection. Pilate therefore condemns Jesus to death.

Then, in a surreal twist, we visit heaven, where Judas is leading the angels in praise of Jesus' superstar status. The implication is that Jesus has finally succeeded in getting himself crucified, so the mission is complete. There is no suggestion as to what that mission might signify. It is also important to note that although Judas is expecting Jesus to join them imminently, there is no resurrection scene in *Jesus Christ Superstar*.

It all ends with the crucifixion, which is portrayed in agonizing detail. Jesus forgives them because they do not know what they are doing, but it seems more like we are being told that Jesus doesn't know what he is doing. Jesus dies on the cross, and the piece concludes with an instrumental movement, entitled 'John 3:16'. Thus we are referred to a text which lies at the heart of the gospel, reminding us that 'God so loved the world that he gave his only Son, so that everyone who believes in him may not perish but may have eternal life' (John 3:16).

The story of Jesus' last days is broadly about betrayal, arrest, torture, death and resurrection. In *Jesus Christ Superstar* we discover another betrayal, which is the betrayal of Christ by modern culture. Here is a work that presents Jesus as a man (nothing more), who believes in himself more than he should, who gets angry rather unreliably, who encourages others to follow him, but refuses to perform miracles, and who is generally a sad, pathetic man, who meets an ignominious but inevitable end. On one level, *Jesus Christ Superstar* mocks faith, deriding those who have 'too much heaven on their minds', and offers an all-inclusive view of heaven at the end, where we can meet up with Jesus the superstar. In this version, he did not rise from the dead, raise Lazarus, have a virgin birth, preach any sermons, heal the sick or tell any parables. While it is unfair to criticize something for what it does not say, we can see what has been deliberately left out. I do not wish to make any assertions or judgments about the creators of *Jesus Christ Superstar*, who also created the superb musical *Joseph and his Technicolour Dreamcoat*. In *Joseph* God is not mentioned; it's just a good story. In *Superstar*, it is the same; God the Trinity hardly features. The passion narrative is just a ripping yarn about a man whom we pity, and who meets a sorry end. There is no theology here, just a moving story.

Jesus Christ Superstar presents Jesus without God. And that is a betrayal of the gospel. A gospel without God, without meaningful salvation, causes us to ask: 'Where is the good news in *Jesus Christ Superstar*?' I am sure we could find some if we wanted to, but the main point is that the story of Jesus has been used to tell a different story. As we enter into the events of holy week we must focus on the true meaning of passion, death and resurrection, rather than be swept up in a postmodern gospel of popular culture, for whom anyone who is popular is a superstar, and for whom superstars are necessarily fallible and weak.

PRAYER

Saving God, who sent your Son into the world that all who believe in him might not perish but have eternal life, keep us on your path of truth as we seek to follow in the way of Christ this holy week, so that we might both grieve over and delight in all he has done for us. Amen.

For further reading: Matthew 26:47–50; 27:3–5
For listening: 'I don't know how to love him', or other songs from *Jesus Christ Superstar* by Andrew Lloyd Webber and Tim Rice

'SHOWN BY THE CROSS'

J.S. BACH—*ST JOHN PASSION*

Then he handed him over to them to be crucified. So they took Jesus; and carrying the cross by himself, he went out to what is called The Place of the Skull, which in Hebrew is called Golgotha. There they crucified him, and with him two others, one on either side, with Jesus between them. Pilate also had an inscription written and put on the cross. It read: 'Jesus of Nazareth, the King of the Jews.' Many of the Jews read this inscription, because the place where Jesus was crucified was near the city; and it was written in Hebrew, in Latin, and in Greek. Then the chief priests of the Jews said to Pilate, 'Do not write, "The King of the Jews," but, "This man said, I am King of the Jews."' Pilate answered, 'What I have written I have written.' When the soldiers had crucified Jesus, they took his clothes and divided them into four parts, one for each soldier. They also took his tunic; now the tunic was seamless, woven in one piece from the top. So they said to one another, 'Let us not tear it, but cast lots for it to see who will get it.' This was to fulfil what the scripture says, 'They divided my clothes among themselves, and for my clothing they cast lots.' And that is what the soldiers did. Meanwhile, standing near the cross of Jesus were his mother, and his mother's sister, Mary the wife of Clopas, and Mary Magdalene.

JOHN 19:16–25

As we enter into the story of Christ's last days before being crucified, we inevitably feel a certain sorrow as we consciously remind ourselves of Jesus' commitment, his prayers, his betrayal, his humiliation and his suffering on the cross. We know the story almost too well. It can so easily go over our heads, as we encounter 'the same old story' year by year, as we sail through holy week, making preparations for the Easter holiday. One day it is Palm Sunday, and suddenly, almost by surprise, we find that Good Friday and soon Easter day have crept up on us, and we have missed our chance to immerse ourselves in Christ's saving passion.

Thus for many, a way to ensure a genuine engagement with the story is to attend a 'performance' of a Passion by J.S. Bach (1685–1750). There are two options—the *St John Passion*, or the *St Matthew Passion*. Both are sublime works, the former is the shorter, the latter perhaps the more famous. It is very likely that Bach set the passion narratives of St Luke and St Mark too, but these have mostly been lost, and it is the other two which have established a place in the heartlands of the European spirit.

The power of music to illustrate and involve hearers in a dramatic event has never been in dispute. Bach did not invent the musical Passion, but he does represent the pinnacle of achievement in that genre. The *St John Passion* was probably the first of the kind he wrote, and it is known to have been written by the year 1723, even though it does not appear to have been performed in that year. Whenever it was performed, it would have been accompanied by sermons, often of up to three hours in length, to which Bach's musical settings were a diversion and complement, and all of which added up to a liturgical event of considerable length. To attend a Bach Passion on Good Friday in Bach's time was certainly an act of great devotion, spiritual discipline, and, inevitably an occasion for Christian teaching and reflection. Today these two traditions have been separated: some churches and cathedrals have on Good Friday 'the preaching of the cross', which may be a three-hour series of connected sermons, perhaps with hymn singing. And then, on a separate occasion, there may be a performance in holy week of one of Bach's Passions. Dividing it in this way enables people to choose to attend one or the other, or both, and also extends the period of reflection further 'back' into holy week. It is a sad yet encouraging fact that in many places where both are provided, the musical event attracts a larger congregation—sad, because the preaching of the word is not as popular as it used to be, but encouraging because people still flock in their thousands to hear Bach's exposition of that word.

For there is no doubt that Bach saw himself as an expositor of biblical truth, and is in one sense to be seen as a teacher of the faith. The text of the *St John Passion* is basically chapters 18 and 19 of John's Gospel, sung by soloists and choir. There are a few verses from St Matthew's Gospel inserted, to help with the flow of the story, and there are also short poetical arias, which are meditations on what is taking place in the narrative. Thus Bach gives us musical time and space in which to reflect, remember, and to pray.

The very opening of the *St John Passion* is a good place to start. The words are by Bach himself, and give us as good a prayer for holy week as any: 'Lord and master... show us by your passion and cross that you are God's true Son, for even in the worst humiliation, you will be glorified.' The orchestra begins the movement with quick but secure semi-quavers, flowing over repeated bass notes, conveying the strength and confident omnipresence of God. And yet, over the top of this we hear the woodwind straining with dissonant, unresolved notes, conveying a sense of unease. Here we have Bach reflecting a contrast which typifies St John's Gospel. On one hand he stresses the ever-present power of God revealed in Christ. St John's Christ is a man of destiny, who knows his role, and who is described variously as 'Lamb of God' (John 1:29, 36), 'light of the world' (John 8:12; 9:5), 'good shepherd' (John 10:11, 14), 'bread of life' (John 6:35, 48) and 'Son of Man' (John 1:51; 3:13–14; 5:27; 6:27; 6:53). Yet, John's Gospel also shows us the human Christ, who is abandoned, denied and betrayed, and who suffers terribly. John blends these two aspects together, and Bach is able to do so in music, even in the opening bars of his two-hour masterpiece.

The opening movement was not written for the first performance, and was added later. Just as operatic composers sometimes wrote their overtures last, so that they could introduce most of the major musical material before the action starts, the opening chorus of the *St John Passion* seems to serve a similar function. The words set a theme of prayer and openness to revelation and renewal through an encounter with the cross of Christ, but so too does the music. As Bach sets the words '*Zeig, uns durch deine Passion* (show, by your Passion)', there is a musical motif which seems to draw out a cross musically on the page. A top E flat drops an octave, defining the downward stroke of the cross, and the music climbs back up, where, about two-thirds of the way up the scale, embellishments around the B flat give a hint of the crosspiece. This may seem like an enthusiastic interpretation, but it would not be surprising to find that Bach had begun his dramatic cantata by making the sign of the cross on the opening pages. Although it should perhaps be acknowledged that Bach was a good Lutheran, and such gestures—in church at any rate—were, and still are more likely found in Catholic contexts! Even so, Bach's music is in one sense inscribed with the cross throughout.

Musically, it is a unity. The crowd scenes, in which the choral singers are asked to play in turn the part of high priests, mob, by-standers and disciples, are often linked. Thus when Bach has the crowd call for 'Jesus of Nazareth' (nos. 3 and 5), when Jesus is arrested in the Garden of Gethsemane, the same music is used, and also much later (no. 25) when Pilate tells the High Priests to judge Jesus themselves, they reply by saying that it is illegal for them to put anyone to death. Similar music also appears when they sing to Pilate that they want Barabbas released, not Jesus (no. 29), and also when they rather deviously tell Pilate that they 'have no King but Caesar' (no. 46). Thus the music helps us to know who the chorus are representing at these points in the drama.

The chorales used by Bach were invariably not composed by him. They were already well known from their use in church worship. In modern performances they are sung by the chorus alone, who on our behalf respond to the events depicted. Thus, after Peter denies Christ, the chorus sing: 'Peter, forgetting, denied his God, but when he sees those earnest eyes, weeps bitterly', and they go on to sing, for us, 'Jesus, turn your eyes on me when I fail to repent. When I continue to sin, awaken my conscience.' The words of this and other chorales are in the first person, and are composed and offered by Bach as vehicles for our reflection, by which we may address God from within the experience of Christ's Passion. To Bach's contemporaries, these would have been well-known chorales, and the congregation would have joined in, entering more fully into the unfolding drama of holy week, making a personal and corporate response. While today we may not know the chorales so well, we are still 'invited in' to the experience by Bach, and can make these words our own, as we walk with Christ to the cross.

The arias in the *St John Passion* reveal another aspect of our response. These are extended musical items, with brief texts which allow Bach to explore the emotional impact of the events which are sometimes described in narrative so swiftly. Thus, after the Evangelist has declared that Jesus 'bowed his head and gave up his spirit' (no. 59), there is traditionally a moment of silence, and then a bass soloist asks at length: 'Now that you are nailed to the cross and have declared your task finished, let me ask—am I saved? Can I inherit eternal life? Is the world redeemed? You cannot speak for pain, but you bow your head silently, and say, "Yes".' It is a moving moment which Bach holds for us in music: the dead Christ cannot speak, but his actions, and the music Bach writes, speak louder than mere words. Unusually in this aria, the chorus also join in, singing as an undercurrent a chorale which reminds us that Jesus has gained life through death for himself and us. As the soloist affirms the salvation Christ has wrought, the choir gently ask Jesus for nothing more than what Christ has won: eternal life. It is a poignant moment.

Bach does not leave us there though, but pushes us on with St Matthew's mention of the temple veil being torn when Jesus dies (Matthew 27:51) and then the burial of Jesus. Only then can we depart, quietly. As the Passion closes we leave Christ in the tomb, but, accompanied by some of Bach's most sublime music, we do not depart in despair. There is no mention in the text of resurrection, but the music is pregnant with Easter expectation. The chorus '*Ruht Wohl*' ('sleep well') is like a lullaby at first, presenting us with a musical pietà, as we may be reminded of Jesus' mother cradling him, not only at birth, but also after the deposition from the cross. Christ is laid in the tomb like a sleeping baby, with the same love, the same tenderness, and with hope for the following morn. It is an unusual, yet powerful and creative emotional sound space into which the dying Christ is placed, and Bach does it in our name: we are the ones who lay Christ to rest so gently, after we have killed him. The music is sublimely beautiful and calm, except that midway through we are reminded that Christ's grave is not a place of death, but a gateway to heaven, and with that hint of the Easter dawn, the music returns to its lullaby.

The *St John Passion* does not quite end there. The story does not end with the death of Christ, nor does it end with Jesus himself. It ends with us. The final chorus sings of the day when awakened from our own death we shall see Christ, and we, with all the saints, will glorify God for ever. On this note of eternity, the work ends, reminding us that although the work of Christ is done, his rule is everlasting, and our praise is endless.

PRAYER

O Jesus Christ, whose glory is revealed the world over, show us by your cross and passion that you are the eternal Son of God, and that even in your greatest humiliation, your name is exalted above all other names, to the glory of God the Father. Amen.

For further reading: John 18—19
For listening: The final chorus and chorale of Bach's *St John Passion*

'HER SOUL, SIGHING, ANGUISHED AND GRIEVING, WAS PIERCED BY A SWORD'

GIOACCHINO ROSSINI—*STABAT MATER*

*The mother stood sorrowing by the cross weeping
while her son hung there.
Her soul, sighing, anguished and grieving, was pierced by a sword.
O how sad and afflicted was that blessed mother
of her only begotten son.
She mourned and lamented and trembled when she saw
the pangs of her glorious son.
Who would not weep to see the mother of Christ thus,
in so much distress?
Who would not be saddened contemplating the mother of Christ
suffering with her son?
She saw Jesus in torment and subjected to scourging
for the sins of his people.
She saw her dear son dying, forsaken, as he gave up his spirit.
O mother, fount of love, make me to feel the strength of your grief,
so that I may mourn with you.
Make my heart burn with love for Christ, my Lord God,
that I may be pleasing to him.
Blessed mother, cause the sufferings of the crucified one
to be fixed deeply in my heart.
Share with me the pains of your wounded son
who is so gracious to suffer for my sake.*

Make me truly weep with you, grieving with him who is crucified,
so that I may live.
To stand with you beside the cross and share your grief is my desire.
Virgin, brightest of virgins, be not cruel to me now:
grant me to weep with you,
Let me bear Christ's death, let me share his passion,
enduring his wounds.
Let me be wounded with his wounds, let that cross inspire me
with love for your Son.
Lest I burn in the flames of hell, let me be defended by you,
O Virgin, on the day of judgment.
Grant that I may be protected by the cross, fortified by the death
of Christ, strengthened by grace.
When my body shall die, grant that my spirit will be given
glory in paradise. Amen.

THE STABAT MATER (TRANS. GJG)

Gioacchino Rossini (1792–1868) was born at Pesaro, and became one of Italy's greatest composers of opera. He is therefore not noted for his religious compositions, of which the *Stabat Mater* and *Petit Messe Solennelle* are the main examples. However, Rossini was a faithful man, and when he wrote the latter he added a prayer in which he describes it as a 'poor little mass', and expresses the view that in spite of his bad music, he might be granted a place in heaven.

His *Stabat Mater* has a slightly unusual history, as initially he did not write all of it, but allowed his pupil Giovanni Tadolini to write the central and concluding movements, when Rossini succumbed to a fierce attack of lumbago in 1831. The commission for the work had come from a Spanish nobleman, and with Tadolini's help, Rossini was just able to deliver it in time, and for doing so he received a gold snuffbox in payment. Rossini insisted that the work never be published, but when the Spaniard died in 1837, Rossini discovered that a publisher was about to proceed. After taking successful legal action, Rossini was persuaded to replace Tadolini's sections with versions of his own. Thus in 1841 a new version was performed and published, and that is what we usually hear today.

The most famous, but possibly the worst part of the *Stabat Mater* is the second movement, *'Cujus animam'* ('her weeping heart'). It is not bad music, but to many its jaunty approach is simply inappropriate. Here Rossini is doing what he knew best: writing an operatic aria, and, to be fair, it is a lovely tune, written for tenor soloist. A lovely tune though, is perhaps not what we expect as we contemplate the mother of Jesus watching him crucified! Thus in this one section of music, the composer is praised and vilified, and this, in a way, characterizes his life. Rossini, while a serious man in many respects, is famous for comic opera and culinary inventions (he wrote a recipe book and invented 'tornedos Rossini'). He led an extravagant life, but had a simple faith.

The very moving text of the *Stabat Mater* is thought by many to have been written by a thirteenth-century Franciscan monk called Jacopone da Todi, or perhaps by Pope Innocent III or St Bonaventure. Whoever the author was, they made a very significant contribution to the spiritual treasury of second-millennium Christianity. In the poem, we find ourselves at the cross with Christ's mother. In this much, we are given a distinctively feminine perspective. Whether male or female, the author takes the reader (or singer) into that realm where no one should have to go, but sadly, where many have had to go over many centuries. No mother should witness the death of her child: there is something fundamentally unnatural about it. Therefore, as we contemplate the feelings of Mary at the cross, watching her son crucified, we are encroaching upon what must have been a terrible, harrowing experience, in which every ounce of pain felt by Christ also tore through her own veins.

Mary's faith was exemplary, ever since that day when, confronted by the angel, she said yes to God, and accepted her unique vocation. Soon afterwards, Simeon told her that 'a sword will pierce your own soul too' (Luke 2:35). As Christ was presented in the Temple according to the Jewish custom, the child's destiny was prophesied. And now, 30 years later, the day that Mary knew about, yet dreaded, had arrived, and no matter how confident she was of the salvation being wrought in blood and sweat upon the cross, it must have caused her unbearable pain, as Jesus is presented to the world once again, this time in agony.

Much is said and written about Christ submitting himself to pain and death on the cross, and how his strength is found in weakness, such that even when humiliated, he maintains and demonstrates a unique form of godly power. But what about Mary, who seems so powerless at the foot of the cross? She is also demonstrating a certain power. She stands there, weeping no doubt, but also aware of the spiritual battle being won. Her refusal to be defeated by her personal tragedy demonstrates not only her strength and bravery, but gives hope to the others present, and to all of us throughout history who watch with her. For we watch with her, not only as we imagine the scene at Calvary, but whenever we turn the television news on. Where there is sorrow, there is often powerlessness, but in Mary's standing at the cross, we may discover an unusual power in defeat, a hope in loss. This power and hope may be personal in the midst of private tragedy (which is why so many find inspiration in Mary), or it may be national or international. As Christ suffers for the world, she watches, and this means that as the world suffers over and over again, she has seen it before, she has borne it before, and has survived. In a world that so often sees destruction, disaster, suffering, violence and war, Mary can be a symbol of hope, reminding us that just as Christ can die daily for everyone, he can also be born again in anyone, any day.

PRAYER

O God and Father of our Lord Jesus Christ, who through Mary caused him to be humanly born only to die upon the cross, grant to us the grace to watch with her as we recall his passion, and the strength to respond to the sufferings of the world of which we are so well aware. This we ask for the sake of the same, Jesus Christ our Saviour. Amen.

For further reading: John 19:19–30
For listening: '*Cujus animam*' from Gioacchino Rossini's *Stabat Mater*

'O DEAR MEMORIAL OF THAT DEATH WHICH LIVES STILL AND ALLOWS US BREATH!'

GERALD FINZI—*LO! THE FULL, FINAL SACRIFICE*

Lo, the full, final sacrifice
On which all figures fix their eyes.
The ransomed Isaac, and his ram;
The Manna and the Paschal Lamb.

Jesu Master, just and true!
Our food, and faithful shepherd too!

O let that love which thus makes thee
Mix with our low Mortality,
Lift our lean souls and set us up
Convictors of thine own full cup,
Coheirs of saints. That so all may
Drink the same wine; and the same way.

Nor change the pasture, but the place
To feed of thee in thine own Face.

O dear memorial of that Death
Which lives still and allows us breath!
Rich, Royal Food! Bountiful Bread!
Whose use denies us to the dead.

Live ever, Bread of loves, and be
My life, my soul, my surer self to me.

Help Lord, my faith, my Hope increase;
And fill my portion in thy peace.
Give love for life, nor let my days
Grow, but in new powers to thy name and praise.

Rise, Royal Sion! rise and sing
Thy soul's kind shepherd, thy heart's King.
Stretch all thy powers; call if you can
Harps of heaven to hands of man.
Thy sovereign subject sits above
The best ambition of thy love.

Lo the Bread of Life; this day's
Triumphant Text provokes thy praise.
The living and life-giving bread,
To the great twelve distributed
When Life, himself, at point to die
Of love, was his own legacy.

O soft self wounding pelican!
Whose breast weeps balm for wounded man.
All this way bend thy benign flood
To a bleeding Heart that gasps for blood.
That blood, whose least drops sovereign be
To wash my worlds of sins from me.
Come love! Come Lord! and that long day
For which I languish, come away.
When this dry soul those eyes shall see,
And drink the unseal'd source of thee.
When glory's sun faith's shades shall chase,
And for thy veil give me thy face. Amen.

FROM RICHARD CRASHAW'S VERSIONS OF THE HYMNS OF
ST THOMAS AQUINAS: 'ADORO TE' AND 'LAUDA SION SALVATOREM'

Although this is one of the most sublime pieces in the choral music repertoire it is not as well-known as it should be. Those who do know it will attest to its beauty, but would also have to admit to the various reasons why Finzi's anthem is not performed often, and therefore is not well-known. The reasons are that it lasts about a quarter of an hour, it is difficult to sing, and that its text is a little opaque in meaning.

Its length marks it out as unusual. An anthem at choral evensong usually lasts about five minutes, perhaps a little longer; this is what congregations expect, and what choirs expect and can be expected to sing. Sometimes *Lo, the full, final sacrifice* is sung on Easter day, not only because it is about the saving work of Christ, but on that day of all days there can be a justification for an anthem that is three times the length of the usual offering. The anthem is rarely heard in a concert, which also restricts its fame.

It is not an easy piece, either. The organist for the piece must be top-notch, for it begins with a two-minute organ solo, and then the organ plays a significant part in the music, far beyond anything that can merely be called 'accompaniment'. A good tenor soloist is required in the choir, as are good singers to carry other solos. The choral parts are quite demanding, requiring some effort even from the most fluent singers.

Gerald Finzi (1901–56) led a difficult life in many respects, and his last five years were spent in the knowledge that he had Hodgkins' disease. In his youth, his father and three brothers all died, as did his music teacher. He was well aware of the fragility of life, and of the pain of grief. As well as being one of Britain's greatest composers, he was also a keen apple grower, and should be credited for having saved some species of English apple from extinction by cultivating them in his orchards. He also had a distinctive enthusiasm for and knowledge of English literature, which enabled him to draw on England's greatest poets for inspiration and textual fuel.

Richard Crashaw (1612–49) was the son of a Puritan preacher but resented his father's strong stance, taking the side of the Royalists during the English Civil War. During that time he was a Fellow at Peterhouse, Cambridge, but when Cromwell triumphed he was deprived of that post. Crashaw fled and ended up in the Italian town of Loreto, having converted to Roman Catholicism. Thus it is not surprising that some of his poetry is rather reactionary, but, like Finzi, we may draw some truth and insight from it.

His poem, based on the writings of Thomas Aquinas, entreats us to reflect upon Jesus: 'himself once offered, a full, perfect and sufficient sacrifice, oblation and satisfaction for the sins of the whole world', as the Anglican eucharist puts it. We are reminded of Abraham and Isaac, the Old Testament prefiguring of the Father and the Son, allying the giving of the manna in the wilderness to Christ the Easter sacrifice. Finzi sets these words in a hushed silence; the organ is mute, having set the mood. Then comes a prayer, that the same love which brought Christ to earth in human form would lift up our hearts so that by sharing in eucharist we become inheritors of the kingdom, with all the saints. Thus we all drink from the same cup, and follow the same way to salvation (see Mark 10:38–39 and John 14:1–6). Then all will be able to share at the heavenly banquet with Christ, where we shall see him face to face (1 John 3:2). Further eucharistic reflection follows, elucidating the point that the offering of Christ, signified in the eucharist, gives us life and protects us from eternal death. There follows an exclamation of praise, and entreaty to the powers of heaven to sing to God, so that we below might join in. 'This day's Triumphant Text' refers to Maundy Thursday, when at the last supper Jesus distributed bread and wine, giving of himself to his disciples (the 'great twelve') and to us thereafter (Luke 22:14–21).

The 'soft self-wounding pelican' is Jesus, and the image draws on the fallacious but prevalent third-century idea that pelicans killed their young and then, repenting of doing so, would pierce their own bodies so that they could restore their young to life. This gives us a picture of Christ, like a mother pelican, feeding his people with his own blood. The idea is that as we bleed to eternal death, we can be restored by the blood of Christ, shed for us. It is graphic imagery, passionately musicalized by Finzi, and reminds us of the eucharistic phrase: 'These gifts of bread and wine may be to us his body and blood', and that in being so, they wash away our sins (see Hebrews 9:12–14).

The final section, which is one of the most beautiful, calls on Christ to return and give again of himself (see Hebrews 9:23–28). Finzi sets the word 'glory' as the climax of the whole work, with a surprise chord that seems to burst upon us like a ray of sunshine through the clouds, reminding us that it is Christ's glory of which we sing, and which we seek until that day when the veil is removed and we see him face to face. Neither Finzi nor Crashaw may have had it in mind, but at this point in the music it is as though this text is revealed as the theme of the piece: 'For it is the God who said, "Let light shine out of darkness", who has shone in our hearts to give the light of the knowledge of the glory of God in the face of Jesus Christ' (2 Corinthians 4:6).

Finally, we should let the last word have the last word. At the end of such a long anthem, there comes a setting of 'Amen', which closes the music and our prayer. It is a loving 'Amen', which is sometimes sung on its own (at least one recent recording of choral music has done this), and although it lasts barely a minute and a half, it ends the piece like the gentle closing of a leather volume. Combined in these final moments is reverence, love, gratitude, and bliss, expressed like a fond farewell. Finzi has captured not only the spirit of Crashaw's poem, but has taken us to another level of contemplation. For those who, like him, suffer so much in life, this must come as balm and rest. While our praises and prayers are in one sense endless, there do come times when we feel it is right to stop, and there can hardly be a better full stop at the end of prayer than Finzi's final 'Amen' from *Lo, the full, final sacrifice*.

PRAYER

For your saving love, shared with us and given to us, O Christ Jesus, we give you all the glory, in which you reign, with the Father and the Spirit, now and for ever. Amen.

For further reading: Hebrews 9:12–28
For listening: *Lo! the full, final sacrifice* by Gerald Finzi

'BAPTIZED INTO CHRIST'S DEATH'

RICHARD WAGNER—*PARSIFAL*

Do you not know that all of us who have been baptized into Christ Jesus were baptized into his death? Therefore we have been buried with him by baptism into death, so that, just as Christ was raised from the dead by the glory of the Father, so we too might walk in newness of life.

For if we have been united with him in a death like his, we will certainly be united with him in a resurrection like his. We know that our old self was crucified with him so that the body of sin might be destroyed, and we might no longer be enslaved to sin. For whoever has died is freed from sin. But if we have died with Christ, we believe that we will also live with him. We know that Christ, being raised from the dead, will never die again; death no longer has dominion over him.

ROMANS 6:3–9

It might be thought strange that on this most holy day, we do not look directly at Christ's suffering on the cross. Instead, we shall consider the impact and significance of the crucifixion by looking at an opera, part of which is set on Good Friday. One of the most famous parts of Wagner's *Parsifal* is known as the 'Good Friday music' (*Karfreitagszauber*). It is a unique passage, towards the end of the work, in which Parsifal, the hero, baptizes Kundry, the outcast.

Richard Wagner (1813–83) was a complex character, who used his great intellect and creative skills in ways that have created controversy ever since. But there can be no doubt that he was an artistic genius. Many volumes have been written on him and his music, and especially on the mythological, religious and cultural significance of his mighty portfolio. His famous 'Ring' cycle baffles and delights audiences still. It is not so much that he wrote a lot of music, but that what he did compose is often long and weighty, bearing philosophical and poetic ideas in extended directions. It is often joked that Wagner's music has some lovely moments, but also some very boring half-hours! It is also often remembered that Wagner is credited with having invented the *leitmotif*—a musical phrase which denotes a particular person, sentiment, activity or object. This makes his operas ('music-dramas' as they should be called) 'readable' in terms of the music, as well as the dialogue, allowing the listener to access the music on various levels, to understand connections and relationships in a deeper way. So careful was Wagner's plotting that these connections are built into the music drama. This makes Wagner's music both challenging and rewarding. Non-German-speakers are inevitably hindered by the language (Wagner wrote his own texts too), but in this age of recordings and videos, we are better placed to engage with the worlds that he creates.

The story of *Parsifal* is drawn from Wolfram von Eschenbach's *Parzival*, which in turn drew its inspiration from Chrétien de Troyes' *Li contes del Graal* ('Tales of the Grail'), in which many of the legends of the Holy Grail first appeared. Later in the thirteenth century the Grail became identified with a cup or chalice which was used to catch Christ's blood as he hung dying. Fans of King Arthur (or even of Monty Python!) will know of the quest for the Holy Grail, and may notice the connection between the name Percival and Parsifal. Legends about the Grail have been popular since at least the thirteenth century. The monks of Glastonbury claimed to have 'discovered' the tomb of King Arthur in 1191, and by the fourteenth century, the story that Joseph of Arimathea had caught some of Christ's blood in a dish or chalice and had brought it to England was widely believed (the tale derives from an account in the so-called 'Gospel of Nicodemus', he who assisted Joseph at the crucifixion). Some legends also associate the Grail with the cup used at the last supper. No one has ever discovered anything substantial, but there are those who value stories such as these.

The power of the Grail lies at the heart of *Parsifal*. In the legend, the Grail, and the holy spear which pierced Christ's side, have been placed in the care of Titurel, and his fellow soldier monks. A sorcerer, Klingsor, failed to reach their standards of membership, and having castrated himself, was rejected by them. In revenge, he created a castle populated by beautiful women, whose task was to seduce the knights, causing them to break their chastity vows. Those who succumbed became his prisoners and soldiers. Titurel abdicated and his son Amfortas succeeded him. Amfortas, in confrontation with Klingsor, was ensnared by Kundry. Amfortas escaped, but not without losing the holy spear to Klingsor, who permanently wounded him with it. As a result, the whole community of Grail knights is damaged, because Amfortas cannot preside at their celebrations. This is the background to Wagner's opera.

The drama opens with a long and exquisite prelude, in which many of the leitmotifs are heard—a foretaste of the musical banquet to follow. Then we hear morning prayer being sung, after which Amfortas takes his daily healing bath in the holy lake (see John 5:2–9). Kundry arrives with ointment (and is thereby associated with the woman who bathes Christ's feet in Matthew 26:6–13). Amfortas can only be healed with the spear, which Klingsor still has. His only hope lies in a prophecy that a 'holy fool', an innocent lad, enlightened through compassion, can rescue the spear and heal him. Parsifal, or Percival, literally means 'holy fool'. As the prophecy is remembered, the stranger, Parsifal, arrives, and kills a swan. He is arrested and reprimanded, but it becomes clear that he has no sense of right or wrong. He also knows very little about himself. One of the knights, Gurnemanz, questions Parsifal and suspects that something of the prophecy may lie in him, and so brings him to the knights' ritual. In this ritual, the Grail is exposed, and the holy blood of Christ enters into Amfortas' sin-laden body, causing him tremendous pain. This is not a eucharist by any means, but there are similarities. Thus, Act One may be characterized as opening with a form of mattins and concluding with a form of eucharist, although both are conducted in an unhappy way.

Act Two takes place in Klingsor's castle, towards which Parsifal is unwittingly heading, having been ejected by the knights. Klingsor instructs Kundry to seduce him. She talks to him of his dead mother, who, she says, died of grief when he left her for his wanderings. This upsets Parsifal and as she consoles him, he nearly succumbs. However, at the last minute Parsifal realizes what he must do: recover the spear and heal Amfortas, thereby restoring the fortunes and the faith of the knights. He therefore rejects Kundry's advances. She is furious, because she has failed, and she curses Parsifal and calls on Klingsor to attack him with the holy spear, which he does. Parsifal, the holy innocent, cannot be harmed though, and when he grasps the spear, Klingsor is defeated and his castle disintegrates.

Act Three takes place on Good Friday many years later and returns us to the knights' lands. The community has almost collapsed because of lack of leadership, and Gurnemanz has become a hermit. He encounters Kundry, in a terrible state; she is now a shadow of the wild woman she once was. Parsifal, dressed in black, arrives, having been cursed by Kundry all those years ago to wander aimlessly. At first, Gurnemanz does not recognize him and rebukes him for being armed on such a holy day. Then he tells him that Titurel has died and Amfortas cannot lead them. Parsifal blames himself for this, and Kundry, again echoing the biblical passage, bathes his feet. Gurnemanz anoints Parsifal as their new leader, and then, in one of the most profound passages of Western music (the 'Good Friday music'), Parsifal baptizes Kundry. Then he returns to the knights as their new leader and heals Amfortas, thus opening up once more to them the saving power of the Grail.

This 'Good Friday music' brings together the histories of all the characters involved. There is Gurnemanz, the faithful warrior who longs for the restoration and salvation of his community. He, like Simeon, witnesses what he has long lived to see (Luke 2: 25–32). There is also Kundry, who, as an archetype, is one of the greatest sinners there could have been. She mocked Christ, rejecting his salvation. She has much to repent of, and now she finally acknowledges her sin, submits herself to Christ and is baptized. And there is Parsifal, the holy innocent, of whom a prophecy has been spoken, fulfilling his calling, and turning the world around for good. Out of the gloomy situation in which the drama is set comes new life, transformed by baptism and renewal. If even Kundry can be saved, then anyone can. And what is crucial here is that the baptism, as St Paul puts it, is into Christ's death, which took place on this day, all those years ago.

The fictitious prophecy about Parsifal reminds us of the need for innocence. In a culture that baptizes children readily, we may be reminded of the story of Jesus having little children brought to him: 'Let the little children come to me, and do not stop them; for it is to such as these that the kingdom of heaven belongs' (Matthew 19:14). When we submit ourselves to Christ we seek the innocence of childhood—not the stupidity of foolishness, but the innocence of sinlessness. It is baptism that washes away sin, and it is Christ's death that makes that possible. Notwithstanding any old legends about a Holy Grail and magic properties it may yield, there is ultimate truth in the idea that it is Christ's blood that washes away sin. This truth is embodied in the eucharist (which is rarely celebrated on Good Friday), and also in baptism, where Christ's gift of living water is freely given through the Holy Spirit (John 3:5 and 4:14). Baptism, eucharist and crucifixion are inextricably linked.

On Good Friday it is easy to forget how crucifixion and baptism go together, for we often focus only on the cross on this most holy day. Good Friday is a solemn day on which we reflect a right and proper grief at the sufferings of our Lord on the cross. But let us never forget what crucifixion was *for*, and the inherent *goodness* of this Friday, through which baptism into the death of Christ, with repentance, means that we, as the children of God, may have restored to us the eternal innocence of sinlessness, which opens up access to our God, now and for ever.

PRAYER

O God of mercy, who through the passion of your Son opens the floodgates of salvation, and through baptism leads us through them, forgive us our continued sin, and lead us ever onward in the stream of blood spilled and living water poured for us, until that resurrection day when all death turns to life in Jesus Christ our Saviour. Amen.

For further reading: John 3:1–16
For listening: The 'Good Friday music' from Richard Wagner's *Parsifal*, Act Three

'SAVE YOURSELF AND US!'

BENJAMIN BRITTEN—*BILLY BUDD*

Jesus said, 'Father, forgive them; for they do not know what they are doing.'... One of the criminals who were hanged there kept deriding him and saying, 'Are you not the Messiah? Save yourself and us!' But the other rebuked him, saying, 'Do you not fear God, since you are under the same sentence of condemnation? And we indeed have been condemned justly, for we are getting what we deserve for our deeds, but this man has done nothing wrong.' Then he said, 'Jesus, remember me when you come into your kingdom.' He replied, 'Truly I tell you, today you will be with me in Paradise.'

LUKE 23:34, 39–43

Sometimes we come across figures who suffer like Christ, either in real life, or in art. One such artistic character is the sailor Billy Budd. He was the creation of Herman Melville (the author of *Moby Dick*), whose *Billy Budd, Sailor* was first published in 1924. This story, which Melville left only partially completed, was taken up by Benjamin Britten for an opera, with the libretto written by the novelist E.M. Forster and Eric Crozier.

The plot is a sad and disturbing one, and resonates loudly with the events of Passiontide. From the very outset we are reminded that this tale is also about good and evil, as well as about an unfortunate sailor whose disability and frustration causes him to accidentally commit a capital crime.

The prologue introduces us to Captain Vere, an old man looking back with regret upon the case of Billy Budd, which causes him to conclude that even goodness is often fatally flawed. In his memory, he carries us back to the HMS *Indomitable* in 1797, the ship of which he was then the commanding officer.

The action begins with the crew hard at work. It is a tough ship, and when a young crew member accidentally bumps into the bosun, he has him flogged. The press gang returns, having 'persuaded' three sailors to join the crew of the warship. One of them is Billy Budd, fit and handsome, but who suffers from a stammer when under stress. The Master-at-Arms, Claggart, recognizes value in him, describing Billy as 'a pearl of great price' (see Matthew 13:45–46). But when Billy calls farewell to his old ship, which is called the *Rights o' Man*, his intentions are misunderstood by the officers, who instruct Claggart to watch him carefully. Claggart orders Corporal Squeak to provoke Billy and get him into trouble. The old seaman Dansker warns Billy about Claggart, but the innocent Billy cannot identify any evil in him, even though Claggart picks on him for wearing a coloured scarf. Then the crew are addressed by Captain Vere, who tells them that they are entering enemy waters and must do their duty. As they swear to fight and die for their captain, Billy's words: 'I'll follow you, I'll serve you, I'll die for you, Starry Vere' take on prophetic dimensions.

Later we find ourselves in Vere's cabin, where the officers are discussing recent mutinies. They decide to be specially vigilant in the stressful times that approach. The same evening, the men relax below decks, singing sea shanties. Billy is popular among his shipmates. He discovers Squeak rummaging through his possessions and attacks him. Claggart has Squeak clapped in irons and congratulates Billy, but once the men are asleep he admits to himself that Billy's popularity, beauty and goodness are driving him mad. He persuades the reluctant young novice sailor, who was flogged, to bribe Billy into leading a mutiny. His efforts fail and Billy stammers under the stress. Billy's friend Dansker realizes what is happening and again warns Billy to beware of Claggart (whom they call 'Jemmy legs'). Billy does not believe Dansker, preferring to anticipate promotion.

A few days later the ship is becalmed and surrounded by mist, and can see no action. Claggart begins to tell Captain Vere his lies about Billy being a mutineer, but a French ship is sighted and the mist clears. They give chase, but the wind drops, and the pursuit is abandoned.

Claggart again speaks to Vere about Billy, but Vere does not believe him, and warns Claggart about the punishment for false witness, and arranges for Billy to confront his accuser. Vere himself prays for the 'light of clear heaven to separate evil from good'.

In his cabin, Vere believes Billy to be innocent, and tells Claggart: 'The boy whom you would destroy is good; you are evil.' Billy enters, believing that he has been summoned in order to be promoted. When Claggart repeats his allegations, Billy is so shocked and upset that his stammer prevents him answering the charge, so he lashes out at Claggart, accidentally killing him. Vere is horrified at the turn of events and calls his officers. He realizes that even though Billy is innocent of murder, a trial will have to be held. He sings: 'It is not his trial; it is mine. It is I whom the devil awaits.'

The trial is held immediately, and Vere gives evidence as the only witness. Billy denies the charge, saying that since he was dumb-founded by his stammer, he responded with a blow. He implores Vere to save him, reminding him that he would have died for him in action. Vere seems unable to act, even though it seems he can save Billy. Billy is led away and the officers pronounce him guilty and sentence him to be hanged from the yard-arm of the ship. Vere is now troubled, because he is face to face with the tension between adherence to inflex-ible rules and instinctive compassion. He says: 'I have beheld the mystery of goodness—and I am afraid', and then he goes to tell Billy the verdict.

The next morning, just before dawn, Billy, in chains, accepts his fate. Dansker, his friend, brings him grog and biscuits, a final breakfast, reminiscent of the bread and wine at the last supper. Encouraged by Dansker, he nevertheless refuses to support a threatened mutiny, for he has sighted a heavenly sail that will bring him peace. Thus at four o'clock, in front of his friends and comrades, Billy is sentenced. With his final words he blesses Vere, and as he is hanged, the crew repeat his phrase: 'Starry Vere, God bless you.'

The stage direction at this point reads: 'Then begins the sound described by Melville as like the freshest wave of a torrent roaring distantly through the woods, expressing a capricious revulsion of feeling in the crew. The sound grows in and grows, and the whole wedged mass of faces slowly turns in rebellion to the quarterdeck.' Britten sets this as a striking, wordless chorus. The rebellion does not take force, however, and the sailors return to their quarters.

The opera concludes with an epilogue, where we see Vere as an old man again. He recalls how they buried Billy at sea, and maintains that he, Vere, might have saved him. Yet the irony is that Billy saved *him*. He had been lost on the infinite sea, a ship without direction or hope: 'But he has saved me, and blessed me, and the love that passes understanding has come to me.' Vere has seen the destination which lies ahead, a heavenly harbour, where Billy went all those years before when he was so unjustly punished, and where Vere himself hopes to go.

Billy Budd is all about redemption. Britten and his writers took Melville's plot and emphasized this aspect, both offering a secular context in which a drama of salvation is played out, but also pinning it to Christianity. Billy wants to be 'saved', and Vere claims to be 'saved'. Yet, ironically, Billy is the innocent one, and Vere is the one who is guilty of letting him suffer. With Christ it is perhaps more clear-cut, when we consider his innocence on the cross, and our guilt of earthly sin, but in *Billy Budd* we find echoes of the same relationship. Billy, the victim, is also the saviour, and it is so often the case that it is our victim who is our saviour. Only those whom we have wronged can forgive us, and therefore release us from our guilt, for many sins, as well as offending God, have human victims too. Those whom we harm are thereby even capable of saving us from ourselves. Christ is the one whom we wrong when we commit any sin, and therefore he is the ultimate Saviour. Christ is also the ultimate victim, because his is the unjust punishment to end all unjust punishments, the sinless victim whose blood removes the sins of past, present and future.

Yet sin continues and, as St Paul says, it continues because of the Law. He means the Law of Moses, of course, but in *Billy Budd*, Captain Vere proclaims that 'earthly laws silenced him'. The crime in the story is not committed when Billy strikes Claggart, but when Billy himself is killed. Sin here does come through the law, even if it is a different, military, naval law. Vere is presented as being inchoately aware of this, as he echoes Paul's exclamation about the clash of sin and law in Romans 7:13–25.

This dilemma exists in all of us, to some extent; in our complex society, which imposes on us numerous rules and regulations, and even in the Church, which has its own rules, we sometimes feel that what the rules say and what is best for all parties do conflict. Often we are forced to make decisions, especially where compromise is not possible, and this was the predicament that Captain Vere experienced. He could not save Billy and condemn him at the same time, and therefore he was rendered helpless. Ironically, only Billy, his victim, could save him. Billy's final words are reminiscent of Christ's final words on the cross: 'Father, forgive them; for they do not know what they are doing' (Luke 23:34).

Sometimes, even the comfort of forgiveness does not remove all the scars of wrong. We take such scars to the grave, and only there, with our bodies, do they decay. The old Captain Vere, even though he believed himself to be saved, still suffered, and it is not entirely clear whether he has truly found peace, or whether he is doomed to relive the most powerful and traumatic event of his life. The lack of musical resolution at the end of the opera suggests that this might be the case. Britten, however, was a master of ambiguous music. In *The Turn of the Screw*, which is a ghost story opera, he manages to hold open the question as to whether the ghosts exist by the way in which he writes. Here, in *Billy Budd*, he holds open the question about redemption and salvation. Can it be achieved in life, or do we need death to seal it?

As we remember Christ, sealed in the stone cold tomb, on this day, we may want to hold this question open for ourselves. But no matter how many scars in life we incur, we can be assured of forgiveness for repentance in this life, and also be assured of the greater redemption which will be made real for us when we depart this life in the faith and fear of our Saviour Jesus Christ.

PRAYER

Christ our Saviour, who for us was the victim of criminal injustice, give us the peace of knowing our salvation, and the knowledge of your healing presence as we sail the sea of doubt and fear towards the haven that is our heavenly home, for you keep us afloat on the waves of your love, and bury all sin and evil beneath us, in this world and the next. Amen.

For further reading: Romans 7:13–25
For listening: 'Starry Vere' and 'We committed his body to the deep' (the final scene and epilogue) from Britten's *Billy Budd*

EASTER SUNDAY

'GLORY TO GOD'

GIACOMO PUCCINI—*MESSA DI GLORIA*

Glory to God in the highest, and peace to his people on earth.
Lord God, heavenly King
almighty God and Father,
we worship you, we give you thanks,
we praise you for your glory.
Lord, Jesus Christ, only Son of the Father,

Lord God, Lamb of God,
you take away the sins of the world;
have mercy on us;
you are seated at the right hand of the Father:
receive our prayer.
For you alone are the Holy One,
you alone are the Lord,
you alone are the Most High,
Jesus Christ, with the Holy Spirit,
in the glory of God the Father.
Amen.

THE PROPER OF THE MASS—'GLORIA'

One of the ways in which the Church marks the contrast between the Lent and Easter periods is by omitting and then restoring the 'Gloria' at celebrations of the eucharist. Thus on Easter Day (or at the vigil service on the evening before) the 'Gloria' is often said or sung with great jubilation, and is all the more effective for having not been heard for many weeks. There is something very fitting in that we are proclaiming the message of Easter by quoting from one of the most famous passages of Christmas readings, although we do not always notice it as we usher in our celebrations of that great moment of joy when we proclaim that Christ is risen. Yet, as we celebrate today, remembering the story of the angels guarding the tomb who proclaim to Mary: 'He is not here, but has risen' (Luke 24:5), we are taken right back to that humble moment of incarnation when God, who as word made flesh lived among us and died for our sins, by his birth, caused the angels to cry 'Glory to God' (Luke 2 :14). At this time of Easter we are reminded of the nativity of Christ, as at Christmas we are reminded of his mission and purpose by so many Christmas carols which mention that he was 'born to die'. We are all born to die, of course, yet Christ's birth and death mean that our life from birth to death is rescued, redeemed:

> *Born that man no more may die*
> *Born to raise the sons of earth,*
> *Born to give them second birth*

'HARK THE HERALD ANGELS SING', BY CHARLES WESLEY

We are not often reminded of how closely are linked the two major Church festivals of Christmas and Easter, but the renewed singing of the 'Gloria' at Easter brings the two together. The use of the 'Gloria' at most celebrations of the eucharist also brings both Christmas and Easter into regular remembrance. The 'Gloria' has been used since at least the fifth century, although the Book of Common Prayer of 1552 and of 1662 place the singing of this hymn of praise at the end of the service, where it is sung in gratitude for the gifts of salvation and communion. Nowadays it is more often found early in the service, where it is also appropriate as an opening hymn of praise. While it derives its title and opening words from Luke 2:14, the author of the rest of the words is unknown.

The text might be described as a Christian psalm. As with those ancient hymns of praise, we find here great outpourings of joy, glorification of God for what he has done for us but also an acknowledgment of the work of Christ, who as Lamb of God has taken away our sins. God as Trinity is praised in the final lines, and it is clear that this is the post-Easter, ascended Christ who is referred to and worshipped.

Angels are messengers of God, and in the Bible we often find them bearing good news ('gospel'). Again, by reminding ourselves of the Christmas story on Easter day we remember that the discovery of the empty tomb and the news of resurrection is the best form of good news there has been, or can be, and it caps the news of birth at Bethlehem, giving that good news purpose and fulfilment. Such gospel revelation merits not only joyous outpouring of celebration, but also reverence and awe, and this is why the 'Gloria' text is so apt for Easter (or any other time!).

In the setting by Giacomo Puccini (1858–1924), we find that a gentle statement of the opening words builds up with triumphant and exuberant music, before a slowing up for the 'peace on earth' phrase. Puccini, who is most famous for his string of popular operas, such as *Tosca*, *La Bohème* and *Madame Butterfly*, employs a quasi-operatic style in this early work, and some people sniff at his over-dramatic word setting as he responds to each phrase in the text. Yet there are varied and rapid emotions expressed in the text, and the colours that Puccini paints musically all serve to illustrate the contrast and depth of meaning found in the 'Gloria'. Comparisons are often made with Verdi's *Requiem* and Rossini's *Stabat Mater*, where religious texts are treated with an intensity that is not familiar to Northern Europeans, for some of whom an outpouring of religious emotion is distasteful.

As we reflect on the universal saving power of Christ revealed in his death and resurrection, which we celebrate especially today, we might remember that the use of liturgical texts through the ages has provided a concert repertoire for choral societies and orchestras, and that through performance, whether they specifically intend it or not, the truth and goodness of God are continually presented in musical form. Conversion and renewal does not have to happen in church, and many are moved at concert performances as well as in worship. It is hard to declare that any particular performance of a work such as Puccini's *Messa di Gloria* is *not* worship, merely because it does not take place in a church. Who knows when and how the Spirit will move an audience just as God moves a congregation?

Puccini himself came from a long line of church composers, and so was brought up well and truly within the faith of the Roman Catholic Church, whose worship and prayer he knew. The *Missa di Gloria*, as we now call it, was never entitled to such a grand title; Puccini himself called it *Mass for four voices with orchestra*, and it was first performed in his home town of Lucca in 1880. Puccini uses some of the techniques of Bach and Palestrina, counterpoint and *fugato*, which we do not find so much in his operas. Some of the music from this youthful work found its way into his operas (thus reversing the Renaissance tradition of plundering secular music for themes for masses), as the *Missa di Gloria* did not immediately find its way into the mainstream repertoire. Now that it is better-known, we can detect more easily the ways in which Puccini resurrects its music elsewhere.

If some of Puccini's music fell silent only to live again in other places, then he is hardly unique among composers. Bach, Handel and Berlioz often re-used their music. In our lives, we often do the same, telling the same stories, repeating the same mistakes, emulating our predecessors (whether we wish to or not). Sometimes we feel bound by 'fate' that we are determined, or even doomed by our genes, our upbringing, or the environmental circumstances in which we live or have lived. We may feel that our behaviour is an inevitable symptom of the times in which we live, or of the restrictions imposed upon us by family and society.

On this Easter Day, when we celebrate the glorious resurrection of Christ, and reflect on it in the context of his life and life-saving ministry, from birth to death and resurrection, we can see a real ray of light illuminating the truth that we are not determined by anything other than the love of God, who in Christ dies and lives, so that we might live and not die.

PRAYER

Christ our risen, redeeming God, help us to see afresh by the light of your glorious resurrection; help us to be renewed by your saving grace and always to live and worship in your presence, so that in any place and in any company we may constantly be inspired by the reality of resurrection and the power of love to change and renew each and every one of your dear people. For you reign in the glory of the Father and in union with the Spirit, ever one God, now and for ever. Amen.

For further reading: Luke 2:8–20
For listening: The 'Gloria' from Puccini's *Messa di Gloria*

'FOR NOW IS CHRIST RISEN FROM THE DEAD'

GEORGE FRIDERIC HANDEL—*MESSIAH*

I know that my redeemer liveth, and that he shall stand at the latter day upon the earth; and though worms destroy this body, yet in my flesh shall I see God. For now is Christ risen from the dead, the first-fruits of them that sleep. Since by man came death, by man came also the resurrection of the dead. For as in Adam all die, even so in Christ shall all be made alive. Behold, I tell you a mystery; we shall not all sleep, but we shall all be changed, in a moment, in the twinkling of an eye, at the last trumpet. The trumpet shall sound, and the dead shall be raised incorruptible, and we shall be changed.

SEE: JOB 19:25, 26; 1 CORINTHIANS 15:20–22, 51–52

It is thanks to Lent that we have what is probably the best-known, most popular and most inspirational of English choral works. Handel's *Messiah* is *the* English oratorio and it is sung, dare one say 'religiously' year in, year out, in cathedrals and concert halls the world over. Christmas is the most popular time, but it has a truly Easter message, as the selections from Part Three above reveal. Handel composed it in three weeks and it was first performed on 13 April 1742 in Dublin. The idea of oratorio was born out of necessity; Handel found that some of his dramatic works could not be performed during Lent, as the then Bishop of London, Edmund Gibson, decreed that opera was inappropriate for a penitential season. In response, Handel invented oratorio, which, although dramatic, often involving individual singers taking character parts, involves no staged action. For Handel, oratorio could be opera without visual action, but this hardly restricted his dramatization of the events and meanings of what was taking place in the story.

In *Messiah*, there are no character parts, nor do there need to be. The drama is the story of salvation, and the main actor is God, supported by Christ, angels, prophets and St Paul! Through narrative singing and choruses, the story of promise, incarnation, rejection, sin, redemption and resurrection is recounted and celebrated. The story of salvation is told through Old Testament prophecies, passages from the Epistles and the Book of Revelation. The only gospel passage concerns the angels' proclamation to the shepherds (Luke 2:8–14).

Charles Jennens, who compiled the texts from biblical sources, did not much like *Messiah*, saying at the time: '... *Messiah* has disappointed me... tho' he said he would... make it the best of all his Compositions. I shall put no more Sacred Words into his hands, to be thus abus'd.' This must surely go down as one of the most famous artistic misjudgments of history! In 1750 Handel began annual performances of *Messiah* at the Foundling Hospital in London. From then on it gained in popularity, and now its acclaimed status is unassailable.

When King George II first heard *Messiah* he enjoyed the 'Hallelujah' chorus so much that he got to his feet. As no one should remain seated under such circumstances, the audience rose with him. Such is the origin of the still much-debated tradition. Although it may have been simply that after nearly two hours of music, the king had cramp and had to stand up!

In 1789, Mozart adapted *Messiah*, adding musical instruments, making it sound like a work of his own period. His version is still performed sometimes, but modern taste seems to prefer Handel's original version.

To discuss the whole work would be impossible here, and David Winter has written a book which takes us through each passage, day by day (*Forty Days with the Messiah*, BRF, 1996). But at Easter, we can turn our attention to the final movements, which, in settings of the parts of the Easter anthems, tell forth the true meaning of Easter as laid out by St Paul.

There is a liturgical tradition established in the Book of Common Prayer of 1662 that for the first eight days of Easter, instead of singing or saying the Venite at Morning Prayer, the Easter anthems should be used. The Prayer Book has few seasonal provisions, so this distraction from the norm is significant, reminding us of just how important the days after Easter are. More recent thinking has made the Easter season extend for 40 days—right up to the Ascension—and so in some places these texts are used for this longer period. The Easter anthems involve 1 Corinthians 5:7; Romans 6:9; and 1 Corinthians 15:20. Jennens and Handel would both have known this liturgical tradition, so it is not surprising that we find an augmented version of these texts towards the end of *Messiah*.

One of Jennens' masterly touches, so beautifully set to music by Handel, is found in the aria 'I know that my Redeemer liveth'. In the blend of Job's statement of hope and St Paul's statement of resurrection achieved is the kernel of *Messiah* itself. For what we have here is an account of prophecy, the prediction and looking forward to a Saviour who will redeem and rescue those enslaved by sin and grief, allied with the fulfilment of that hope in Christ. This is the big message of *Messiah*, but it is also expressed in microcosm by this clever juxtaposition of the texts from Job and 1 Corinthians. Hope and fulfilment come together in an aria that is surely one of the most beautiful and sublime songs in the English language. The fusion of words and music parallels the fusion of Old and New Testament exquisitely.

The aria is followed by the hushed, unaccompanied choir extolling the inexorable logic of passion and suffering: 'Since by man came death, by man came also the resurrection of the dead. For as in Adam all die, even so in Christ shall all be made alive' (see 1 Corinthians 15:21–22). It is sung as though it were a secret, something to be kept quiet, but then the full choir bursts forth with joy, proclaiming that all shall be made alive. The tension between awe and rejoicing is balanced superbly by Handel, for surely both responses to the miracle of resurrection are appropriate. It is a mystery indeed, as the next aria goes on to tell us, but it is also a mystery worth shouting about!

With 'Behold, I tell you a mystery', there is a sense that we are arriving home. The prophecy has reached fulfilment; Christ has been sent, has arrived, has lived and ministered among us, and has been crucified and is now risen. Now the music tells us that we are on our way home along the new road that has been made for us, the new highway in the desert, as it were, with which the *Messiah* opens ('Comfort ye', Isaiah 40:1–3). We are being led towards change, eternal change when the last trumpet sounds, and the dead are raised. Soon we shall be arriving at the great final 'Amen', when God's work is done, the eighth day of creation, when all is redeemed. It is towards this that the *Messiah* races in Part Three, hindered only by the musical beauty of each movement.

As we reach the Easter period, there is also a sense that we are arriving home. We have walked on a journey through some dark days, remembering our sin and our mortality, and have been miserable in the proper sense of the word (we have been, and still are, people in need of mercy). But now that we have reached Easter, the destination of Lent, we can truly feel that we have arrived. The resurrection is a good place to call home, because through resurrection we reach our eternal home, the spiritual and physical place of rest and peace, where we meet with Father, Son and Holy Spirit, in the glory of the new heaven and earth (Revelation 21:1–5).

Just as there is closure at the end of a piece of music, a cadence on which the music comes to rest, so there is cadence when we move through Christ's passion to resurrection. We reach a spiritual place where we can pause to breathe the air and enjoy the view, and to hear the music. That place is a place of renewal, and it is located in the Easter period, when we can celebrate, not only because we have journeyed through Lent, but because Christ is risen indeed! Such a movement is a microcosm of our own lives, as we pass from death to life, that major moment of renewal, for which all our many life pilgrimages have been rehearsals, as we tune up for heaven.

PRAYER

Risen Christ, who, in bursting forth from the tomb, opens for us a new highway to glory, lead us forward to our heavenly home, so that as we rehearse the harmony of heaven in prayer and worship, we may be filled with your resurrection hope, until that final day, when with angels singing and trumpets blazing we may join in the great hallelujah, for ever and ever. Amen.

For further reading: Revelation 21:1–5
For listening: Movements from George Frideric Handel's *Messiah*

Death is not the end; Christ's resurrection shows us this, and opens up for us a new melody as we journey on to greater glory. With the full and perfect harmony of saints and angels accompanying us, we can look forward to a life beyond the imperfect cadence with which our earthly lives are brought to an end when our time comes. Thus, at our end comes a new beginning, whether we are thinking of our own lives, the story of Lent and Easter, or even as we reach the end of a Lenten discipline, such as the reading of a Lent book.

So now we bid a fond farewell at the end of our journey, parting company, like pilgrims who have arrived at their destination, having accompanied each other like members of an orchestra, a travelling band, attempting to sing together, in harmony with each other and with our Lord. As we go forward into the Easter season, let us be like bright lights bursting from the empty tomb, filled with Christ's presence and his risen glory. And let us remember those words of St Augustine with which we began:

So, my friends, let us sing 'Alleluia' … Let us sing as travellers sing on a journey; but keep on walking. Lighten your toil by singing, and never be idle. Sing, but keep on walking… Advance in virtue, in true faith and in right conduct. Sing up—and keep on walking!

NOTES FOR WEEKLY GROUPS

There is a very commendable tradition in many churches of meeting weekly in Lent to discuss, reflect and share together. Here are some suggestions as to what might be done in a group together, but these are by no means written in stone. It may be that there is too much material here. Do not feel pressured to use it all! Explore the music and the readings as is most appropriate and possible for you. It may well be the case that the weekly gathering is an opportunity to listen to some of the music together, especially if someone has good access to recordings or even video material. Do make sure that no one is inconvenienced by not having a sense of the meaning of any foreign language texts.

FIRST SESSION: REPENTANCE

Listen to all of Allegri's *Miserere*. The text is Psalm 51.

- What is the use of being miserable?
- Is it possible to feel truly forgiven?

Look at 2 Samuel 11:2—12: 13. It is a long passage, but it is the story of David's sin that prompted him to write Psalm 51.

- Is David's sin the kind of thing that people do today? What happens to them if they do?
- Is forgiveness something that we see in the world around us very much?
- Is there something in this week's news that speaks of forgiveness?

If possible, also listen to the two arias, 'Dove Sono' and 'Porgi Amor' from Mozart's *Figaro*. (There are videos available too.)

Look at Luke 15:11–32. Some people call this the 'Parable of the Prodigal Son', while others would rather see it as being all about the 'Forgiving Father'. Which is the most appropriate title?

- How easy is it to keep forgiving someone? Share stories of forgiveness if you can.
- In a small act of worship, call to mind sins to repent, write them down on a piece of paper. Read 1 Timothy 1:15–17 out loud, and carefully destroy the papers.

If appropriate or possible, sing the hymn: 'Immortal, Invisible, God only wise'.

SECOND SESSION: CREATION

Listen to the opening of Haydn's *Creation*. The text is Genesis 1:1–5. Also listen to other movements if you like (such as 'The Heavens are telling').

- What do we make of this Old Testament account of creation today?
- Science cannot account for the beauty of artistic creation—can it account for the beauty of divine creation?
- What are we to make of the great diversity within creation, and also of the apparent injustices inherent in creation?

Read Acts 8:4–24.

- What should our attitude to magic and sorcery be?
- Can the power of music be dangerous or misleading?

Listen to all or some of Britten's *Young Person's Guide to the Orchestra*.

- What does his use of individual instruments and ensemble playing say to us about the world we live in?

- If we were writing a 'Young Person's Guide to life and faith', what would we include—which voices should be heard?
- What good things have happened this week—at home, in the local community, in the world?

Read Genesis 1:24–31 and share with each other different things that make this a good world and celebrate them in a brief act of worship.

If appropriate or possible, sing the hymn: 'All creatures of our God and King'. It is based on words written by St Francis of Assisi.

THIRD SESSION: *REQUIEM*

Listen to the 'Dies irae' from Verdi's *Requiem*. Then listen to the 'In Paradisum' from Fauré's *Requiem*.

- What differences between these pieces of music strike you?
- What do these pieces say to us about death?
- On Ash Wednesday we encountered those words: 'Remember you are dust and to dust you shall return'. Do you find this phrase striking?
- At funerals we use the phrase 'Ashes to ashes, dust to dust' as the body (or cremated remains) are laid to earth. This phrase is used many times in a single day, all over the world. In the midst of life we are surrounded by death. What does it feel like to remember this fact, which for much of our lives we happily ignore?
- Christians are buried or cremated 'in sure and certain hope of the resurrection to eternal life in our Lord Jesus Christ'. Is this only for Christians? How do we know?
- What should be our attitude to the death of those who reject or ignore the call of Christ?

(It may be that someone in the group is recently bereaved, and that others present may not know it. Pastoral sensitivity is therefore required from all present. An opportunity for quiet reflection, and also perhaps for sharing experiences, fears or feelings in pairs may be a good idea.)

If there is time, also listen to 'Ich habe traurichkeit' from Brahms' *German Requiem*.

If there is to be worship, read Revelation 21:1–5 and perhaps sing 'The day thou gavest, Lord is ended'.

FOURTH SESSION: WAR AND PEACE

Begin by reading Genesis 22:1–13. Listen to the section of Britten's *War Requiem* that uses Wilfred Owen's poem 'The Parable of the Old Man and the Young' (the 'Offertorium').

- What do you think about the juxtaposition of these two ideas? Is the story of Abraham and Isaac about war?
- In what way can the 'sacrifice' in war be likened to the sacrifice of Christ on the cross?
- How do you feel about warfare? Is it ever justified? Can you think of cases where it might be, or could never be?

Read all of Psalm 137.

- Are these sentiments justifiable?
- Are the people who wrote these words any different to people today, in their attitudes and their circumstances? Can we sympathize with their attitude towards their enemies?
- How do you feel about your enemies, whether they be personal enemies or national enemies, or enemies of society?

Listen to the slow movement of Bernstein's *Chichester Psalms*—and other movements, if there is time.

- If violent, we risk hypocrisy; if peaceful, we risk being ignored or dismissed. Should our reaction to violence be violent itself, or gentle?
- What does peacekeeping mean? Should we think in terms of people like Gandhi, or should we heed the words of Christ found in Matthew 10:34–39, 26:51–52 and Luke 22:35–38.
- Sometimes it seems that Jesus is happy with violence and weapons —or does it?
- Are Christians called to be pacifists in this day and age? Is it possible to be a pacifist? You might like to think about this in relation to the events of the past 12 months or so: remember what was happening in Lent 2003…

If there is to be worship, read Matthew 5:38–48 and perhaps sing: 'I vow to thee my country'. Some people do not like this hymn and think it controversial, but the verses offer a striking contrast to each other.

FIFTH SESSION: SIN AND POWER

Listen to the 'Soldiers' Chorus' from Gounod's *Faust*. (If you cannot find a rendition in English, read out a translation first.)

- Are there people today whom we might think have sold their souls to Satan?

Read Revelation 13:11–18.

- Sin is often easily confused with goodness; the gap between them may not be so great. The number 666 is close to 777, which is three sevens—a perfect number of perfect numbers. Can you think of examples where something that looks good turns out to be evil?
- Think about the story of Samson. Was he a good man?
- What about Delilah? Is it right to think of her as a wicked temptress who betrays him? Should she have betrayed her family instead?

Listen to or watch a video of Saint-Saëns' opera.

- Do you think she loved him? Why?
- Do Handel and Saint-Saëns have anything to add to the story, or are we better off thinking of Samson as a rebel hero, or as some kind of terrorist? Does his story help us understand the situation in the Middle East and the Gulf in recent years?
- What about Salome and John the Baptist—what insight for modern politics do they give us?
- Do the stories of other biblical figures help us to think about sin, judgment and forgiveness? Who are the heroes, and who are the zeros?

If there is to be worship, read Matthew 5:6–12 and perhaps sing: 'Blest are the pure in heart'.

SIXTH SESSION: MASS APPEAL

Listen to the 'Kyrie' from Bach's *B Minor Mass*.

- Why is there a plea for mercy at the beginning of the eucharist?
- Does Bach convey the right mood? Does the music convey a proper sense of mystery, guilt, shame, awe or fear and does it remind us that while we seek forgiveness we also have assurance of mercy?
- Why do we seek mercy if we have already been granted it?

Read the account of Jesus' triumphal entry into Jerusalem (Luke 28–40). Listen to Palestrina's setting of the 'Benedictus'.

- How does the use of this text in the middle of the eucharist strike you? Sometimes it is omitted—is it used in your church, and why is it used (or not)?

Listen to *Panis Angelicus* by Franck. It is a very popular piece, well-known and appealing. But many people have no idea of what it is about. This could be because many non-churchgoers do not have a grasp of what the eucharist is about.

- Imagine you have to explain what communion is, using this piece as a starting-point! How easy is it?
- Much music for the eucharist is in Latin because until fairly recently the Roman Catholic mass was celebrated in that language. Reformed churches have used the vernacular for hundreds of years. Should the music of Bach, Palestrina and Beethoven be translated? Or can we think of Latin, a 'dead' language, as a uniting language that crosses boundaries because it is no one's native tongue?

Listen to the final section of the 'Agnus Dei' from Bach's *B Minor Mass*.

- How are the 'Kyrie' and 'Agnus Dei' linked? Can you hear the similarity?

If there is to be worship, sing: 'Alleluia, sing to Jesus' and read Revelation 15:1–4.

SEVENTH SESSION: SALVATION

Now in our final week, we consider Christ's passion, death and resurrection.

Begin by listening to the song 'I don't know how to love him' from *Jesus Christ Superstar*.

- Is Passiontide confusing—do we know how to love Jesus? Is it possible to get 'loving Jesus' right?
- Discuss the portrayal of the events of holy week in *Jesus Christ Superstar* in depth if you have the resources (there is a film available on video). What does it have to say to or about faith? Is it a good thing for people to be introduced to Jesus through this work?

Read the account of the crucifixion from John's Gospel (John 19:16–30). Listen to the opening section of the *St John Passion* by Bach. (There are recordings in English.)

- What are the differences between the way that Bach sets the story and *Jesus Christ Superstar*? Which do you prefer and why?

Read the account of Jesus' burial (John 19:31–42). Listen to the final chorus and chorale from the *St John Passion*.

- What can we feel? What should we feel? In response to the cross, people often feel that silence can say more than words, for there are no words that are adequate. Are there situations in the world today that elicit the same response? Can music help us?
- If we are silent, is it the silence of avoidance and denial, or is it the silence of respect and grief?

Perform John Cage's *4'33"* together. Spend some minutes in silence together. Pray, but also listen to the sounds of your own life (heart, breath, stomach even!). Imagine what it must be like not to sense these—to have no life. Imagine Christ dead.

Break the silence with 'I know that my redeemer liveth' from Handel's *Messiah*. Does music such as this make it more true that 'Jesus lives'?

If there is to be worship (and this week you may not feel the need), read 1 Corinthians 15:42–57 and sing the hymn 'Jesus lives'.